The Which? Guide to Computers

About the author

Since working for a decade in the software industry Richard Wentk has been a freelance writer, computer trainer and consultant, with a particular interest in making computer technology accessible to non-technical people. He is also the author of *The Which? Guide to the Internet* and *The Which? Guide to Computers for Small Businesses*.

The Which? Guide to Computers

Richard Wentk

 CONSUMERS' ASSOCIATION

Which? Books are commissioned and researched by
Consumers' Association and published by
Which? Ltd, 2 Marylebone Road, London NW1 4DF

Distributed by The Penguin Group:
Penguin Books Ltd, 27 Wrights Lane, London W8 5TZ

First published September 1995
Reprinted January, March 1996
Revised edition September 1996
Reprinted September, October 1997
Revised edition May 1998
Reprinted November 1998
Revised edition September 1999

British Library Cataloguing in Publication Data
Wentk, Richard
    Which? Guide to Computers – (Which?
    Consumer Guides)
    I. Title II. Series
    004

ISBN 0 85202 773 7

For a full list of Which? books, please write to Which? Books, Castlemead,
Gascoyne Way, Hertford X. SG14 1LH, or access our web site at
http://www.which.net

With thanks to John Docherty, Sara Edlington, Caroline Ellerby, Ivor Garfinkle,
Martin Harney, Jacqueline Hewitt, Fionna Johnson, Ian Kilminster, Marie Lorimer,
Bruce Tober, John Wheelwright.
Illustration on pages 10–11 Kevin Jones Associates as used in *PC Guide* (Future Publishing)
Issue 1, July 1995
Cover and text design by Kysen Creative Consultants
Typeset by Business ColorPrint, Welshpool, Powys
Printed and bound in England by Clays Ltd, Bungay, Suffolk

Contents

Introduction

During the 1990s computers moved from being a technical tool to an almost essential consumer item with a rapidity unmatched by any other technology. Where once information technology could be bought only after protracted negotiations with teams of professional sales people, now much-improved versions of similar technology can be bought over the counter in the high street. As a result, for many people computers have become an essential part of everyday life, and both at home and at work basic computer skills have become almost as important as the ability to use a telephone.

The astonishing growth of the Internet, which relies on computer technology for its success, has made it possible for people with little or no computer expertise to shop, chat and manage their finances at any hour of the day or night. More information is now transferred electronically every day than by more traditional methods, and electronic mail (email) has become as widely used for social purposes as the telephone, letter or postcard. Even music and photographs are beginning to move out of the CD rack and the photo album on to the Internet, where they can be swapped and commented on more conveniently than ever before, by those that have access to the technology.

These less technical uses for the technology are reflected in the way that computers are now being sold. At the beginning of the 1990s the selling of computers began to shift from specialist high-technology outlets into the high street. Today consumer spending on computer products rivals that on many established high-street goods and services. The value of software sales in Europe in 1998 has been estimated at just under £10 billion, and interest in electronic information services such as the Internet has been raised to fever pitch by the computer press. Price wars have sent the cost of components spiralling downwards and made it possible for almost anyone to afford technology that in the mid-1980s would have been beyond the reach of all but the largest organisations. A typical mid-price computer today, costing £500, is far more powerful than a £1 million machine of the 1980s. More expensive – but still affordable – machines are beginning to approach the speed and power of what would have been known as a 'supercomputer' a decade and a half ago.

But for all the technological advances, the biggest obstacle facing anyone thinking of buying a computer is still the dearth of simple, easy-to-understand information. Surprisingly, perhaps, this is not just a question of jargon but also of approach. Although computers are now very much a part of everyday life, both at home and in the office, and manufacturers are making efforts to ensure that their products are easier to use, far too much useful information is still presented in the form of technical specifications. To most people such details are meaningless. They want to know whether the computer can help them achieve what they want to achieve in their work; how much a system is likely to cost; and where they can get help if they run into problems.

This lack of accessible information, combined with the wide availability of computer technology, can lead to problems for both home and business users. A 1999 survey by MORI showed that over 50 per cent of the people interviewed felt very stressed by computer problems. 'Computer rage' – the physical or verbal abuse of computers which are not working properly – is a common occurrence, especially in the workplace. Another source of frustration is the time it takes for some suppliers to rectify problems.

Certainly there are risks involved in buying and using a computer, and a number of businesses have come to grief by misjudging their computer requirements. Such risks can be minimised, however, and for those willing to ignore the hype and base their choice of computer on a realistic assessment of their needs the benefits can be enormous. Most companies which take the plunge and computerise some areas of their operation discover they are able to streamline and simplify much of the day-to-day maintenance of their business and make significant savings. Similarly, families who take the time to think about what they really want from a computer before buying one for use in the home can find that they have acquired something that is a superb arithmetical aid, a reference library, an extra dimension to any hobby or interest, and provides entertainment for the children all at the same time.

This book has been written for the non-technical person who would like to know more about buying a computer as a practical tool, rather than as a grey box with an attached set of performance statistics. In the pages that follow you will find simple explanations of what a computer can do for you at home and for your small business, how to choose between competing products, how to estimate the real costs of a computer system, and how to make sure that you and your business are protected if things go wrong. Also included are suggestions to help you guard against the common pitfalls of computer purchase, together with hints and tips on how to save money by negotiating better prices and buying wisely. Many of the common jargon words are explained, to enable you to read and understand advertisements and articles in computer magazines. Other areas covered include the pros and cons of the Internet and other electronic information services, the legal implications of maintaining a computer system, especially in the light of the Data Protection Act 1998) information on how to finance your purchase, how a computer affects your tax position, and how to ensure that continuous use of computer equipment and accessories will not damage your health.

If you are to get the best from your investment, your computer system has to be matched to your individual requirements. The information presented here will help you clarify what you want, and give you the knowledge and confidence to deal with computer dealers competently. Whether you are running a medium-sized business or simply looking for a better way to write letters, do your personal accounts or amuse your children, you will find everything you need in this book to help you.

Anatomy of a personal computer

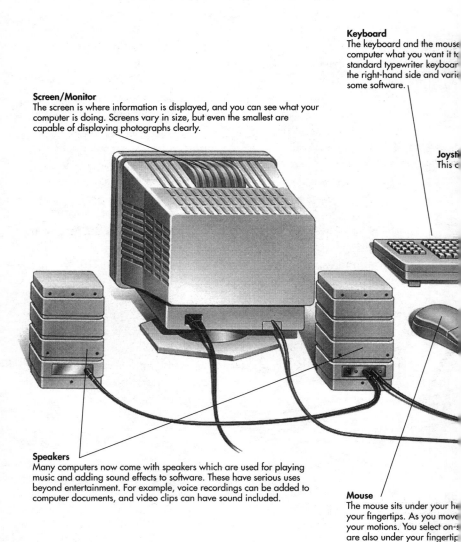

Screen/Monitor
The screen is where information is displayed, and you can see what your computer is doing. Screens vary in size, but even the smallest are capable of displaying photographs clearly.

Keyboard
The keyboard and the mouse
computer what you want it to
standard typewriter keyboar
the right-hand side and varie
some software.

Joysti
This c

Speakers
Many computers now come with speakers which are used for playing music and adding sound effects to software. These have serious uses beyond entertainment. For example, voice recordings can be added to computer documents, and video clips can have sound included.

Mouse
The mouse sits under your he
your fingertips. As you move
your motions. You select on-s
are also under your fingertip

still the main way of telling your
The keyboard is very much like the
h an extra set of keys for numbers on
her special keys which are used by

al extra is used solely for games.

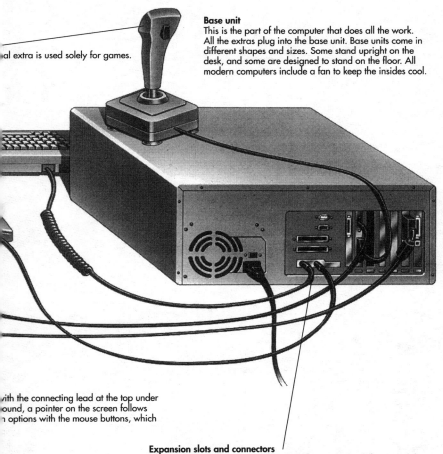

Base unit
This is the part of the computer that does all the work.
All the extras plug into the base unit. Base units come in
different shapes and sizes. Some stand upright on the
desk, and some are designed to stand on the floor. All
modern computers include a fan to keep the insides cool.

ith the connecting lead at the top under
ound, a pointer on the screen follows
 options with the mouse buttons, which

Expansion slots and connectors
All modern computers have a set of sockets on the back for essential
extras such as a keyboard, screen and mouse. These are designed so
that you cannot plug the wrong item into the wrong socket.

Chapter 1

What a computer can do for you

A computer is the perfect tool for manipulating information. In the office it can replace the ageing typewriter, act as a very fast adding machine and provide easy access to the books and other records. In the home it can be used for writing letters, entertaining and educating children, playing games and managing personal finances.

However, any modern machine, even a modest one, can be used for much more than these tasks. In fact, a computer can be used to help with almost anything, from automating a bakery to keeping track of stock in a bookshop or displaying examples of different hairstyles to customers with their own features superimposed electronically.

The term 'information' is very wide; it covers words, sounds, photographs and numbers. Images such as maps and technical drawings can easily be stored and manipulated on modern computers. Novel uses, such as photographic editing and retouching, interior design and automated route planning are just some of the sophisticated applications now widely available.

A computer is a sizeable investment. Used wisely, it can streamline the running of any business. Unfortunately, it can also become more of a problem than a solution. It is possible to cripple a business by making the wrong decision in purchasing and using a computer system. Using real-life examples this book illustrates the sorts of mistakes people make regularly and how you can avoid them.

CASE HISTORY: Jenny

Jenny Shipway, who runs a clothing business, was looking for a computer to help with business administration.

'A friend suggested I got a computer to help with the books. This sounded like a great idea, so we started to look around at what was available and eventually decided on a PC.

'So I got the computer first. Now I know that was my first mistake. I should have got the software sorted out and then found the right computer for it. I had an idea that somehow the computer on its own would make everything easier. I hadn't even thought about software for it at all. There was some free stuff that came with it, but it didn't seem to do much. It certainly wasn't what I wanted.

'On my friend's suggestion I had a look round some of the computer shops in Tottenham Court Road, London. In a lot of them the sales people leapt on you the second you walked through the door. I felt pretty intimidated.

'Eventually I found one shop that was slightly more relaxed. I explained that I was running a business and needed some software for it. I was steered in the direction of a software package described as an "office suite", which I was told was perfect for businesses. Exactly what I was looking for. It cost nearly £450. That sounded a lot, but I thought that if it did the job it would be worth it.

'It didn't do the job, and it wasn't worth it. I found it was much too complicated. I eventually got the word processor and the electronic organiser working, but the rest of it was beyond me. It wasn't what I wanted at all. I'm sure if I was running a big company it would be just the thing, but for my kind of small business, doing the sales, bought ledger and VAT, it just wasn't right.

'In desperation I bought a few computer magazines. I didn't understand much of the editorial content, but I saw what I'd just bought being advertised for £250! That was the going rate, because of something called a "competitive upgrade". I'd paid the full recommended retail price, when I could have saved myself nearly half of that. Never mind that it didn't do what I wanted anyway.

'Of course I was furious, but there was nothing I could do. I realise it was my own fault, as I wasn't clear about what I needed and I didn't think things through. Computers have this aura of infallibility, and it's easy to feel intimidated and make decisions you'd never dream of in another context.

'I tried contacting the shop, but of course they said they couldn't take the software back. I'd broken the seal and started using it, and that, as far as they were concerned, was that. I even contacted my lawyer, but he said that in the circumstances I'd be pushing my luck trying to take action.

'I think that was the worst moment. At that point I'd spent the best part of £2,000 and had nothing to show for it, apart from some letters printed out more stylishly than I could have achieved on a typewriter and a slightly better organised address book. Someone suggested I tried ringing around computer consultants listed in *Yellow Pages*. A few were off-hand and said that they only dealt with larger companies. One or two simply didn't return my calls. But eventually I got through to someone who very patiently listened to what I wanted, gave me some options, and we settled for a proper accounts system. It cost all of £100, and it does everything – accounts, tax, VAT, PAYE, the lot. He even helped me get it working, showed me how to use it and helped me sell the "office suite" to someone else. Apparently I hadn't registered it, so I wasn't even the official owner. We managed to get nearly £200 for it. Unfortunately, that money went on his fee. That hurt a bit, but I do think it was worth it.

'I realise now that it's easy to waste a fortune in this game. If I was doing it all again I'd make damn sure I did my homework, or I'd get real expert help from someone who's been down the same path. That's just so important – otherwise I'd have wasted the best part of £2,000 and been left with nothing to show for it at all.'

Software first

A quick look through some computer magazines shows that most advertising concentrates on hardware. Computers are sold as boxes, rather than useful tools. The industry works on the basis that hardware is exciting, doubly so if it works faster than last year's hardware. Software, which is what turns the hardware into a useful tool, appears to be something of an afterthought.

When deciding on a computer system, it is important to approach things from the other end: software, then hardware. You have tasks that need to be carried out. A computer may be able to help you with them. So take a look at the software available and decide which package you might find useful for which tasks.

Managing your money

A computer can be an invaluable tool for managing your money. At its simplest it can help you balance the books and perform cheque-book reconciliations. With the help of a computer you can keep a history of all your transactions which is at least as detailed as that kept by your bank. This can make domestic budgeting easier – you can, for example, keep a detailed record of heating and lighting bills on a quarterly basis, and be ready for the next set of bills well before they arrive. Another possible use is to check annual percentage rate and mortgage calculations, so that you can work out exactly how expensive a loan will be and find the most cost-effective way to pay it off.

CASE HISTORY: Steven

Steven Adams works from home as a freelance journalist. Before he got a computer, he had problems keeping on top of his financial situation.

'I'm not a very organised person. I love working from home, and also having the opportunity to get out there and chase stories rather than being stuck in an office. But I always used to get my accounts in late, and I'd usually be charged interest by the Inland Revenue. I was hopeless at keeping track of invoices, too. Sometimes I wouldn't even bother sending them in. But it's a bad habit to get into, as you have no idea where your money is coming from or who owes you what. It was getting so bad that my accountant took me to one side at one point and politely suggested that I needed to get my act together.

'Even though it should only take maybe a half-hour a week to sort out all my expenses, somehow I just couldn't seem to find the time. So I started to wonder if my computer could help. I knew that all I needed was some software.

'The first thing I tried was a spreadsheet. This wasn't what I wanted at all. For a financial whizz it would be perfect, but for me it was just too involved. It was too open-ended and I didn't fancy having to program it myself before I could start using it.

'So I had a good, long think about what I needed. I decided it had to be something that was designed from the start to do the things I wanted. It should be able to track my invoices and then remind me when payments were late. I also needed help keeping track of the expenses that come up on each job. If I don't note these down I end up paying tax on the money that's refunded to me. Then I needed some general accounting and bookkeeping help, and also something that could work out expenses incurred as part of my job in a more general way, like petrol, phone bills and so on. Finally I needed something that was easy to set up and use. I'm not VAT-registered, so that wasn't a problem. But a VAT option would be useful.

'The next step was to go into a newsagent and buy a pile of computer magazines. Most of the adverts were hardware-based. But there were a few software products listed too.

'Eventually I tried a demonstration copy of some bookkeeping software that came free with a magazine. It was a limited version, but I tried it out and found that it did almost everything the way I wanted it done. The full version was only £100, so I got that, and got organised. I bought the version with the VAT option and now that work is picking up, I don't have to worry about hiring an accountant every so often to sort things out. It's great, because the software paid for itself right away.'

Bookkeeping

For most businesses keeping the books is something of a chore. A computer can automate the work, as well as producing professional end-of-year accounts. Keeping up with VAT calculations can also be made much less time-consuming. It is relatively simple to automate VAT accounting, including any rate changes and zero-rated items. It is also possible to produce a single printout at the end of the accounting period which can be sent straight to HM Customs and Excise with a covering letter.

CASE HISTORY: Stella

Stella Beck runs a stationery supply company.

'Bookkeeping has never interested me, but it's never seemed cost-effective to employ someone to do it. I used to be very disorganised about it, and sometimes I'd lose bills and forget to chase payments.

'I bought a simple accounts and money management package, and it has really helped. I'm disciplined enough now to make sure that all the sales and payments go through the system, and at the end of the day it tells me exactly where I stand. It's been a godsend for the VAT, because that used to take forever. Now, I just have a printout I can wave at the Customs and Excise people. They're happy because they don't need to hassle me, I'm happy because it takes an hour to sort everything out instead of a couple of days of panic. The business is happier too. I have more time to deal with people, which is the part I really enjoy.'

Sole traders can use a computer to keep track of their creditors and debtors. This can be combined with invoice- and cheque-printing systems, to provide an all-in-one cash flow control system. It is possible to set up a system whereby bad debts are chased with letters, as well as making sure that bills are paid as late as possible to help with cash flow. One advantage of a system like this is that it enables you to estimate accurately the financial position of your business a month or two ahead, based on sales projections.

Advanced accounting systems can handle credits and debits in foreign currencies, and allow for exchange-rate fluctuations. Of current interest is the ability to deal with transactions in Euros; at the time of writing some businesses have to accept payments in pounds as well as Euros, and suitable software can make it easier to maintain a summary of these transactions. The job of calculating payroll contributions is also relatively straightforward. The computer can be made to allow for budget and tax changes and even refer to them on a year-by-year basis. Keeping track of payroll outgoings, PAYE and National Insurance contributions becomes much simpler.

Financial planning

For financial planning the spreadsheet is now an indispensable tool of the trade. It presents you with a grid of boxes, called 'cells', each of which contains either a number or a formula. You can specify something as simple as 'add up all the numbers entered above and print the total here', or as complex as the total payment for a loan, based on a principal, a period and an interest rate.

CASE HISTORY: Martin

Martin Smith, a chartered accountant, was wary of computers until one of his clients showed him a spreadsheet in action.

'I was hooked. It was just the perfect tool for the job. Most people who use spreadsheets don't have a financial background, so they only use simple applications like profit and loss accounts. I found I could do much more than that, because it's easy to do things like profit management, payback analysis and answer other 'what-if?' questions.

'Most of my work used to be tax-based. Now I get a fair bit of work helping with business plans. With the spreadsheet I can track interest rates and watch what effect they'll have on a new project. New businesses can be very sensitive to these, so I can warn clients just how much of a risk they're taking. The fact that I can draw graphs helps as well – they can put a message over in a very direct, accessible form.'

As Martin's story shows, spreadsheets are ideal for speculative calculations. It is easy to set up a table of potential income against interest payments and then vary the interest rate to see what happens. Without a computer you would have to recalculate each entry. With a computer you can change a single number – in this case the interest rate – and the spreadsheet does the rest. The information can be presented graphically as well as in tabular form. This is useful for trend-spotting and can also help with producing financial reports for directors and shareholders.

Money on-line

Most banks now offer schemes whereby statements can be sent direct from the bank's computer to the business's computer without having to be printed on paper first. These schemes also offer the chance to make payments electronically. Money can be transferred from one account to another – which may be abroad – by typing a few commands on the computer's keyboard. These payments can be arranged at any time of the day or night.

A computer also makes it easier to keep track of stocks and shares. There are now a number of electronic news services which offer more or less up-to-the-minute details of stock prices. Combined with trend analysis software these can give you your own personal electronic connection to the Stock Exchange with 'buy' or 'sell' suggestions.

Finally, many high-street banks now offer electronic banking services over the Internet (see page 64). These are the equivalent of high-street banking, and, as with their business equivalent, make it possible to transfer money and pay bills at any time, even outside of normal office hours. Note that they cannot yet be used to pay in cheques or cash, or make cash withdrawals (although this may become possible in the future). However, some banks do make it possible to arrange loans and even mortgages on-line.

Stock control

For applications which require a more in-depth approach to information management, the best available tool is the database. A database can be used to keep track of any kind of information and pick out trends and details from it. For example, when managing a sales team it is possible to collate sales by area, by product, by salesman or by season.

Keeping track of hundreds of different items in a warehouse while working out the optimum use of space is something of a challenge by hand. But a database can be used to tackle the problem easily, as well as making it possible to play with 'what-if' scenarios.

CASE HISTORY: George

George Becker runs a car spares service. He uses a computer to keep track of stock levels and to manage his inventory in an intelligent way.

'I got someone in to set up a database for me. It keeps track of all the parts I sell, warns me when stocks are low and reminds me to re-order. It's not foolproof – every so often we'll get a run on some part or other out of the blue and I run out. But it's made my life a lot easier.

'The reports are great. I can keep track of exactly what the stock is worth and cut down on slow-selling lines so I don't have goods lying around taking up space.

'It helps with the selling too. It's all been marked up so that if one part needs an extra, that comes up on the screen. We don't get people coming back a day later saying "Can I have one of these as well?" any more.'

Another efficient use of a database is in personnel. It is easy to set up a database of employees, with photographs, to include all the details of appraisals and indications of an employee's work record. This makes it possible to arrange a 'skills bank' that can be used when employees are being selected for new projects.

Managing personal information

An electronic personal organiser can completely replace a paper one. It is a convenient way to store information such as 'to-do' lists, anniversaries, currency–conversion factors, appointment and meeting reminders and general notes. Electronic organisers can also be set up to provide an audible reminder or alarm at a certain time, and to keep links between different kinds of information. All the contact details of everyone involved on a certain project can be kept together, and appointments can be linked with telephone numbers so that any changes can be communicated quickly and easily.

CASE HISTORY: Trevor

Trevor Knight sells advertising for a magazine publishing company. He used to use a paper 'organiser' but recently switched to a computer-based system.

'I can honestly say it's changed my life. Now everything – appointments, follow-up calls, names, addresses, phone numbers, fax numbers – are all systematically stored away instead of being in an overstuffed ringbound notebook with pages and business cards spilling out of it. The computer can find anything in a fraction of a second. The fun part is getting it to dial the phone numbers and log the calls for me too.'

Communications

A computer can also be used to transmit information as well as storing it. With the addition of a simple and affordable extra called a **modem**, your computer can dial telephone numbers for you (see Appendix II). This turns a computer into an automated telephone book which can save you hours during the course of a working week.

A modem can also be used to send and receive faxes. These can be read on screen and printed out only if necessary for future reference. While many budget fax machines still use fax paper which is prone to curling, fading and yellowing, computer-printed faxes are always printed on plain paper.

CASE HISTORY: Ryan

Ryan Williams is a freelance journalist with a particular interest in learning how computers can be used to communicate.

'I bought a modem to send and receive faxes. Most of what I sent came straight from my computer anyway, so I didn't need to print it out.

'Then one of my editors told me about electronic mail. The company already used an internal mail system and was enlarging it so that outsiders could send mail as well. It meant I could send copy straight to the office without even faxing. The text would go directly from my computer to the office system.'

Within an office, computers can be connected together on a **network** so that information and messages can be passed among them. **Electronic mail (email)** can take the place of paper memos, and the network can also be used to share resources such as printers and external fax machines. The biggest advantage of a network is that it makes it easy to keep track of people and make sure that everyone works together smoothly.

The **Internet** offers the same kinds of facilities but on a much larger scale. The Internet is an international computer network that allows mail to be exchanged between any computer anywhere. For example, you can mail someone on the other side of the world with a list of prices and services. Unlike ordinary mail, the information arrives almost instantaneously. Costs are based on national, and most probably local, call charges, no matter where the destination. Collaborative projects can also be managed and undertaken across the Internet.

The Internet can be an excellent source of computer support and advice. Aside from Internet connection charges – usually quite reasonable – this support is free and is provided by experts.

Presentation

Business presentations play an important role in many corporate environments, and here too the computer can offer effective help.

As with desktop publishing tools and word processors, many presentation applications offer a range of templates which can be used to add impact to a presentation. They also include libraries of graphics and symbols. The most sophisticated tools offer simple animation features which include video effects such as dissolves and cross-fades, and also animated graphs and symbols. Pre-recorded music clips and sound effects can also be used to add emphasis and interest to the presentation.

Until the 1980s all stationery was printed by professional printers. However with the advent of desktop publishing, pioneered by the Apple Computer Corporation with its Macintosh range, it is now possible for a business or an individual to produce professional-quality leaflets, flyers, posters, advertising material, business cards and so on. Desktop publishing software is available for all makes of computer, and in many cases is sold with off-the-peg design templates. These guarantee professional results and help to overcome the lack of design and layout skills which blighted many early amateur desktop publishing efforts.

CASE HISTORY: Sally

Sally Griffiths runs a computer training company.

'A big part of the job is getting information across as clearly as possible, and computers can be really good for that. Today's software makes it easy to design striking presentations, and we use those to communicate with as much impact as possible. It helps our clients to pick things up more quickly. They're also impressed when they see what a computer can do.

'We tend to work a lot with corporate teams, and they often need to use the same technology themselves. So it's a bonus that presentation software is one of the easier kinds of software to use. They can get superb results very quickly. It helps with confidence – some people are still a bit intimidated by computers – and it helps them practically too.

'We also consult on presentation and image in general, and there are some very interesting things that businesses can do with a simple black and white laser printer and pre-printed stationery'.

The automated mail-shot is another useful facility that can help with presentation. This takes a standard letter, a list of addresses and other relevant details and automatically produces a string of personalised letters (complete with printed envelopes). Targeted carefully and used creatively, mail-shots can be very effective.

At the moment, budget colour printers are very affordable but cannot yet compete with the quality and sharpness of black-and-white printers. Over the next few years high-quality colour printers will become more widely available and affordable, but for now it is still possible to produce strikingly professional results by using pre-printed paper. These offer graphic backgrounds as an effective backdrop for text that can be added later. They can be used to produce professional-looking leaflets, letters and business cards from your own home or office for a much smaller outlay than something that has been designed and printed by a print-house.

Electronic presentation is becoming increasingly popular. Instead of creating paper reports, many larger businesses now place information on local computer networks, called intranets, where they can be read and searched by anyone who needs them. Apart from saving on printing costs, electronic presentations can include animations, sounds and video, and can also be produced in colour.

Businesses can use the same kinds of facilities to promote themselves internationally on the World Wide Web (known simply as the Web)– a popular part of the Internet. This kind of electronic presentation has now become commonplace, and in some cases will even have taken the place of paper-based presentations.

Professional tools for specialist work

Computers can also be used to help with specific professional applications. Job-specific software is readily available for a wide range of professions including law, medicine, architecture, design and various kinds of engineering.

CASE HISTORY: Fionna

Fionna Johnson works from home as an illustrator and graphic designer.

'Like a lot of creative people, I was very wary of computers. To be honest I thought they were rather dull. But when a friend demonstrated what he could do on his computer with graphic design software, I was smitten. Now I have similar equipment, it enables me to try out all sorts of different approaches in a fraction of the time it would take to produce alternative designs conventionally. So I can supply a far better, more flexible service to clients at a low cost.

'I now use a graphics tablet and stylus instead of a pen and paper, and "draw" into the computer directly. I can simulate any kind of brush – airbrush, watercolour, pencil, whatever – and even make the "paper" as wet or dry as I'd like. The range of colours is all but infinite. And it's easy to add extras such as fragments of photographs or news clippings, and then, if you want, distort them to produce a special effect.

'I've had a huge amount of extra work as a result, and it's really freed me up creatively. I can do things I never even dreamed of doing with ink and paper, and I still haven't reached the limits of what I can do. I don't even need to worry about mistakes. I can undo the last thing I did, and the computer takes me back to where I was before.

'The only problem is getting things printed. Detailed full-colour artwork can cost a small fortune to print out if you use a bureau, but more and more publishers now handle designs and artwork on data cartridges, or even sent in over a phone connection or the Internet.'

Computer-aided design (CAD)

This software can be invaluable for visualising two-dimensional and three-dimensional objects. CAD software is rather like an advanced version of the traditional drawing board, except that it can be used to design in three dimensions as well as two. The drawings – which can include mechanical parts, buildings, items of furniture and so on – are held inside the computer's memory. They can then be viewed on the screen from any angle and altered quickly and easily. CAD can help with engineering, architecture, interior design and any other kind of work that can benefit from the chance to look at a plan or layout before it is drawn or built. Advanced CAD tools can be used to place computer-generated images of items on a photographic background. This is ideal for architectural work, enabling the effect of a building on its surroundings to be assessed before the building is built.

Image manipulation

More and more artists and graphic designers are using computers. Many advertising hoardings now carry work that was designed – at least in part – on a computer, and computer animations are routinely used in television advertising, including spectacular '**morphing**' effects where one object appears to change into another. Computer animators such as William Latham are working with the branch of mathematics known as fractals to create intriguing new images. Computers offer designers many advantages over conventional media, including the ability to create new special effects that are not possible any other way.

Other examples

Computer technology is also influencing photography. Photographers have always used studio and darkroom techniques to enhance their work, but with a computer these kinds of adjustments or image manipulation can be made more easily using **photographic tools**.

For haulage firms and countless businesses for which getting from A to B in the fastest possible time is an important consideration, one of the most useful computer tools of recent years has been the **electronic route-planner**. This works out a route between two places based on a number of criteria (shortest, cheapest, quickest and so on). The route can be tailored to take into account typical speeds and miles-per-gallon ratings of different vehicles. Planners for roads in Europe and the United States are also available.

Another practical application is the preparation of **timetables for schools**. In the past this has been an onerous and time-consuming task, but a computer can keep track of all the information with ease.

Legal firms can now access case histories and precedents electronically. **Legal databases** are available which detail previous judgements and make it easy to track related cases. This can save many hours of research.

Even **catering and hotel management** can benefit from computerisation. Many hotels now use computers to keep track of room bookings, maintain a list of their guests' spending and calculate an itemised bill at the end of their stay.

Leisure uses

Since the late 1980s the home computer has gradually been integrated with other home entertainment and leisure products. A plug-in extra called a TV tuner is now available which transforms a computer into a television set. Many computers can now play music compact discs

(CDs) through a pair of attached speakers. The same CD player can also be used to view videos, which are also supplied in CD form. Software is also being supplied on special CDs called CD-ROMs (compact disc, read-only memory). These look like ordinary music CDs but contain information instead of music. CD-ROMs have a vast storage capacity, and new kinds of **multimedia** software (which includes pictures, sounds and video clips as well as words) have been developed to take advantage of this. CD-ROMs are slowly being replaced by DVDs (Digital Versatile Discs). These were originally designed to provide high-quality video playback, but are now also being used to provide software and multimedia information. DVDs work very much like CD-ROMs, but can store up to around ten times as much information.

Other leisure uses include art and music. With all creative applications the power of the computer is demonstrated in the ease with which beginners can correct mistakes. A musician can record a performance and then correct individual notes. The corrections can be as obvious as changing wrong notes, or as subtle as tiny changes in phrasing or rhythm. An artist can remove the last brush stroke, rub out sections of a picture without leaving any traces, or change the colours after a picture is finished. Those with slightly more dedication and enthusiasm can explore the world of computer animation and photo-realistic image creation.

There is also a small but growing market in educational software. These applications range from simple counting and reading games for pre- and primary school children, to more advanced 'adventures' in science. Some of these have obvious uses as a worthwhile and educational distraction for children whose harassed parents would like a break.

A number of educational and general interest titles are aimed at adults: for example, various encyclopedias are now available in CD-ROM format. Unlike a paper encyclopedia these include snatches of sound, music and video to enhance the presentation of information.

Lastly computer games are developing into an art form in their own right, and the latest games are now designed and created by the same studios that produce Hollywood films (see Chapter 7).

Choosing the right software for the job

Software comes in two types. The first is the dedicated application, specialised for a single job: for example, an accounts package, which is designed to keep the books and cannot be used for anything else. To use this kind of software you just type in your information. All the setting up has already been done for you. The second is the general-purpose package, which gives you a framework in which to work. These have to be tailored to your needs before you can use them. In this group are all the large business software packages. A spreadsheet can be used not only for accounts but for tax, financial projections, balance sheets, and mortgage and loan calculations as well. Before you attempt any of these tasks, however, you have to create a template for each one. This kind of software gives you two jobs instead of one – first you create a framework for the information, and then you add the information itself – but it has the advantage that you can organise information to suit specific needs. However, setting up the software will take extra time.

The type of software you choose will depend on the kind of work you want to do. If you want a specific job done or if you are worried about the amount of time it will take you to master a computer, then a tailor-made package is a good choice. This will give you a return much more quickly and will be easier to use and set up in the short term.

If you would like to explore what a computer can do for you in a more general way and would prefer a more flexible approach, then one of the larger business packages such as Microsoft's Office Professional may suit your needs better. Some of these are very powerful indeed, and there is often some overlap between the applications they include. For example, you could work out quarterly sales figures by geographical region using either a spreadsheet or a database. Neither is 'right' for the job; you will simply approach the problem in two different ways, depending on which you use.

If you decide on the second type you will have the added advantage of integration. Large business packages are often designed to work with each other, so you will have the ability to move information from a database to a spreadsheet, and perhaps create some charts which could then be 'pasted' into a word processor for a business report.

Is a computer essential?

Every year the computer industry spends millions of pounds in an attempt to persuade you to buy its products. For all this, you may find you do not need a computer at all.

CASE HISTORY: Jill

Jill Taylor runs a small newsagent's shop. She considered getting a computer to help manage the accounts and organise paper deliveries, but decided against it.

'We don't make a fortune, so we didn't have much to spend. We made a few enquiries and looked at a few computers, but in the end decided it just wasn't worth it. My husband has been doing the books for years, and he is quite happy with the way things are. He might get them done more quickly with a computer, but he says he enjoys the work. And he double-checks everything, so mistakes aren't a worry.

'As for the paper round, that takes half an hour a day to sort out. I have to write all the addresses on the papers by hand anyway, and it wouldn't be a lot quicker to use printed sticky labels. Keeping track of the payments is a bit of a chore, but I've been managing the job for a long time now and I'm used to it.

'Once we thought about it, it was obvious that we could get by without a computer. We'd have to spend over £500 to get something that was up to the job, and there seemed better things to spend the money on. In the end we just decided to leave it – and I can't honestly say I've regretted that.'

It is tempting to buy a computer 'just because'. If you look at your needs closely, however, you may decide that you do not need one at all. If you have less than £500 to spend and intend to use your computer mainly for writing letters, then it may be better to look at some of the all-in-one word processors currently available. These cost between £200 and £400, and offer you many of the features of a computer-based system. They have the advantage of being easier to use, easier to move from one place to another and easier to learn.

If you want to dabble in the basics of computing, but are not concerned about doing any serious work or keeping up with the very latest developments, then consider a second-hand machine. These are adequate for light-duty work, will introduce you to all the basic concepts and can cost as little as £100. They will not be able to work with the latest software and hardware, so you should assume that you are buying a closed system. In other words, what you buy is what you get. Extras are not an option. For someone on a strict budget a second-hand machine can prove an excellent, low-risk introductory buy.

If you are planning to use your computer for more business-oriented tasks, you can expect to pay £500 for a basic modern machine to over £10,000 for a no-expense-spared system. In general, you get the best compromise between cost and performance at around £1,000 to £1,500, for a complete system including printer and software. This will give you a modern machine that you can expand as your funds grow and will have a life of two to three years. (At the end of that period it will still be useful, but you will need to reassess your needs in light of technological advances.)

When it comes to looking at the individual facets of your business, the best approach to computerisation is to ask yourself how much time you spend on certain activities and how organised you are already. If you are perfectly happy keeping addresses and phone numbers in a card file, then you should think long and hard before buying an electronic system to replace them. In general, activities that you perform occasionally are best done by hand. Activities that are time-consuming, repetitive and a chore are best done by computer, but if you have a system that works for you now without a computer, there is no good reason why you should feel any need to buy one.

As a rough guide, you can start by working out how much time you waste over the course of a year on tasks that add nothing to the value of your business. Next, calculate how much this time is worth at a suitable hourly rate. Estimate how much time these activities will take if you get a computer to help you. For some kinds of work – VAT, payroll calculations and so on – this should be relatively straightforward. You can guesstimate how long it would take to type the relevant information into the computer, and then add a week or so as 'learning time'. Other kinds of work will be much harder to quantify, and you may need to arrange a demonstration at a reputable computer store before you can get an idea. Once done, you can work out the time and cost saving of installing a computer by comparing these two figures.

This is only useful as a rough guide; the installation of a computer sometimes results in improved productivity and new business opportunities which are not always foreseeable. Sometimes it doesn't. By doing this comparison, you will at least have some idea of whether you are buying on a whim or taking a calculated risk.

Now that you have an overview of what is possible, it is time to look at your options in more detail and examine more closely what you should look for when considering each one.

Chapter 2

Buying a computer – an overview

To get the most from a computer you need to remember that you are not just buying a collection of gadgets and widgets, but a complete system – something that is very much greater than the sum of its parts. Computer advertising often tries to lure novice users into spending more than they need by tempting them with vague promises of speed and power. In practice, these factors can have surprisingly little to do with long-term usefulness and reliability. Buying the fastest computer in the world is a waste of time and money if you spend all your time struggling with it. Similarly, a computer that breaks down or leaves you baffled can be more of a liability than an asset.

To avoid this kind of difficulty, it is important to leave the glossy advertising to one side and look realistically at the different elements of a computer system.

Hardware describes the physical parts of the computer – keyboard, screen, main system unit and any other extras you decide to buy. Think of it as an extension to your office. Inside the computer's case you will find the equivalent of a filing cabinet for storing information and a desk-like area where you can choose from a selection of useful tools. The more you spend on hardware the more quickly these tools will do their work for you, and the more room there will be in your new 'office' for both tools and information. There are many different kinds of computer but the two most popular lines are the IBM-compatible PC (known as the PC) and the Apple Macintosh (known as the Mac).

Software describes the tools or programs which run on the hardware, and more often than not you will need to buy them separately. There are hundreds, perhaps even thousands, of different software products available today, all tailor-made to help you with specific kinds of work. For example, if you want to write letters or create text you need to buy word-processing software; to keep track of finances, you buy an accounting package.

Software, much more than hardware, determines how productive your computer will be. Good software is so easy to use that you forget that it is there. It is also easy to learn (**user-friendly**), which means you can start doing useful work with it very quickly. Bad software can be a hindrance, and will force you to work around it rather than work with it. It can also cause difficulties when you start to use it: for example, when your computer does something unexpected and you are left floundering and confused with no idea what to do next.

Choose your software first. This is one of the golden rules of computer-buying. Work out what you want to do, decide which software will work best, and then find the hardware to match.

The hardware and software are the most obvious parts of a computer system, but there are a number of other options you also need to consider.

Support means help with maintenance and problem-solving. If you rely on your computer on a daily basis you need to be sure that the support will be efficient and quick – being left without your computer for a week or a month can be disastrous.

The other kind of support is needed for those times when you are unable to work out what to do next. You may perhaps be using a word processor that claims you can print lettering in italics, but even though you have looked at the instruction manual you still can't see how to do this. At times like these it is a very good idea to have someone or something you can refer to – otherwise you can find yourself wasting a lot of time or using your software at a tiny fraction of its potential.

Training is closely related to support and provides you with the help you need to get started. There are numerous training resources available, some very affordable. Courses or personal tuition can prove expensive, so you may want to consider books, videos and computer-based training software. Magazines can also be a supplementary source of introductory hints and tips.

Insurance is vital to ensure that if something goes wrong, you have the financial resources to put it right. If your computer fails or is stolen you may be left without access to the information essential to the running of your business. In the short term such a loss can be crippling; in the long term it can be catastrophic. Fortunately, you can protect yourself from these kinds of risks. You can insure your system to protect the information as well as the system itself. You can also keep the information safe by making regular safety copies or backups.

Security becomes an issue when your information is confidential, or you are not the only person with access to it. There are also legal considerations to be aware of if you start to collect information about your customers or your employees (see Appendix XII). There are ways to protect information and ensure that it can be read only by selected users.

The other kind of security is much simpler and cruder – you need to protect your computer against theft. This is a growing problem, especially in large towns and cities. Again, there are basic steps you can take to make sure that your equipment is as unattractive to thieves as possible. This is discussed in Chapter 11.

Space Is there sufficient or a convenient space in your existing work area? Computers, like children, can be more demanding than anyone expects. If you find that your existing office is not adequate to cope with a large new arrival, you will need to budget for extra space or furniture to cope with it.

The buying process

Once you have decided what you need and looked at the options, you can start the buying process. Don't rush into it, however. There are good ways and bad ways to buy a computer. Briefly, you are likely to have the following options:

- hire a consultant
- buy a complete package from a dealer or by mail-order
- do the research and buying yourself
- buy a second-hand system
- ask a computer-literate friend or colleague to guide you through the process.

A consultant

Hiring a consultant is by far the easiest and the least time-consuming way to buy a computer. It should also – in theory, at least – give you the best results. Unfortunately, in the short term it is by far the most expensive approach.

Consultancy fees can vary from £25 to £250 an hour; the rate depends on the consultant's experience and the size of project. Computerising a sole trader's business is relatively straightforward. Computerising a medium-sized company which has offices in different parts of the country requires a much higher level of expertise.

A good consultant should be able to:

- talk to you in detail about your requirements
- analyse your needs
- let you know if your expectations are unrealistic and discuss alternatives
- choose the best and most cost-effective solution, and settle on a firm price
- install a fully tested and working system
- provide training and advice on how to use the system most effectively, or make recommendations on the best sources for training from outside
- be on call to provide support if anything goes wrong, or arrange for professional support from another source.

One of the best ways to find a consultant is by personal recommendation. Ask friends and colleagues. Remember, however, someone who works well with a friend may not be the right person to work with you.

If you need to start 'cold', you will find that some consultants advertise in the trade press and *Yellow Pages*. They may also run shops and small dealerships of their own. Your local dealer may know of a tried and trusted consultant.

Unfortunately, there is as yet no professional organisation which can guarantee a level of service. This means that when you are looking for a consultant you are largely on your own, and you need to apply the same instincts you would use when hiring any employee.

These are some points to consider:

Professionalism You need to feel confident that your consultant will keep appointments, be professional and be on call at any reasonable time. A few consultants are technically brilliant but can be abrasive with those less knowledgeable than themselves. Avoid them unless you specifically need the services of an unusually gifted specialist.

Some parts of the computer trade can be quite informal; if the consultant turns up to your first meeting dressed casually, do not assume that he or she is not professional. Don't allow first impressions to put you off – if your consultant is able, it will show in the references and attitude, not necessarily in the choice of clothes.

Honesty and directness There is a small chance that you will be your consultant's first client – which he or she should divulge in any initial interview. In this case it is advisable to be especially attentive to your consultant's previous work record. A good consultant will be happy to offer credentials.

It is prudent to discuss exactly what the terms of your working relationship will be and, if possible, draw up a full contract, so that if there are any problems you are covered legally, and both of you know exactly where you stand.

Previous work experience A good consultant will be happy to provide details of previous clients who can offer references. Asking for these will give you an idea of the consultant's capabilities and personality – both from the answers you get to your questions and the stories previous clients have to tell.

You should also ask about the consultant's areas of expertise. A specialist may not have the skills needed to take on more general work.

Communication skills A good consultant should be able to speak plain English without intimidating you or making you feel that you are working at cross-purposes. The consultant should demonstrate a clear grasp of your requirements. Be very wary of someone who tries to blind you with science or talks entirely in computer jargon.

The words 'feasibility study' should also be treated with suspicion. Putting together a computer system for a small business to handle accounts, payroll work, word processing and some desktop publishing does not require a feasibility study – although the computerising of a medium-sized country-wide business might. If in doubt, get a second opinion.

Although a consultant can be expensive – perhaps doubling the price of your computer system – the long-term benefits could justify the initial outlay. If your computer is vital to the efficient running of your business and you are unsure of your own technical abilities then a consultant can be a very cost-effective option.

Buying from a dealer

Buying from a dealer can be a risk. Computer dealers range from small shops run by enthusiasts to large multinational companies. They also vary widely in terms of quality of service, reliability, professionalism and support. The ideal is a friendly local dealer who has a strong interest in retaining your business, enjoys working in the trade and has plenty of experience to draw on.

Unfortunately, some dealers are less than scrupulous – it is no exaggeration to say that a handful are little more than used-car salesmen who, aware of the potential of a new market, have been quick to take advantage of it. If you fall foul of one of these you can find yourself being deliberately misled by someone who wants to off-load obsolete stock at an inflated price and has no interest in your needs or long-term custom.

To ascertain whether you are dealing with a saint or a shark simply visit your local dealer in person, explain roughly what you are looking for and listen closely to the response. Vague sales pitches such as 'This is the very best', 'Everybody uses this one' or 'Really fast machines, these' should be treated with suspicion. Try applying the same criteria as you would when assessing a consultant. Does there seem to be a genuine understanding of what your needs are? Is there a wide range of options to choose from, or are you being steered towards stock that is piled high in the shop front? Does the shop assistant demonstrate knowledge of the subject and a professional attitude? If you feel confident about the level of aptitude and service, then you have probably found your source. You may pay more in the beginning this way, but you may also find yourself with a free source of help and advice – both of which can be invaluable for inexperienced users.

If you are unable to find a good local dealer, you have the option of buying by mail-order from computer magazines. Take the same approach again – telephone the computer company, talk to the sales department, explain what you want, ask a few awkward questions and note down the replies. The tone, precision and usefulness of the responses will tell you a lot about the way that particular dealer does business. You cannot realistically expect the same level of service from a mail-order dealer – especially a large one – as you would from a small local shop.

It is tacitly acknowledged in the industry that the high-street consumer electronics stores are likely to offer you the worst of both worlds. Prices are often significantly higher than elsewhere, and the level of support and help that the staff can offer tends to be minimal. At best you may be steered towards big-name products that happen to be in stock at the time. At worst you may find that you know more about the computers than the staff on the other side of the counter. Some high-street retailers offer telephone support – at a price. If you want help – and you will need it if you are new to computers – you will probably be asked to pay for it by the minute on an 0891 number. This can be stressful and expensive, and you have no guarantee that your problem will be solved.

High-street stores often charge a much higher annual percentage rate (APR) than a bank or other credit source might. As a result, you can find yourself spending the kind of sums that might have bought you the services of a consultant, yet you could still be left with something that you cannot use properly, which does not quite do the job you want, and which you do not understand.

In 1998 the Tesco supermarket chain started selling PCs in its stores, and it's possible that other chains may follow suit in the next few years. Sold this way, PCs become something of an impulse purchase, and, realistically, this is often the worst possible way for beginners to buy. A more effective approach is to evaluate these 'deals' in the same way as all the other computer-buying options – with the difference that checking on after-sales service and support becomes even more important than usual.

Do it yourself

Doing the background research and buying a computer yourself is the most time-consuming option and the most demanding in terms of your personal resources. Buying a computer 'blind' with no research at all is very unlikely to get you a good deal. In fact, it may not even get you something you can use effectively.

If you have the time, it can be worth learning the basics of the subject from the hundreds of books, magazines and courses that are available. This can be a good investment, as dealers tend to respect knowledgeable customers more than complete novices. The difficulty is that not everyone has the time, inclination, interest or mental aptitude needed to master the field.

This approach can only be recommended if you are not in a hurry, if your computer is not going to be central to the running of your business and if you feel you have the abilities to take on the subject in depth. The rewards can be high, however. You will be able to save on hardware costs, because you will know how and what to buy and at a much lower price. You will also be less dependent on outside help. Just like someone who knows how to repair his or her own car, you can enjoy the benefits of cost-saving and independence. The disadvantage is that it takes time to learn all you need to know to reach this standard.

Buying second-hand

At first sight, the second-hand approach may seem appealing for several reasons. You will be buying a tried-and-tested system which someone else has already been using. In theory all the teething troubles should have been sorted out, and you will be able to work with something that does the job straight away.

However, there are a few caveats. It is important to remember that computer equipment depreciates quickly. This means that second-hand 'bargains' are rarely what they appear, and, in many cases, you will be able to buy a new, much better system for the same price as a second-hand one.

Another problem is that for legal reasons software cannot usually be sold to a third party, even when it has been paid for in full by the original owner. This means you will not be eligible for any help the manufacturer may offer to users, and you will not be able to take advantage of any improved versions (**upgrades**) of the software that the manufacturer decides to release, unless you buy them at the full price.

Finally, you cannot be sure that someone else's system matches your needs. Another person's set-up may be perfect for him or her, but it may not be right for you.

Second-hand computer equipment does have its uses, though. If you are working to a very tight budget – a few hundred pounds, perhaps – then you will have to buy second-hand. In this part of the market the equipment has depreciated as much as it is going to, making it less of a long-term risk, but there are still pitfalls to watch for. The most worrying is that spare parts and consumables may no longer be available. Before buying, check that you can still get these for the second-hand machine. For example, some models of the Amstrad word processor family of small computers used a special kind of plastic diskette to store information. These are no longer widely available. If you can find a source locally or perhaps buy up a large stock from somewhere else, you will find that these machines offer good value for simple word-processing and accounting tasks. Without a source of these consumables, however, they are only slightly more useful than a doorstop.

With a little help from your friends

In theory this is the best and cheapest way to get help. In practice, you should make absolutely sure that your friends and colleagues fully understand your computer requirements and have set up a similar system for themselves before you act on their advice. Unless you have a friend who is prepared to help you put a system together from start to finish, you should treat the advice of friends and colleagues as a source of useful, but not definitive, information.

New is not always best

Innovation is a permanent feature of the computer industry. If you are doing your own research and making your own purchasing decisions you may encounter **advance product announcements**. The product may look worth waiting for but as a rule of thumb it is best not to wait. *Be wary of any major innovation.* If a product has been on sale for less than a year, there is still a chance that there may be something wrong with it. Many new products simply are not reliable. This may sound incredible, but time and again this has proved to be the case. Manufacturers of both hardware and software are under great pressure to keep ahead of their competitors, and products are often released before they have been fully tested in the field. If your computer needs are conservative, and you need reliability far more than the very latest, fastest and best of everything, then it is prudent to avoid becoming a manufacturer's guinea-pig.

If you do need the very latest and best – and particularly if you are likely to lose work to your competitors without it – then you may need to take the risk. This can put you in a more vulnerable position than someone who is buying established technology. To minimise your risk, hold out as long as you can and watch for any problem reports in computer magazines.

Another reason to avoid waiting for new products is because sometimes they simply fail to appear: this phenomenon is known as **vapourware**.

A typical piece of vapourware is announced; it misses its first release date, its second, and perhaps even its third and fourth. A year or more may have passed since the first announcement. Sometimes vapourware does eventually appear as a genuine product, but not invariably. There is no way of knowing in advance how it will turn out.

Computer manufacturers have been known to use colourful and creative tactics to put the competition at a disadvantage. Advance product announcements are among these. Manufacturer A is about to release an impressive new product. Manufacturer B, whose sales will be hurt by this, hears about the new product and immediately announces to the world that brand-new B product is better and will be available very soon. Some buyers wait for product B. The release date comes and goes. Manufacturer B announces that there are a few problems. However, not only are these being sorted out, but the extra time is being used to incorporate some exciting new features. The second release date passes. Buyers are now confused – should they buy product A, which is known to work and is available now, or product B which sounds much more impressive but is not yet available?

A product that you can use now is worth more to you than one that is not yet available – no matter what claims are being made for it. As a small business or home user your needs are modest and you can safely ignore the scheming, plotting and salesmanship. If in doubt, get something that is known to work. If it does what you want, and you are confident you will be comfortable using it, then buy it. If something better comes out later you can always change it – if you still need to.

Free PCs?

In the US it is now possible to receive a PC for nothing. In return for their computer, users agree to connect the PC to the Internet and view advertising. There are no similar schemes available in the UK at the time of writing – possibly because Internet access phone charges are not free here, as they are in the US – but as this changes it is possible that similar deals may be offered. Receiving a free PC is clearly rather different to buying one, and the usual strictures about careful buying can be relaxed.

Equally clearly, the system may not suit everyone, and questions still need to be asked about the long term. What happens if a PC breaks down, for example? At the very least anyone who takes advantage of such a deal should be sure to keep safety copies of any important information away from their PC, just in case they decide the advertising wastes too much of their time and attention and want to transfer to a paid-for machine at a later date. Business users who return a machine may also want to make sure that any sensitive information it contains is deleted beforehand. In any case, anyone signing up for a free PC deal should read the small print of any contract carefully, to be sure exactly what it is that they are required to provide in return, and also what happens if their PC breaks down.

GREAT EXPECTATIONS?

However you buy your computer, assume that you will not be able to work with it straight away. The software and the hardware both require a learning curve – a period of time which you will need to familiarise yourself with the system.

It is a good idea to start with simpler software, such as a word processor, to gain basic experience and confidence before moving on to more complicated packages.

Chapter 3

Presentation, DTP and graphics

The quality and visual appeal of your stationery can tell those with whom you correspond a lot about your business. With a computer it is possible to produce print-shop-quality results at a fraction of the price. The production of letters, diagrams and leaflets can be streamlined so that they can be created to order much more quickly. What follows is an introduction to the possibilities offered by computer-based word processing, desktop publishing and presentation software.

Basic word processing

Why use a word processor when a typewriter will do? If you have been using a typewriter for many years without problems, why pay the extra for a word-processing system? For some kinds of work a typewriter is still perfectly adequate: a cheap, reliable way to produce high-quality letters. For something more versatile, however, it is worth considering a computer-based word-processing system.

. The chief advantage of electronic systems is that you can correct mistakes before you print them. You can make as many changes as you like in the document before the print touches the paper. Paragraphs are managed automatically. If you delete a word in a sentence the remaining words move to fill in the gap.

Word processing also gives a range of broader editing options. Words, sentences and paragraphs can be moved around. Text can be copied from one document to another. Footnotes and headers can be added and pages can be numbered automatically. You can also keep electronic copies of your work, so that letters can be stored inside the computer or on floppy disks and re-used later with minor changes. It is also possible to build up a library of blank letter headings addressed to different clients which will save typing in their details every time.

A very useful word-processor feature which has been available for some time is the **mail merge facility**. Mail merge works by taking a standard letter with carefully ordered blanks, and then filling in the details from a separate list. It can also be used to print envelopes. It is possible to include simple individual details which can make a letter look more personal.

Layout

At the next level of sophistication a word processor gives you detailed control over the visual appearance and layout of the text. Lettering has always been available in different styles (called **fonts**) and sizes (measured in **points**). Most word processors are supplied with a selection of basic fonts. Extra fonts are available as libraries, almost always at additional cost. The main text of this book is typeset using a font called Bembo with letters that are 10½ points in size. Other examples of fonts and point sizes include:

This is 9 point Times

This is 12 point Arial

This is 14 point Zaph Chancery

This is 16 point Garamond

Fonts can add extra impact to a piece of work when used with restraint and discretion. For letter-writing it is more practical to use one font, although you may want to add a letterhead in a different style to make the letter more eye-catching. The addition of font styles, such as **bold** or *italic* can emphasise points in the text and make headings distinctive. Underlined, superscript, and subscript lettering can also be used.

For example, a standard letter could be improved by using different lettering styles and sizes: the name and address of both the sender and the recipient could be in bold text, and the name of the signatory could be underlined. All of these details could be stored in the computer with the text of the standard letter.

Professional word-processing software includes a set of style sheets for applications such as memos, faxes, business letters and presentations. These contain no text, only the information needed to lay out the different areas of text on the page. They are easy to use and excellent results are possible.

Spelling and grammar checkers

Spell check is a facility on most word processors. It scans a document and queries unusual words. Most have a dictionary option so that you can add words of your own. Spell checkers are invaluable but not infallible. They have no way of noting common mistakes, such as misspelling 'their' or 'there' for 'they're', where the words are spelled correctly but the proper use depends on context.

It is important that you get a checker with an English dictionary. Early examples used American spellings ('color' for 'colour', and so on), and these proved more of a hindrance than a help for UK users. Most professional packages on sale in the UK now include UK spellings, but if you buy a cheaper package it is a good idea to check this.

Many word processors also include a **thesaurus**. This works like the paper equivalent, except that it can benefit from the computer's speed and suggest alternatives more quickly. Computer-based spell checkers and thesauri are limited in the number of words they have in their vocabularies; most contain as many words as a small dictionary. A computer version of the *Oxford English Dictionary* is available – but it is expensive, and the current version does not integrate seamlessly with any of the popular professional word-processing packages.

Grammar checkers are more subtle and often less useful tools. A grammar checker scans a piece of text for grammatical errors, such as split infinitives and dangling participles. It gauges the impenetrability of the prose according to a variety of measures, one of which is estimated reading age. Grammar checkers are entertaining to play with and can offer some advice on how to improve writing style. However, the subtleties of the English language are still beyond the grasp of even the most powerful computer, and many of the suggested 'improvements' will be irrelevant, misleading or hilarious.

Outline managers and other text tools

Professional word processors also offer options which make the management of text much easier: for example, they can literally count the number of words in a document. Other information, such as the document creation date, is also likely to be available.

Outline managers can transform a list of notes into a neatly laid out outline that can form the skeleton of a writing project. The word processor can also prepare a contents list or an index, maintain a list of revisions, or keep track of a table of authorities for listing references in a legal or other professional context.

Macros

Most professional word processors include a **macro** facility. This provides an easy way to automate regularly repeated actions. A macro is a recorded set of actions that can be 'played' manually or automatically when you start using the word processor. If, for example, you want the last two documents you were working on to reappear on screen when you start up your word processor, you can create a macro that loads and displays them for you.

Macros can be as basic or as complicated as you care to make them. Most word processors are supplied with a range of macros that add extra features to the package. For example, the Lotus Word Pro word processor comes with around 200 macros that can be used for cross-referencing text, clearing the screen, finding old documents and so on.

CASE HISTORY: William

William Henley, who writes for a national magazine, recalls his first encounter with a powerful word processor.

'As a writer all I have to worry about is the text, and it's the production editor who looks after the layouts and the graphics. But even basic editing has been made a million times easier with a word processor; it's really useful to be able to go back and rewrite and add to work after it's been typed in.

'The magazine has contributors who supply their work on disks over the Internet, or (less often now) on floppy disks. One problem is the number of different formats, so the production department asks for plain uncoded text – known as ASCII [American Standard Code for Information Interchange] – which is the lowest common denominator and doesn't include extras like italics, but will work on any system. Even then there are compatibility problems. Sometimes there are strange characters at the start of each paragraph and so on.

'To sort this out I use a macro that goes through a document and deletes everything that isn't standard. I used to do this by hand, and it could take minutes to go through a piece and delete the stuff that wasn't wanted. Now it takes a few seconds. I have other macros which help with basic layouts, so I can produce copy that doesn't need much fiddling around with when it's laid out. And the word-count tool is a godsend. We have to write to length, and it makes that a whole lot easier.'

Desktop publishing

Whereas word processing is text–oriented and ideal for letters, memos and faxes, **desktop publishing (DTP)** is used whenever text and graphics have to be laid out on a page. Typical uses include newsletters, price lists, advertising flyers and posters.

DTP continues where top-end word processors leave off, by adding features such as the ability to split text between columns and pages, to make it flow around complicated shapes, to print it upside down, sideways, at an angle or along a curved line, and to include photographs and other images on the page. Font handling is much more sophisticated, making it easy to produce banner headlines, paragraph headings and quote boxes. Lines, ovals, boxes and frames can be added to draw attention to areas of text, and textures and borders can be created to make a document look more ornate. Unlike word-processing software, which is almost exclusively used to print black letters on white paper, all but the very cheapest DTP software can work with colour, although you will need access to a colour printer to print out the results.

Even a budget DTP package is capable of far more striking results than a word processor. The two are often used together, with the latter providing basic text–editing features and the former more sophisticated page layout facilities. Most DTP software includes filters which can import text directly from a range of popular word-processing packages. This ensures that special effects such as italics are maintained.

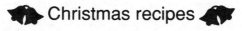 Christmas recipes

Three delicious and labour-saving ideas to rest the cook and cheer the company, all based on Rutherglen Liqueur Muscat from Victoria, Australia

We once christened liqueur Muscat 'sticky toffee pudding in a glass': pour it out and savour the complex Muscat aroma, the richly concentrated flavours (prunes, walnuts, vanilla, treacle), the refreshing tang and irresistible sweetness. The wines are fortified, aged in wood and blended on the solera system, imbuing them with enough character to make a dessert on their own – and also to stand up to Christmas pud, and even chocolate. (They're no slouch with Stilton, either.)

Plum pudding ice-cream makes a change from the traditional pud, while remaining close to it in spirit. To softened vanilla ice-cream add any (or all) of crumbled macaroons, mincemeat, glacéd fruits, candied peel and pistachio nuts. Stir in a spoonful or two of liqueur Muscat, with an optional extra spoonful of brandy. As a flamboyant gesture, freeze it in a bowl which will turn out a good hemispherical shape, and garnish with real cranberries or artificial holly.

Soak sultanas overnight in a glass of liqueur Muscat and fold them into vanilla ice-cream an hour or two before serving. To gild the lily, use coffee ice-cream.

At a recent tasting of Rutherglen Liqueur Muscats, we particularly enjoyed **Chambers** (*Selfridges £8.75; Wizard £8.99; The Australian Wine Centre £9.49; Tastevin £9.50; La Réserve £9.95; La Vigneronne £10.50*); and **Stanton & Killeen** (*Majestic Wine Warehouses £8.99*; Selfridges £9.25; The Australian Wine Centre* and *Thos Peatling £9.99; Tastevin* and *La Vigneronne £10.50; Fortnum and Mason £10.75*). During December, the shippers (Walter S Siegel) are giving retailers a free bottle with every case of wine so that their customers can taste the lovely sticky stuff before buying. Look out for the special label.

Champagne

The Hungerford Wine Company is meeting the problem of rising champagne prices (see page 3) head on. Managing director Nick Davies enlisted the help of Tom Stevenson and other experts to taste 186 champagnes, from which they have selected 41 for 'The Amazing Champagne Offer', valid till Christmas or as long as stocks last. They guarantee that if you find one of the identical wines cheaper elsewhere, they will match the price or cancel your order.

We were amongst the lucky few invited to taste the magic 41, with the Davies and Stevenson verdicts on hand for comparison. In the **non-vintage category**, they rated Ruinart Brut (*£18.50*) best and best value. Our top marks went jointly to Philipponnat Royal Reserve Brut (*£15.99*) and Louis Roederer Brut Premier (*£18.95*). Amongst the **rosés**, we agreed with the house vote for Dom Ruinart Rosé 1981 (*£36.50*) in top place, with Laurent Perrier Rosé Alexandra 1982 (*£63*) close behind – both wonderfully fresh. Hungerford suggest as best value Heidsieck Monopole Rosé 1985 (*£18.99*)

In the **vintage** category (a dozen wines), we again voted with the house for Krug 1982

13

This text from *Which? Wine Monthly* was created and edited using a word-processing package called WordPerfect 5.1 and laid out using DTP software called PageMaker

Graphics can be imported in a similar way. These can be clip art (see below) or graphs or tables that have been created using other software.

Two examples of clip art.

Clip art is a selection of basic cartoons, images, drawings and sketches that is often supplied with a DTP package. As with fonts, extra images are available at additional cost. Note that clip art collections with hundreds of thousands, or even more than a million images are now widely available. While this may seem impressive, consider that it may take you hours or even days to search through a collection like this. When looking at these collections, it is worth checking whether or not they have any kind of search facility to make it easier to find a specific type of image.

Remember that installing a very large number of fonts in a computer can slow it down significantly especially when it it started up. Even commercial designers tend to limit the number of fonts they work with – perhaps 200 – rather than keeping thousands of different fonts available simultaneously.

CASE HISTORY: Jessica

Jessica Macbeth is a teacher and personal skills trainer who also works as a writer. She uses her DTP system to produce limited editions of books which she sells at her classes.

'I use a laptop computer with Adobe PageMaker DTP software to work on my books. I also have a scanner and a cheapish bubble-jet printer. You can get books of clip art with all kinds of different images, and I scan these in and use them to add spice to my work. For the page layouts, I have about 50 different fonts installed, although I tend to use the same handful again and again. They have a huge effect on the look of a page.

'The results I get when I print them out are good enough to take to a printer. He scans in the pages and prints them out using a professional printing press. I supply the artwork double-sized, and he reduces it. This reduction takes away some of the rougher edges. For my next project I've found a printer who can take my disk directly.

'It's a lot of fun and very satisfying too. Anyone who has basic layout skills can do it. This is what DTP was supposed to be about, before it was hijacked by the corporate world. It doesn't have to be used for business reports; people can have fun with it too.'

Hypertext and multimedia

Today, most documents are produced on paper. However, for some users words and graphics are not enough. Many top-end word processors now include a facility which allows sound and video clips to be added, though they can only be viewed on another suitably equipped computer. These multimedia documents are an indication of how information will be exchanged in the future, when words, sounds, pictures, video clips and other information will be integrated seamlessly.

Multimedia documents lend themselves to the creation of **hypertext**, which does not follow the traditional linear format of the printed page. A typical hypertext document includes areas of the screen that respond to the user's enquiries. Some words may be highlighted: when selected, further information on the topic in question is revealed. These 'hidden' pages may contain links of their own, and so on. The result is an 'intelligent' document that can be browsed through, following words and ideas that take your interest, rather than as a linear sequence of words that has to be read from start to finish.

One application of hypertext is the electronic CV (curriculum vitae), which has proved popular in creative fields such as advertising and design. As well as plain text, an electronic CV can include voice clips, photographs, examples of previous work and snatches of music. This lends itself to all kinds of intriguing creative possibilities.

A more mundane application of hypertext is the creation of computer-based help for computer-users, which has become the standard for new software. Users are presented with a list of basic options, from which they select the 'help' option. From here, they can explore different topics in more detail. Because these are linked to each other in an intelligent way, there will always be a list of relevant options available on screen at any point in the process.

Some companies in the United States now present their annual reports as a hypertext document which is distributed on CD and includes video clips of the directors and animations showing the financial results. The non-linear nature of hypertext makes it easy for investors to access the information they want.

A company called Adobe is also pioneering its Acrobat system, which is a computer-independent way of presenting electronic documents. The Acrobat reader software is available free, and allows users of any kind of computer to read documents prepared with the Acrobat system, which can contain text, graphics and other information. Acrobat is an indication of the likely direction of electronic publishing in the medium term.

Apple computer-users have had access to a hypertext product known as Hypercard since the late 1980s. IBM-compatible users have access to OLE (Object Linking and Embedding), which was developed by the Microsoft Corporation. Both of these products can handle the demands of a full hypertext system. OLE takes hypertext a stage further by including links between applications, as well as information. Because all the links are maintained automatically it is possible for different people to contribute to the same document. One person can be responsible for graphics, another for text and a third for sound. They can work independently, but whenever one person makes a change the document as a whole is updated.

Electronic publishing on the Internet

Because it is easy now for anyone to publish information on the Internet, a range of packages to help with this have become available. Many word processors include an Internet-ready option which can convert a page of text into HTML (HyperText Markup Language). Despite the fearsome name, this is simply the special code that is used to lay out pages of information on the Web. Word processors that create HTML are very easy to use – the user simply chooses a 'Save as HTML' option, and the word processor does the rest of the work. To make the information appear on the Internet, it is copied to a special computer called a server. Many Internet Service Providers (the companies that allow home users and small business users to use the Internet with a small computer) offer these servers, and will frequently allow access to them for free.

One drawback with this approach is that word processors are still best at word processing; even the best examples lack the more sophisticated tools (such as various Internet-specific page layout options, and options for animations or other special effects) that are needed to create a really professional-looking electronic document. So buyers also have the option of using a web-page editing package instead. These offer much cruder word-processing facilities, but are designed to make all the other tasks involved in creating pages for the Web much more straightforward. In the end they, too, create HTML, but users have much more control over the way their pages are laid out and are better able to manage the link-words that are a vital part of the Internet's HyperText facilities.

Dedicated enthusiasts can create web pages armed with just a simple text editor and a manual describing how HTML works. While a knowledge of HTML is often useful to fine-tune page layouts, this approach is not recommended for beginners. In fact, even experienced users are likely to find it heavy going.

Business presentations

Presentations have become an accepted part of the business scene over the last few years, whether to ask a bank for money, pitch for business or investment, or to pass on information within a company.

Computers can play a major role in the preparation of a presentation. Apart from word processing and DTP for the production of high-quality handouts and slides, there is a set of tools specially developed for presentations. These packages are geared to the creation of punchy images with banners, slogans and other details. Most of these can support graphs, charts, video-like animations (such as cuts and crossfades between pages), sound effects and video clips, as well as straight text.

Like word processors, most packages include templates which make it easy to build a complete presentation. They also contain libraries of backgrounds, foregrounds, clip art and other graphics which can be used to customise the presentation. A complete beginner can produce a professional presentation within a day or so; experienced users can do the same much more quickly.

You can make presentations directly from your computer. A useful, if expensive, option is the overhead projector screen. This plugs into the back of your computer and fits over a standard overhead projector base. The screen is translucent, and whatever appears on it is projected in the usual way. As a result, you can prepare a presentation on your computer, and then project it to your audience while controlling the presentation from your computer's keyboard. Remote control options are also available, allowing you to walk around the room and make your presentation at the same time.

Portable computers, discussed in Chapter 10 and Appendix VII, are often used for this purpose. These allow you to add full hypertext links to a document. With the addition of some speakers, or access to a small PA system, you can use your computer to create a full sound and video experience.

Pre-printed paper

Unless you work with hypertext, text and pictures are designed to be printed. To be able to do justice to the physical appearance of any work you produce you need to use the right kind of printer (see Appendix II). Even with a cheap printer there are things you can do to make your work more attractive.

CASE HISTORY: Isabel

Isabel Davis, who works for a firm of accountants, was given the job of producing an information pack for new clients. She considered using printed colour brochures designed on a DTP system, but discovered there was a cheaper way to create a similar effect.

'Someone sent us a catalogue of pre-printed papers, and I was very impressed. They come in a huge selection of colours and designs, and some even come with templates you can use with your existing software.

'I sent off for some samples and decided on a basic style, which is available for various formats – business cards, letterheads, presentation covers and so on. I used the DTP system we have to add some fancy lettering, and saved that as a letterhead. Now, whenever anyone prints a document, the heading appears at the top, fitted into a blank space on the special paper. It looks very eye-catching.

'People have started to look at us as a dynamic company that gets things done, so we've had quite a bit of extra business.'

Pre-printed paper is available from specialist outlets (see Addresses). At its simplest it can be used as a striking background for posters and other displays. Commercially produced paper that is designed specifically to be used in a business setting – folded flyers, letterheads, business cards and compliments slips – is not customised: areas are left blank so that details of individual businesses can be added. Some companies also supply templates which can be used with the most popular word processors. This makes it even easier to design high-quality output on-screen, before committing it to paper, and at a very low cost.

For some kinds of work, however, only the very highest quality is acceptable. Professional-quality colour printers are available for around £1,500. These will come down in price over the next few years, but at the moment are out of reach of all but businesses with a substantial colour printing requirement.

Print bureaux

Print bureaux can take text and graphics created on the computer and print them on commercial-scale machines. One possible application is the creation of slides for a business presentation. You design these at home or at the office and then give the information on disk to a print bureau. The bureau will turn this into pin-sharp slides which can be used in the normal way. Your local print shop may already offer this service. If not, you can find details in *Yellow Pages*.

Voice dictation systems

A recent development in the word-processor market is the voice dictation system. Instead of typing your words, you speak them into a microphone. You can make words appear on the screen, and to a limited extent you can also control your computer this way.

Current voice-based systems are moderately sophisticated. Prices have fallen dramatically, so that a 'continuous-speech' system that can recognise spoken English with no unnatural gaps costs between £50 and £200. Accuracy is variable. Most systems have to be 'trained' first – a time–consuming process that typically requires the reading of a set text. Vocabularies are usually large enough for general use. Systems that can work with more specialised professional vocabularies are usually only available to special order, though, and can be very much more expensive.

Perfect accuracy is still some way off. Current systems make regular mistakes, which need to be corrected afterwards, and punctuation still needs to be spelled out in full, rather than understood implicitly. But people who are used to dictating, or who find typing awkward, will still find that these systems can save time overall. Some also offer voice control of the computer as a whole, so that other software can be started, documents can be printed, and so on. Names to watch for include Dragon Dictation Systems and IBM's ViaVoice system.

PACKAGES TO WATCH FOR

The word-processing market is dominated by Microsoft Word, Lotus Word Pro and Corel's WordPerfect. Each of these packages offers a huge range of features and can be used for almost anything. Word Pro is only available for the PC. For Apple Mac users comparable packages are Mac Write Pro and Nisus. Personal preference will dictate your choice.

DTP is dominated at the budget end of the market by Microsoft's Publisher, which is powerful but extremely easy to use, and includes hints and sample page layouts to get you started. At the top end, the choice is between Quark XPress and Adobe PageMaker. PageMaker is the original DTP package, but Quark XPress is used by many magazine companies and publishing houses. Both include a full complement of professional features.

For presentations Lotus' Freelance is very quick and easy to use, even by a complete beginner, and includes a huge collection of backgrounds and page styles.

For electronic publishing on the World Wide Web, Microsoft's FrontPage, Adobe's PageMill and Corel's WebMaster are all popular choices.

Chapter 4

Keeping track of your money

Repetitive and tedious chores such as accounting, bookkeeping and VAT are perfect tasks for a computer. It will make the dull jobs easier, thus saving you time, and it can help you be more organised.

CASE HISTORY: Ray

Ray Thomas recently decided to computerise his business, a garage and used-car dealership, having found that keeping up with PAYE, tax, VAT, billing and other financial matters was getting beyond him.

'We were just coming out of the recession. We'd survived pretty well and I'd kept all my mechanics. Business was picking up again, but I was spending more time on paperwork than I wanted. I used to employ someone to come in and do the books and sort out everyone's pay at the end of the month. But he retired, and getting anyone else in would have been costly. I started to wonder whether a computer might help me out.'

Ray was able to get help by asking his local TEC [Training and Enterprise Council] for details of someone who could put a system together for him. They also suggested he went to the local college to get some basic training.

'I was worried about this, but it wasn't nearly as bad as I thought. It took a while to work out what was what, but by the end of the course I'd got the basics under my belt. The TEC also suggested some names of people who could help me out. We bought the kit from a local firm, and they've been really good about the problems we've had – but there haven't been many. Gary, one of the mechanics who knows a bit about computers, sorted out the software side of things with a bit of help from them. And now it works like a dream. The computer does everything my old accountant used to do. It looks after the VAT returns, works out all the PAYE deductions – and so on. It even prints the cheques. We use stationery that works with the software. When the tax codes change and allowances change, Gary just keys in the new ones. It takes a couple of hours, and we're set for another year.

'Gary suggested doing some leaflets on the computer. It hardly cost us anything because he used some software that came free with a magazine. And when we did a leaflet run locally it got us some new trade.

'All told I think the system cost about £2,000 to set up. Now that's a one-off payment, but we were paying the accountant more than that each year. I'm thinking of opening a car-hire business now, so we've started working out how the computer can help with that too.'

Buying financial software

There is no lack of suitable software for managing money, as the advertisements in computer magazines show. Many excellent packages are available at very reasonable prices, and unless you are running a very large business you should be able to pick up a system that does everything you need for £500 – much less if you are a sole trader.

Most **accounting packages** contain a minimum of purchase ledger support, sales ledger support with account tracking (so you can watch for late payments), cashbook calculations to look after petty cash and double-check bank statements, VAT tracking, balance sheets and profit-and-loss reports, and support for multiple bank accounts. An important feature is error correction – if you discover a mistake you should be able to correct it without having to retype every entry. Security may also be important, and some packages include password access. They may also offer the facility to design individual invoices, as well as support for different kinds of invoice (pro-forma, quotation and so on). One useful feature is the ability to set up discounts for individual clients.

As well as keeping track of employees, their hours and their payment schedules, **payroll software** should also cope with special circumstances such as one-off contracts, sick pay and maternity leave. It should be possible to set up regular payment schedules – weekly, monthly, four-weekly and annual – and rearrange these to deal with variable hours and payment rates. Good support for overtime calculations is essential. Some packages can deal with National Insurance (NI) payments for directors and the way in which company cars can affect NI and tax. You should also be able to produce a single report of PAYE details for the Inland Revenue and print this information directly on to the relevant forms.

Stock control software is more specialised. Features to look for include advance warnings of low stock, tracking of the total value of different items and a report of the total value of the stock as a whole. The software should be capable of optimising stock levels as well as keeping track of them; a range of simple analysis options and reports will help you with this. Useful extra features include the capacity to add additional information to the stock description of each item, so, for example, items which need to be sold together can be flagged as such at the counter, and a measure of the amount of warehouse space taken by different stocks.

Some packages are tailored to the needs of specific businesses. These are advertised in trade journals and offer a comprehensive all-in-one solution for the typical small business user. They tend to be more expensive than off-the-shelf products and can also be less flexible. On the other hand, they are written specifically for a certain market and incorporate terms and concepts with which that market is already familiar. Such packages do one kind of job very well indeed and require less setting up. In general, however, standard business packages can do the same kind of work for less money.

As with other products, it is useful to check for specific features when deciding which software to buy. With financial products watch out for the following:

Ease of use Software should not be hard to use. There is no need to follow the conventions of accountancy – such as double-entry bookkeeping – if you find these confusing and they do not fit your requirements.

Professional recommendations A product that is recommended by an official body, such as the Institute of Chartered Accountants, or the Inland Revenue and HM Customs & Excise, is more likely to be productive. The Inland Revenue will accept direct printouts from certain brands of software, and this will avoid the need for the further services of an accountant.

Printing facilities and stationery Some packages offer their own printed stationery, including cheques and invoice forms. Others support stationery from other sources, such as printed P35 annual returns. Since it is your computer's job to save you time, the more pre-printed stationery you can buy, the better. Otherwise you may be left with software that produces results on the screen, but leaves you to write out 200 cheques by hand at the end of the month. Check which stationery you can use, how much it costs and how easily you can get hold of it.

Features Most of the common accounts packages offer all the basics you need. However, if you run a medium-sized business that trades overseas and has many different bank accounts you will need to check for extras such as multi-currency support and cross-account calculation options. In general, it is advisable to make a checklist of tasks – for example, maternity leave for PAYE calculations – and ensure that your software supports all of these. Good software will also offer further options; for example, support for BACS (Bankers' Automated Clearing Service), which can pay money straight into a recipient's account (see below). Euro support is also an important option to consider.

When checking features, make sure you ask what kinds of reports are available. As well as a balance sheet and a profit-and-loss statement, you will also need to be able to track customer accounts, flag late payments and track creditor payments. As before, you should assess your needs carefully and make sure that the software can produce all the reports you need.

Support As with all software, you should check to see what kind of support the manufacturer or main distributor offers. Will you be able to telephone with queries if you get into difficulties?

Price Some sophisticated financial packages cost thousands of pounds. These are aimed at finance professionals and larger businesses and may not be ideal for the smaller trader. You should be able to get a very good package for much less than this.

Options Some packages integrate with other software from the same manufacturer and make it easy for you to share information between them. Some features – such as tax returns, invoice-tracking and financial analysis – are available as options. Make sure you get details of every product each manufacturer offers, so you can plan ahead for options. For example, you may not need to worry about VAT now, but if the business takes off you may be forced to start including this in your bookkeeping. It is always a good idea to plan ahead and get software that can cope with anything that might happen.

Updates Some financial software is available with an annual update option which contains the latest information on tax codes, allowances and other details. You can add this information yourself, but if your time is valuable check to see if your software includes these updates.

Personal finance

There are a number of financial packages aimed specifically at the home user. These include features such as:

- bank statement reconciliation
- mortgage and loan planning
- credit card reconciliation
- bill-minding
- budgeting
- calculating expenses by category
- simple investment management
- overall net worth calculations.

These packages are recommended if you like to keep a tight rein on your finances and oversee exactly how your money is being spent. They are also an efficient way to check for bank and credit card errors.

For sole traders with a modest turnover, a personal money manager can be an excellent alternative to a larger accounts package. It will handle all the information you need to keep track of your income and expenses. The latter can be itemised according to category, so you can keep track of your spending and produce a single printout at the end of the tax year with all your expenses shown in detail. Categories are user-defined, so you can go into as much or as little detail as you like, and you may be able to supply the printout as part of your tax return.

Sophisticated money managers allow the user to track late payments and list when creditors should be paid. Some can even handle VAT, usually on the accrual system, which means that VAT becomes due when an invoice is issued, not when payment is received.

If your business needs are modest, it is a very good idea to look at these personal finance packages first rather than the larger business accounts packages. Many of the former include business-ready features such as invoice-tracking and VAT calculations. They are easier to set up and use than their larger siblings, and are often less intimidating to work with – which means you are more likely to take the time to keep your finances up to date. They may well be cheaper too.

For domestic use, these packages can take quite a bit of your time. To keep an accurate record you have to make each transaction twice – once in the real world and once in your computer. Given that many people use standing orders, direct debits, automated credits, debit cards, credit cards, cheques and cash to move their money around you might find that the time you need to spend to maintain an accurate picture is not worth it. This is something that depends on personal preference – some people like to keep track of every last penny, while others have an instinct for how much it is safe to spend and when, and are not concerned about the details.

Perhaps the most useful features of a personal money manager are bill management, loan estimation and cheque-book reconciliation. With accurate financial records it is easy to work out which bills are due and how much they are likely to be. This can give you warning of cash flow hiccups. Cheque-book reconciliation checks the figures in case your bank has made a mistake. Loan estimation can help you work out interest payments in unusual situations not covered by loan agents' tables.

CASE HISTORY: Terry and Sarah

Terry and Sarah McGinnes use a money manager to help them plan their long-term spending.

'We've been using it to work out whether or not we can afford to go on holiday somewhere exotic this year. Terry has been promised a salary rise, and we've been looking to see how that affects how much we can spend. He won't get the rise until we get back, so we're planning to take out a long-term loan now, and to pay it back more quickly than we would normally. We can get the loan because we can afford the monthly payments now, but it will cost us less when we pay it off quickly.'

A relatively new development is the combination of computers, modems and banking systems. Many high-street banks now offer an electronic home banking service, which makes it easy to check balances, arrange instant, or near-instant transfers and even to pay bills from home. This can be done outside of opening hours, which can be useful for people who find it hard to get to a bank during the day because of work restrictions.

Tax planners

A useful extension to the idea of the domestic money manager is the tax planner. These packages are updated every year and include all the details you need to fill in your tax return. The results can be printed on ordinary plain paper. Some packages have Inland Revenue approval for this, which means you can send in the sheet with a covering letter and do not need to copy the numbers across to your tax return form.

Tax planners can be a good way to estimate your tax liability, but they cannot give you the same level of advice as a trained accountant can. If your tax affairs are straightforward they can make the task of filling in your return much simpler. For the self-employed, some of whom will need to check whether specific expenses are deductible, it can be worth spending the money on hiring an accountant.

Portfolio managers

The management of stocks and shares is a task that is tailor-made for a computer. Not only can it keep track of prices, earnings and dividends, but it can also analyse market trends and make 'buy' or 'sell' suggestions based on proven analysis techniques.

It is perhaps surprising that there are not many investment management software packages. Personal finance managers include simple options which can allow you to keep track of your net worth, based on current stock prices. However, none of these packages includes any of the powerful predictive tools that professional brokers use.

Shareware (a try-before-you-buy system discussed in Chapter 9) is a good way to try out a range of low-cost investment managers. One of the best is PFROI, which offers a complete set of investment tracking and management functions with features such as valuation versus investment plots and portfolio totals. PFROI is available from the larger shareware libraries, along with a good range of other titles.

The other major use of computer technology is in on-line share dealing. This uses the Internet as a way to evaluate the performance of shares and manage a portfolio. The attraction here is fast access to the latest prices. While it is still impossible to deal directly on the Stock Exchange, having the latest information at one's fingertips can make portfolio management much easier.

Apart from share-related information, a number of online brokerage services are available. These offer very reasonable rates of commission. Adventurous traders can even use the Internet to buy and sell on foreign exchanges, particularly Wall Street. Details of the various share-related services sometimes appear in the computer press.

Spreadsheets

A spreadsheet is a general-purpose calculation tool. It provides a grid of cells that you can fill with information: a number, a date, a word or a formula. Most cells contain a number but they can also contain a formula that works with the numbers – a total, an average, a percentage and so on. The formulas can be simple or complex. Many spreadsheets are used as adding machines, providing a total for a set of figures in a column and then a grand total for the row of subtotals across the bottom. The range of possibilities is huge, however, and covers everything from simple arithmetic to complicated financial calculations such as loan repayment schedules, pricing based on profit margins, and useful figures such as the internal rate of return. Some spreadsheets include formulas to help with statistical analysis and engineering, and can handle general mathematical problems such as matrix manipulations and equation-solving.

The biggest advantage of a spreadsheet is the ease with which it can recalculate results. If one entry is changed in a column, the total at the bottom changes. No matter how complex or convoluted the calculations, the spreadsheet will keep track of all the links between the numbers and formulas entered and work out the final result.

If you decide you need a spreadsheet, it is a good idea to look first at those included as part of an 'office suite'. These all-in-one packages include a spreadsheet, word processor, database and other optional extras, such as presentation software and perhaps a personal information manager or a contact manager. A suite-based spreadsheet gives you *integration* between these different programs, so that information can be exchanged between them all quickly and easily.

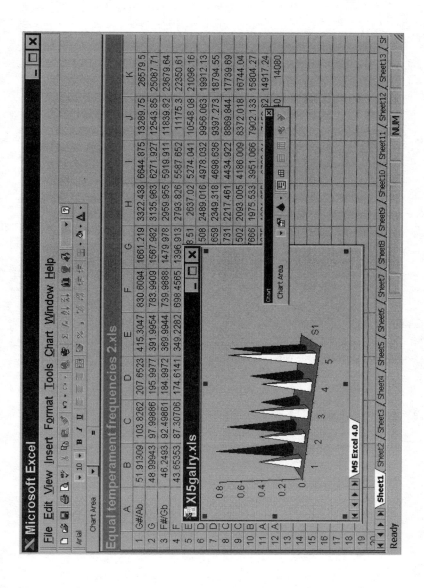

An example of a spreadsheet created using Microsoft Excel and illustrating some of the graph-drawing capabilities.

Many spreadsheets can present information graphically. Pie charts, bar charts, line graphs and maps are all common. So, for example, you could prepare the financial aspects of a business plan in a spreadsheet, and then transfer the graphs and tables over to a word processor or DTP package to present them professionally.

CASE HISTORY: Laurie

Laurie Leonard used a spreadsheet to help him create a business plan for his new business and was able to use some of the more advanced features to good effect.

'I started off knowing nothing about business plans and less about accountancy, but after reading a few books I started to get an idea of what my bank manager was going to ask me when I asked for the loan.

'The best thing about the spreadsheet I used was the way that many of the measures I had to calculate, like gearing and the internal rate of return, were already included as formulas. It was easy to estimate sales figures, guess interest rates, work out loan repayments and so on. I could also play with the numbers to see what would happen if interest rates suddenly went up.

'I did a printout of the results, and took along my portable computer as well. Because of the "what-if" features I was ready for the difficult questions, and I got the computer to recalculate the new figures on the spot. I think my bank manager was impressed that I'd done my homework – and even more impressed at the built-in safety margins I was offering – and I got the loan I needed.'

Your money on-line

Many banks are now offering on-line services. These are now advertised widely, and counter staff should be familiar with them. These services can be a useful way of keeping track of your money, especially out of normal business hours, and can also save you time by eliminating the need to make regular trips to your branch.

Each bank's system works the same way. You are given a special number for your modem to dial and software that manages the connection. Security is maintained with passwords, and in some cases you will also be given a secret personal identification number (PIN); if you are using a business-oriented system you may be given a 'smart card' (which is rather like a credit card), together with a reader through which you swipe the card. Business systems include usage logs, so you can check for unauthorised access attempts.

At their most basic these systems give you a chance to check your balance and look at a recent mini-statement on screen. Systems for home and light business use effectively offer you access from home or the office to the information available to counter staff at a branch. They are another way of arranging transfers, paying bills, and keeping track of balances.

Business users with more demanding banking requirements have a number of other options, although these only become cost-effective once more than 150 payments are made regularly every month. This makes them ideal for payrolls, although once in place they offer all the usual electronic banking advantages as well.

There are two fund-transfer schemes operating in the UK: BACS and CHAPS. BACS offers an on-line cheque payment service. Instead of writing out a cheque, the details are supplied to the bank in some other way, but the transaction is treated as a cheque and suffers from the same delays. Unlike a cheque, however, the money is not *debited* from your account until it is transferred. BACS is ideal for payroll use, and with an on-line BACS system you can completely automate payroll payments and make all those end-of-month salary cheques redundant with a single phone call.

Some banks offer a simpler, non-electronic version of BACS called BOBS (branch oriented BACS service), which works like a semi-automated standing order. You supply the bank with a list of people whom you pay regularly. Then, once a month, you supply a list of amounts to be paid to them. This can be presented as information on a floppy disk, as a computer printout or even as a handwritten slip. The bank then transfers the money according to your instructions. BOBS does not rely on modems and remote computer access, but it is slower and more cumbersome than purely electronic forms of transfer.

CHAPS (Clearing Houses' Automated Payment System) is a same-day version of BACS. CHAPS payment requests go directly to the inter-bank clearing network and are usually credited (and cleared) on the day the request is made. In effect, CHAPS offers an electronic banker's draft service.

Some on-line banking schemes also include options that allow payments to be made abroad. Most UK banks subscribe to the international SWIFT (Society for Worldwide International Financial Telecommunications) network. On-line payment requests can be routed through this network to move money out of the country. Some countries are not on the SWIFT network, and payments made to these will be transferred by telex message. You may also come across TAPS (Trans-continental Automated Payment Service) which is another international network.

Access to the CHAPS, SWIFT and TAPS networks is useful for larger businesses that regularly trade abroad, and for anyone who needs to make guaranteed payments quickly. Most smaller businesses will not need to use these features, but for those that do access to on-line payments can give a competitive edge.

On the whole, all banks offer a similar selection of services across a comparable fee-scale. But some add extras which can make a choice easier. Barclays, for example, includes options which give you details of current exchange and interest rates. Others, such as the HOBS (Home and Office Banking Service) scheme from the Bank of Scotland, give you access to a special high-interest deposit account. By storing surplus funds in this account overnight you can gain extra interest.

FINANCIAL PACKAGES TO WATCH FOR
For the small business TAS Books (Megatech Software), Quick Books (Intuit), Sage Instant Accounts (Sage), Money Manager (Connect Software) and Pegasus Solo Accounting (Pegasus) are all excellent accounts packages. Many of these can be combined with extra modules to add features such as full reporting, job costing and so on.

For domestic users the most popular packages are Money (Microsoft), Quicken (Intuit) and Moneybox (MoneyBox Software).

Popular tax planners include QuickTax (Intuit) and the Consumers' Association's own tax-planning software, TaxCalc, which is updated anually.

The most widely used spreadsheets include the immensely powerful Lotus 1-2-3 (Lotus) and Excel (Microsoft).

Chapter 5

Keeping track of information

Small business courses traditionally emphasise the importance of bookkeeping and cash flow. But keeping track of information can be just as important to a business as keeping track of money. By using and storing information effectively you can benefit your business. For example, if you are dealing with hundreds of people, you can use your information store as a memory jogger to add personal details to the conversation, or you can keep track of what each conversation was about, and use the computer to remind you when another call is due. Computers excel at this kind of work and offer a much more efficient way of organising information than pen- and paper-based methods.

Personal information managers (PIMs)

A Personal Information Manager is a computer-based version of the popular ring-bound paper organiser. A typical PIM will offer you:

- an address book
- an appointment diary
- a 'to-do' list
- a year planner
- a space for general notes, useful tables and other information.

The computer-based PIM makes it a lot easier to keep the information up to date. Maintaining a list of addresses requires no messy alterations. When someone's address changes, you simply type in the new one (if you're likely to need the old one later you can always keep a safety copy).

Another very useful option is an **auto-dialler** feature. If you have a modem (an electronic phone-line link discussed in more detail in

Appendix II), some PIMs will automatically dial a telephone number for you. Support for dial prefixes (such as 9, for an external call through a switchboard, or 132 to access the Cable & Wireless network) is also provided. Unfortunately, this support can be rather basic. You will be able to specify your local STD code, so that local numbers are dialled without it, but usually Cable & Wireless users will need to keep track of local codes (which do not require the 132 code) by hand.

Another useful feature is the telephone log. Most organisers maintain a list of calls made using the auto-dialler. This can be helpful in estimating a telephone bill or in charging someone by the hour. Incoming calls can also be logged in a similar way, although this is a slightly more clumsy process, as the logging has to be started by hand when the call comes in.

Many PIMs include an alarm feature. You can set up your computer so it gives an audible reminder of an appointment before it happens.

The latest PIMs are beginning to include network-related features. (Networks are covered in Chapter 6.) This means everyone's appointments can be linked together. Team members can schedule appointments with their colleagues automatically, or you can use the network to find a time when everyone is free for a meeting. Another popular use is task assignment – a group manager can assign jobs to team members. The team leader can leave the fine points of the work to the team members and concentrate on scheduling a project as a whole.

CASE HISTORY: Kenneth

Kenneth Hesket discovered PIMs five years ago and has never regretted it.

'I got my PC way back when, and someone told me about a program called Sidekick. I tried it out and loved it right away. For the first time I could keep all my information organised in the PC and get at it in any way I could think of. I no longer keep a pile of scrap paper for addresses next to the phone. Now it all goes into the PIM. I've got into the habit of using the "to-do" lists as a memory jogger and, all told, I get about half as much again done now as I used to. I don't spend time looking for things and I'm rarely late for appointments any more. It's one of the most useful productivity aids I've ever come across.'

Choosing a PIM

Some PIMs are simply electronic versions of paper organisers; others take a much more free-form approach and let you organise information as you wish. It is important to choose the PIM that suits your way of working.

Here is a list of features to look for.

Flexibility You should be able to design your own address book pages and specify what kind of information you want to include. You may, for example, want to allow space for home and business contact details for some clients, and perhaps electronic mail addresses as well. Some PIMs are inflexible, and the information must be entered in a set way. Others are more open-ended, and you can decide which details to include in the different sections. An extreme example of this is InfoCentral, which can store any kind of information and make any kind of connection between each item.

Connections between sections If you enter an anniversary or a birthday, it should appear in the diary section as well. Items put into a 'to-do' list should also appear on the diary pages.

Display options You should be able to switch between one day per page to at least one week per page.

Priorities You should be able to schedule tasks according to priority. Tasks that are overdue should be flagged in some way and carried over to the next day.

Specific dates As well as birthdays and other important dates, you should also be able to specify dates such as 'the third Wednesday in every month' or even just 'the 3rd of every month'. If the third happens to fall over a weekend then the PIM should warn you or move the date to the following Monday.

Alarms and tickles Alarms are to remind you of meetings. Tickles are reminders that a task is due for completion. You should be able to set the alarm to go off at a given time *before* an event.

Time logging Some PIMs include features to help you keep track of the time you have spent on different projects or talking to clients. Some of these can even produce a final billing record. Phone logs can be used to track both incoming and outgoing calls.

Search options PIMs tend to handle address information inflexibly. There is often not the option of setting up a company contact name and address and then listing other contact details, such as internal exchange numbers, for the people who work there. A search feature can work around this by giving a list of people who work for the company, even though their names and addresses may be scattered around your address book.

Security Some information in your PIM will be personal, some you may need to share with colleagues – and some may be changed by colleagues too, who may need to reschedule an appointment for you or add a task to your list. A PIM should include security features which control access to different areas. Most PIMs use a password system – one for you, one to grant *read only* access for colleagues and public access for those areas that are public and can be changed by anyone.

Communication features An auto-dialler is very useful if you have a modem. If you use email, then records of email address details will also be essential. Check also that the PIM can be organised to cope with multiple addresses.

Workgroup features These are most useful for sharing information within a team but redundant for those who work alone at home.

Speed and reliability The PIM should be able to get results quickly and reliably. It should have the capability to search for and present contact names quickly. Some PIMs may offer useful features, but if it takes minutes for the information to appear on screen you might as well be using a pen and paper.

Contact managers

PIMs tend to be calendar-oriented, with an address book section which is kept separate. Contact Managers (CMs) integrate these two

PIMS to watch for

Lotus Organiser (Lotus Corporation) has scored consistently high marks in usability studies. It is very similar to a paper organiser but includes some simple linking, so that, for example, an entry in the 'to-do' list can call up a relevant telephone number. One drawback with Organiser can be that it is very structured, although some users find this reassuring as they can start using it right away. Starfish Software's Sidekick and Symantec's ACT! are two other popular products.

Packrat (Action Computers) is a do-it-all PIM with more features than you could ever need. All information templates can be customised and there is full network support. Packrat also includes features which overlap with larger and more expensive project managers. It can even be integrated into other pieces of software, so that Packrat's options appear on screen when you are using your word processor or other software.

InfoCentral (Novell) is a different kind of PIM. Instead of the usual address book and calendar format, InfoCentral works more like an outliner. You can enter any kind of information and then build links between different items. This approach takes some getting used to, but users who make the effort to learn it are enthusiastic about what it can do for them.

kinds of information more closely. If you need to keep track of the letters, faxes or memos you have sent to different people a CM is a better choice. A good CM can produce reminders when you need to get in touch with someone again, and can also produce personalised letters and faxes from the information you store in it. This can save you the task of typing out the same letter hundreds of times with only minor changes.

CMs can be very useful in a larger company which uses a computer network. The CM allows each department to share the same information, but in a different way. For example, if a customer calls technical support and is put through to sales, his or her details can be transferred at the same time and every aspect of the call can be logged. An advanced CM includes features such as sales forecasting, support for price lists, instant profit calculations, and 'meeting generators' for use on networks (you specify a list of attendees and the CM compiles a list of times that they are all free).

When choosing a CM you should look for the following:

Fax support Fax communications should be integrated seamlessly.

Network support You should at least be able to schedule meetings with colleagues on the network. Support for email both inside and outside the company is another option.

History logging This is vital for a good CM. You should be able to log all your actions together with the responses they generate, and also be able to schedule reminders for yourself.

Document support and mail–merge These enable you to prepare standard letters, personalise them automatically and print them.

Query generation and reports You should be able to list information by company, by area and by any search criterion you choose. You should also be able to generate reports summarising your work.

Palmtop support Some CMs are designed to integrate well with palmtop computers. You can manage all your appointments on a big desktop computer, and then use the palmtop when out on the road. (For more information on palmtop computers and electronic organisers see Appendix VII.)

Databases

Databases are used to organise information in a user-defined way. They are powerful complex programs and can be used to extract summaries of information as well as keeping it together. Databases are completely open–ended, so you can organise your information in any way you like. You can also filter the information in different ways by presenting the database with a query. This produces a broad picture, known as a **report**, which conveniently summarises the facts and can help you spot trends, anomalies and other patterns. If, for example, you are maintaining a list of sales, you can create a report which totals the sales you have made to each customer. You could also total sales by geographical area, by specific towns, or even from all customers whose surnames begin with 'W'. It is this flexibility that makes databases so powerful and useful.

Basic databases allow you to keep track of any kind of information that can be represented as text or numbers such as client contact details, sales records and so on. More advanced databases can also handle graphics – including photographs – and other kinds of information. There are two kinds of database:

Flatfile databases store information in a single table, and are more or less the computer equivalent of a card index. The 'cards' can be very complicated, with hundreds of entries on each one, but each card uses the same template for the information.

Relational databases spread information across different tables, while maintaining links between them, so you do not need to copy information unnecessarily. To understand this better, imagine a series of orders, each of which includes a customer's name and address. A flatfile database would require you to type in the name and address *for every single order received from that customer*. With a relational database you can assign each customer a number or code instead. The customer's details are kept in one place, and the order details make a reference to them. If the customer moves, you only have to type in the new address once. This is obviously quicker and more likely to be accurate than retyping the same information every time.

An important feature to look for when choosing a database is *referential integrity*. This means the software ensures that you never enter information without all the details filled in (for example, you cannot create a purchase order without a set of customer details to go with it). Not all databases check for this, and without this feature you can experience problems as links between different kinds of information become confused.

Relational databases can be used for much more than maintaining names and addresses and keeping track of sales.

Database DIY

Unlike PIMs and CMs, databases need to be set up before you can use them. You have to decide what kind of information you want to keep

CASE HISTORY: Andrew

Andrew Kemble runs an advertising agency and uses a database to keep track of sales leads.

'We used to use a card index system and a set of diaries, and we had problems all the time. The system didn't work well if someone ran more than one company, but had one account with us. That kind of thing caused confusion. Organising follow-up calls was a pain too. If someone was off sick we couldn't always make sense of what they'd written in their diary.

'We got someone to install a database for all this. Now we can search for people by their personal details, company name, or any other way. It's a lot easier to keep track of what they've used us for in the past. We can include details of the kind of work they've had from us in the past and build up a picture of what they'll be interested in in the future.

'But it's the follow-up calls that have really paid for the system. Now we just use the computer to print out a list of all the calls that need to be made that day. And it was a godsend last Christmas – it printed all our envelopes for Christmas cards.'

and then create the templates (known as **forms**) needed to keep it. This can be a challenging task, especially for a beginner. Not only will you need to work through the software so that you understand what it does and how to use it, you will also need to think clearly about how to organise the information.

If your needs are fairly simple then form design will be obvious. Most database products include examples to help you, and you should be able to modify these.

Creating a more complex database, however – one which keeps track of sales, accounts and other information for a medium-sized company – is a job for a specialist programmer. Database design is one of the few instances where it will not be possible to buy something that is right for the job straight off the shelf.

Some databases include their own versions of a programming language, which is usually based on the popular BASIC (Beginners All-purpose Symbolic Instruction Code). This allows you to make detailed changes to information after it has been stored in the database.

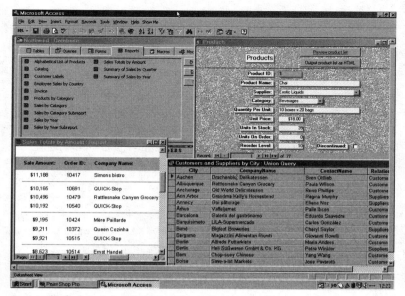

An example of a form design within a popular database

Database systems that work on a network of computers are proving popular with medium-sized businesses. They are sometimes integrated with a range of other networked options such as email, and perhaps even conversion systems which allow small personal computers to be connected easily with more powerful business-oriented machines.

An example of such a system is Microsoft's BackOffice. This creates a framework in which a company can manage and maintain large amounts of information and make it accessible to everyone in the company who needs it. BackOffice uses an advanced database management system called SQL (Structured Query Language), which has become a standardised way of getting information out of large databases.

The following example illustrates the power of the database as an information management tool. It also shows that experience, skill and a natural talent for organising information are essential to get the best from this tool.

Choosing a database

In the same way that a spreadsheet is often sold as part of an 'office suite', databases are usually integrated with other products from the

75

CASE HISTORY: Mary

Mary Hardwick is network manager for a telesales company.

'We now have hundreds of thousands of telephone numbers in our database. Originally I developed a system that would change over the numbers for Phoneday. But now that BT has taken to changing area codes on a more regular basis – and more changes are planned – my bosses decided it would be useful to extend that work to create a more general tool. Quite a few places are still using five-figure numbers, and these are gradually being updated to six-figure ones.

'We're still using the same database system, although it's a new version of the software. The system includes a simple programming language that can be used to alter any or all of the information we hold in an intelligent way. All I have to do is write a simple program that looks at the numbers and makes the modifications. So in the case of the original Phoneday it was easy to change all the 081 numbers to 0181 automatically. For the others we either get details from BT beforehand, or in some cases our reps tell us when an area code has changed. In either case it takes a few hours at most for all the information to be updated. It would take far longer if it had to be done by hand.

'In the near future it looks like we won't have to do this any more; BT will sell us their own number database. But as we started out targeting specific customers rather than selling to the general public, we've had to develop in this rather awkward way.'

same manufacturer. It is possible to create your own collection of business applications from different manufacturers. However, this is a much more expensive option and makes it much harder to exchange information effectively between the different applications. Unfortunately, it is highly unlikely that you will be able to get hold of a demonstration version of a database from the larger manufacturers. Some databases are available as shareware but in the main you will need to rely heavily on reviews in computer magazines. Features of a database to consider include:

Ease of use Watch out for reviews that emphasise usability, preferably with untrained or only slightly experienced users. Read their comments to get an idea of how well you might do when trying to use the software. Older databases are text-based, and these are harder to use. The latest examples allow you to design forms by moving boxes and other options around on the screen. These are much easier to use and usually produce better results too.

Flatfile or relational? The larger and more popular database packages are relational. You can use them as a flatfiler if you want to and explore the relational features later as you become more confident. You cannot work the other way, however. A flatfile system cannot be expanded to give you relational features. You will have more space and room for expansion with a relational database.

Form design options If you need to include photographs or graphics, ensure that the database can handle this. Some products include options to make forms look more appealing on screen, such as fonts and graphics which are purely decorative. Others take a much more workmanlike approach. If you need your forms to look good – and remember they can be printed, as well as appearing on screen – then check what kind of presentation control features you can use.

Speed Watch out for speed ratings (sometimes these are known as *benchmarks*). If you buy a slow database because it is easy to use, but need access to thousands of records, you may need to invest in hardware that is faster than average.

Hardware requirements Some databases are more demanding than others. Make sure that your computer has enough memory and disk space to be able to handle the database efficiently.

Help features Most modern software comes with help that you can access while working, so you will not need to refer to the manual once you have mastered the basics. But watch out also for templates and design hints to make your job easier, especially when you are just starting out.

Query features How easy is it to get information out of the database?

Do I need a database?

If all you need is a simple contact list then a PIM or a CM is a better – and cheaper – solution. However, if you need to do any of the following, a database will be more appropriate:

- include photographs and diagrams along with text and numbers
- create one-to-many links between information, and be able to list the details in different ways – for example, list all patients assigned to a certain doctor, or all patients taking medication bought from a certain company
- analyse information in many different ways – for example use sales figures to work out the most profitable product lines or geographical areas
- customise the way information is stored to suit your own special needs.

PACKAGES TO WATCH FOR

Microsoft's Access is currently the most popular and highly rated database product on the market. It includes cue cards which make it easy for you to design forms from scratch, even if you have minimal experience. Access is supplied as part of Microsoft's Office Professional Suite.

Lotus' Approach is another popular choice. This has also scored highly in usability ratings but has a reputation for being slow when asked to deal with large amounts of information.

Chapter 6

Exchanging information

If you are planning to use more than one computer, you should consider installing a **network** – a system that allows your computers to exchange information with each other and also to share printers and other facilities.

Networks

Networks come in three forms. The cheapest is known somewhat irreverently as 'sneakernet'. Sneakernet is not a true network. Information is transferred manually on floppy disks from one machine to another. This is time-consuming and disruptive and can result in more than one version of the same information. In an office where everyone is working on different parts of the same document, information needs to be carefully managed to prevent this. Despite its disadvantages, 'sneakernet' is still used in some offices, where work is rarely shared and someone takes responsibility for preventing multiple versions.

Sneakernet works best if all the machines are the same type. It is now possible to transfer information between PCs and Macs quite easily. This was not always the case and if you have older machines you may be faced with compatibility problems.

The printer-sharing problem can be overcome with a **printer switch** that connects one of a group of computers to one or more printers. It is a simple and cheap solution. More complicated versions are available which can be switched remotely from the computer itself.

For groups of between five and twenty computers, the best option is the **peer-to-peer network**. This connects all the machines to each other. No one machine is more important than the rest – hence the 'peer' title. Each computer has a special 'public' area for information, and any computer on the network can read or write data to this area. This makes it ideal for situations where work needs to be passed from place to place. Security is maintained because only the public areas are shared. Private work can only be accessed from each individual machine.

A peer-to-peer network allows extras, such as backup systems and printers, to be shared between a group of users. Its biggest drawback is the disruption that can occur when new software is added to the system. The software has to be installed on each machine which can prove very time-consuming.

For larger work groups a **file-server system** is more efficient. This is built around a single central computer which serves as a repository of all the information in the company. The information on the server can be accessed by each satellite computer, which may or may not have its own hard disk, depending on the kind of work it is expected to do.

Server systems are complex and need to be installed by experts. They also require formal office organisation. A designated network manager ensures that the system runs smoothly and efficiently and that sensitive information is not available to all users.

Peer-to-peer networks and file-server systems rely on **network cards** – plug-in circuit cards that can link computers together – which need to be connected with a suitable cabling system. The details vary from system to system but a common standard is **Ethernet**, a reliable high-speed connection that can be used to link together all the computers in a large building.

Any network that is used exclusively by a single business is now becoming known as an **intranet**. In theory an intranet offers business users the kind of facilities available on the Internet (see later in this chapter for more about the Internet), but with a scope that is limited to the business itself. In other words, electronic mail and other information are passed freely from computer to computer within the company irrespective of whether the computers are in the same building or in different countries, but the information is disconnected from the rest of the Internet for security. A true intranet is more efficient and secure than the Internet, but it is also more expensive to set up, especially for multinational companies. However, this new jargon word is now often used to describe any inter-office network, irrespective of the facilities it offers.

A recent development is the Virtual Private Network (VPN). This uses the simplicity and convenience of an Internet connection to link different offices, perhaps in different countries. Information is sent over the Internet in code, so that it can only be read by authorised recipients. While Internet connections are still expensive, they are very much cheaper than a completely private international network linking parts of the same organisation.

An even more advanced option is an all-in-one network that uses similar technology to provide internal and external telephone services. Many phone companies are now using Internet-like systems for their own networks, and this makes it easy and cheap for a large company to create a single integrated network which can handle computer information, telephone calls, voice mail, and fax messages. The details of these systems are outside the scope of this book, but they are mentioned here because by around 2005 the same technology is likely to start becoming available for domestic users.

Network software

To get the most from a network you need to use the best possible software. Some software options become possible only once a network has been installed.

The biggest practical benefit of a network is **email**. Messages are typed on one computer and appear almost instantaneously on the screen of another. Email is an excellent way to improve office efficiency and is beginning to replace paper memos as the standard way of passing information between computer-users.

CASE HISTORY: Howard

Howard Hawker works as a programmer for a small company that produces computer games, and he found that the email system was ideal for communicating with his colleagues.

'We use email for a variety of things – to schedule meetings, pass on company news and deal with queries. It's a lot more immediate than typing a memo, but not as intrusive as making a phone call. People can read their email when they feel like it, so it doesn't clamour for attention in the same way the phone does or interrupt concentration and work flow. It's helped our project to progress, and everyone seems to be getting a lot more done. Now I'm not sure I'd want to live without it.'

Networks are ideal for group management. Colleagues can contribute ideas and comment on projects without having to spend time in meetings. Some PIMs now include network-ready functions (see page 68).

A network is also an ideal tool for formal project management. (Chapter 8 includes a brief introduction to project management software and many of the available software packages include integrated network features.)

In a large company it is common for customer details to be stored in a single database that anyone can access. Customer correspondence, however, will usually still be scattered around different departments, and it can take a whole morning of telephoning around to track down one letter.

Lotus Notes, a document database system, was designed to solve this problem by maintaining a list of all the relevant documents used in a company no matter in which department, building or site they are. The system is fully network-ready, so that if, for example, a customer sends a fax, the fax itself – with accompanying notes, if necessary – is stored in the database. In multi-site audit work, for example, different teams can build up a complete audit picture by using the package to integrate their individual contributions.

Lotus Notes is not a replacement for a conventional database; it lacks some of the advanced features these offer. Its great strength is that it is not limited to text. Any kind of information, including spreadsheets, graphics, sounds, images, fax messages and voicemail messages can be maintained. Notes has proved successful and so far remains the only product of its kind.

Network hardware

Fax machines and answering machines are a common sight in small offices. Both of these can be replaced by their computerised versions, saving space and sometimes paper. In fact, by offering these services on a network it is possible to serve the needs of an office with much less equipment than might otherwise be required.

There are two ways to create a network. LANs use network cards combined with suitable software to physically connect computers together. Once a connection is made, information can be copied between machines very conveniently, perhaps using some version of the public/shared system described on page 79–80.

For connections to the Internet or a bulletin board (see page 89), a special extra known as a **modem** is required. Modems connect to the telephone line and allow your computer to send information to any other modem-equipped computer in the world. Most modern modems also include a fax facility. With the right software – which is often included when you buy the modem – you can send a fax directly from your computer without having to print it out on paper first. The computer can easily maintain a 'fax address book' for common destinations and can also send copies of the same fax to many different addresses automatically. Your computer can also receive faxes. These can be viewed on screen, or printed out if you have a printer attached.

Some modems also offer voice recording. With the right software these can be used as an electronic **voice mailbox** service. Outsiders can dial in and leave voice messages for different people on a single telephone line. Their respective mailboxes can be password-protected to make sure only the intended recipients hear their messages.

At the lower end of the market, voice-recording technology can be quite crude, and the software may not be up to professional standards. But a fully working professional system – which may cost only slightly more – can boost the image of a small business. For companies that do not have their own switchboards, voice mail can be used as a kind of automatic receptionist. The computer is able to store callers' messages and even to maintain separate password-protected 'mailboxes' for each employee. Voice mail prevents interruptions in meetings and prevents a build-up of stress when calls interfere with important work. It can also save money, as one computer can do the work of a number of answering machines.

The voice mail system can also be used with pagers. Users can dial in and send a pager message via the computer. The computer can pass the message on to the appropriate pager number.

One problem with fax modems is that they can only transmit information generated by your computer. If you are a designer or artist and need to fax hand-drawn work on a regular basis, or you work with cuttings or other kinds of printed material, you will need to invest in a **scanner**.

A scanner takes an image, be it a sketch or a photograph, and converts it into a form that the computer can use. Once the image has been scanned in, it can be sent as a fax. Some scanners include software for **optical character recognition** (**OCR**). This enables the scanner to read printed text and to convert it into text on screen. This can save retyping. Budget scanners tend not to be very reliable, so OCR – even when it comes as a free package – should be treated only as an interesting optional extra. More expensive OCR packages do a much better job and some are used professionally in the publishing trade to scan in copy supplied from faxes and manuscripts for later editing. It is not yet possible to scan in handwritten text, so do not expect to get good results from anything other than high-quality printed text, and always proof-read the text afterwards. Some fax software includes OCR facilities, so that a fax can be instantly converted into text.

The Internet

The networks discussed so far have been Local Area Networks (LANs), limited to a single site. Wide Area Networks (WANs) offer the same kinds of facilities but across a much wider distance. Many WANs are owned and operated by companies, but one – the Internet – is open to anyone.

The Internet is a public-access network with some unusual features. No one owns the Internet, and there is no overall organising or administrative body. Instead, it works more as a loose affiliation of users, computer system managers, governments and commercial interests. It can be used to exchange information, software and mail between computer-users worldwide. Current estimates suggest the Internet is used by over 100 million users worldwide.

The public parts of the Internet have a very definite culture of their own, with their own vocabulary, ideas and social conventions. In these areas users debate issues, gossip and exchange information, often in quite a rough and ready manner. In other, more professionally oriented areas the tone is more restrained. As a computer-user the latter areas can be most useful to you, as it is here that advice and computer support are exchanged.

To access the Internet you need a telephone and a modem. You can then open an account with an Internet Service Provider (see Appendix VIII for more details). You pay for this in much the same way that you pay for your existing telephone line, with a monthly subscription. In return you are given access to the Internet. Usually this access is via your modem over a telephone link – your computer dials the provider's computer, and a connection between the two is made. What happens next depends on the kind of service your provider offers. Some act as an electronic *poste restante*, collecting mail and other information for you, holding it until you dial in and then forwarding it to you along the telephone lines. Others act as a gateway that connects your computer directly to the Internet. This kind of connection is much more useful, but it can also be harder to set up and use. However, it is not necessarily any more expensive, and once it is up and running it can give you many more options and much better access to the services that the Internet offers.

Some service providers also charge you by the minute for any time spent using their services. A few, such as CompuServe, have a complicated pricing scheme where some services (such as access to certain stock-market prices) cost more per minute than others. There may also be extra charges for email on a per-message basis.

Access to the Internet offers a number of useful services:

email Messages can be passed from computer to computer directly. Unlike network email, however, the two computers can be anywhere in the world. If you are doing business abroad you can send a couple of pages of text overseas for far less than the cost of a telephone call or fax. You also have the benefit of knowing that your email goes directly to your intended recipient. The transfer of mail is almost instantaneous. In extreme cases it may take an hour or two, but usually it arrives at its destination in minutes.

At the moment email suffers from two drawbacks. It is best suited to plain text communications. It is possible to transfer sounds, pictures and even video clips electronically, but this can be an awkward, time-consuming and sometimes expensive process. As the technology of the Internet improves, these restrictions will lift.

The second disadvantage, and for business purposes the greater, is that email is not a secure way to communicate. There have been instances where email messages were intercepted without the permission of either sender or recipient and used as evidence in court cases. To get around this email can be **encrypted**. This turns the text into gibberish which makes no sense to anyone except the recipient who has a software key to unlock the original message. The best encryption system – PGP (Pretty Good Privacy) – is available as shareware (a try-before-you-buy system discussed further in Chapter 9). It can be slightly confusing to use, but once installed properly it offers near-total security.

Free access to software and other information A large number of software archives around the world offer unlimited free access to thousands of shareware and freeware (see Chapter 9) software packages. Other kinds of information, such as current weather satellite images, recipes, travel information and hints and tips for almost every sport and hobby, are also widely available.

Free access to services which can help you find this information Knowing that the information is available is only part of the story. With the total number of computers on the Internet in the millions, it can be impossible to track down what you want without help. A number of free services (with colourful names like Gopher and Veronica) make this easier. These are fast 'intelligent' search tools that scan the Internet looking for information on a key word basis. A search based on the word 'mail', for example, would find a list of email-related software and information, and supply you with details of the computers you would need to access to retrieve this data. There are also services which can help you find someone's email address if you know the name and approximate location.

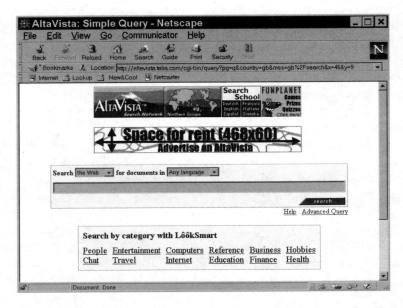

AltaVista is a free on-line indexing service that helps Internet users find information on the Web.

News groups These are the public discussion areas mentioned earlier. There are over 40,000 groups available, and the numbers are increasing every day. They are arranged according to subject matter, which includes everything from computer topics to poodle-breeding and music fan clubs. Most service providers only supply a selection of the more popular and useful English language groups. The computer-oriented groups – and there are many – are a good place to find free support.

The World Wide Web Part magazine, part art form, part encyclopedia, the Web is a global hypertext system. (For more information on hypertext, see pages 49-50.) Pages of text and pictures contain highlighted words which link to relevant information stored elsewhere either as part of the same document or part of a different document on another computer in a different country. Although the Web is visually appealing and easy to use, it is also slow (some pages can take minutes to appear on screen), and therefore can be expensive.

The most useful thing the Web can offer the user is international advertising space. Many organisations and individuals now have their own web pages and it is an excellent way to reach millions of potential customers.

News wire services These offer direct access to Reuters, Associated Press and other news agencies. A number of electronic news services (such as ClariNet) are also available. For the most part, the cost of these services is in addition to the normal Internet connection. The advantage of subscribing is that you get the news as soon as it happens. Several news-filtering services, the equivalent of press-cutting agencies, are starting to become available.

Do I need the Internet?

You should seriously consider an Internet connection if:

- you deal regularly with overseas businesses with email contact addresses
- you need access to the latest news and stock-market prices
- you already have a basic level of computer literacy and would like easy access to expert help on a wide range of subjects.

CompuServe was one of the first on-line services and is still available today.

As a means of obtaining computer support, however, the Internet is not a cheap option. Even the cheapest services cost about £100 a year, not including telephone bills, and this in no way guarantees support. If you ask for computer advice in one of the public discussion areas your query may well be read by thousands, perhaps even tens of thousands of users, but it is always possible that none of them will reply or even know the answer.

However, if you are considering an Internet connection for other reasons, such as email, this can be an excellent way to get help. On the whole users do reply to genuine questions. The situation is even better on on-line services such as CompuServe (see example of typical on-line service provider software above), which give you direct, more formal access to manufacturers' support teams and other users of their hardware and software.

The Internet and children

The unrestricted nature of information on the Internet means that some of it is frank and explicit, and therefore unsuitable for children. Some on-line services, such as AOL, include parental control options which mark certain areas 'out of bounds'. For those with more direct access, a number of products have become available which attempt to restrict what children can and cannot find on the Internet, filter out offensive language and optionally keep a list of Internet accesses so that parents have a record to refer to. None of these products is totally foolproof. Although they will deter and protect younger Internet users, many computer-literate teenagers will be able to work around them in short order.

This is one of the most politically difficult areas surrounding Internet access, and a workable solution is still some years away. In the meantime, parents should be aware of the dangers and should look out for reviews of the relevant products in the more home- and family-oriented computer press. This is discussed further on pages 93–5.

Bulletin boards and on-line mail-order

Some companies offer their own bulletin board system (BBS). This is a public access information and message area that anyone with a modem can dial into. The software for this is very affordable.

You can use the board as a billboard for free advertising and as a way of keeping in closer touch with your clients. Clients can place orders at any hour of the day or night.

If you work far from home and use a portable computer but still need access to your main office system or if you need to share information acquired in the field with colleagues working back at the office it is worth setting up your own BBS. (You can use the Internet to do this, but it is not ideal if you need to work with pictures or diagrams.)

CASE HISTORY: Emma

Emma Summers works as an architect in a busy London practice. She uses the company's bulletin board to help with last-minute changes to presentations.

'A client will often change his or her mind about an element of the project at the eleventh hour. When that happens I phone the office and colleagues create a new set of drawings or visualisations using their powerful computers, and I upload these to my computer via the phone line in my hotel room. Then I can present these to the client later the same day. We've done this a couple of times now, and it's got us something of a reputation, as well as getting us the contract.'

Bulletin boards are slowly being replaced by the Internet, which offers better facilities for public access. However, for information that is intended to remain confidential within a company, BBS systems can often be more efficient, because information can be sent directly between modems much more quickly than it can be sent over the Internet.

POPULAR INTERNET SOFTWARE

For the Web, the choice is between Netscape's Communicator and older Navigator software, and Microsoft's Internet Explorer. Netscape's products seem to be marginally more reliable. A version of Internet Explorer is built into Windows 98. This demands more powerful hardware than Communicator, although many users are pleased with its advanced facilities. Both the Netscape and the Microsoft products offer news and email facilities, although these are not as good as new and email-specific packages such as Forte's Agent and Qualcomm's Eudora. Explorer and Communicator are free, can be copied from the Internet, or, more conveniently, are often supplied on the cover CD-ROMs of Internet magazines. Agent and Eudora are also available free from the same sources. However, more advanced versions which add extra features can be bought directly over the Internet. Eudora is also sold in many computer stores.

Chapter 7

Computers and the family

Computers are well on their way to becoming household objects. As a result, the market in computer applications intended for home rather than business users is burgeoning. As with buying a machine for business use, a computer for home use can easily turn into an expensive white elephant. Software and support make all the difference. This chapter introduces the more popular domestic uses of computers, and examines the pros and cons of home computer ownership.

Education and childcare

Aside from games, two of the most popular uses of a home computer are in education and childcare. Computers can be used as electronic babysitters, as substitute teachers, as creative play areas (where any messes made remain virtual and harmless), and as exam revision tutors.

CASE HISTORY: John

John Alsop, an editor for a computer magazine, uses the computer to entertain his two children.

'We have an Apple Mac at home, which so far has had mixed reactions from the kids. Gemma, who is four, was playing with the mouse almost as soon as she could walk, and she'd spend hours playing with some basic toy art and sound software. We've moved on to more complicated packages now – some stories and simple games – and she's happy to work her own way through them. She's quite content to play with the same software over and over again as long as it involves plenty of input from her.

'Simon is a year younger, and just beginning to show signs of more serious interest. One problem is that his sister gets first go most of the time, so we may have to start rationing their time on the computer, or making more of an effort to find software they can use together.

'If we want some peace and quiet we set up the software and leave either or both of them to get on with it. As a distraction it's just fantastic.

'I often get asked whether or not it helps their education prospects or whether it teaches them computer literacy. I think the answer is no. To other parents I'd say – treat it like a toy, not an educational work-out. It can keep your kids busy, creative and curious. The best thing about computers is their endless flexibility. I think putting kids in that kind of environment is going to be worth more in tomorrow's job market than a more rigid idea of computer literacy.'

While computers may not teach computer literacy, they can help with teaching the basic concepts of English and maths. There is now a wide range of primary-school-level software available which teaches these basic concepts by presenting them as games. The range of titles is quite large, and no one series stands out above the others, but companies to watch out for include Dorling Kindersley, Ablac Learning Works and The Learning Company. For a current list of available software it's best to refer to one of the leisure-oriented computer titles listed in Appendix XIII.

Later on in their schooling, children can find computers helpful in other ways. Many schools now accept word-processed essays and – neatness aside – these obviously require keyboard and computer skills. Beyond these basic uses, there are three other sources of academic help.

Educational software is specifically designed to support some part of the National Curriculum. The standard of this software varies. Some examples are dull computer 'slide-shows' which collect together a few photographs and other graphics on a CD-ROM and link them together with a simple commentary. At the other extreme are the creative interactive packages which give pupils a hands-on experience of a subject. For example, chemistry software may work with complex animations of how various atoms link together to produce compounds, or mathematical software may draw graphs to show how different mathematical principles work. These more colourful and lively packages can be very valuable.

High-quality educational software can be hard to find. However, it is reviewed regularly – although not usually comprehensively – in the more family-oriented computer magazines, such as *Parents & Computers*. Depending on the resources of the school, teachers may also be able to help with recommendations.

'Edutainment' software aims to be entertaining as well as informative. It is much more widely available and more popular. The distinguishing features are impressive graphics, animations, interesting sound effects, clever use of humour and relatively basic content – while interesting, it isn't usually matched to the National Curriculum and is less academically rigorous.

These packages can be very useful because they sustain interest by appearing to be more like games than 'serious' educational items. In fact, many packages include games of one sort or another. These almost always have an educational slant – for example, revision of the facts summarised, or animated exercises in various kinds of problem-solving.

Edutainment's main drawback is its expense. Although some packages are available for around £10, most titles cost between £30 and £40 – as much as two or three good educational books.

The Internet is an almost infinite resource for research and study. While it would be an exaggeration to say that the answer to any possible homework question is available on-line, an astonishing amount of information can be found with relatively little effort. Mastering the searching and index system used on the Web is no mean feat, but anyone who has surfed can find information on almost any subject – or access to experts who may be able to help. Until children do this – and they will need to be taught, as there are few, if any, on-line tutorials designed specifically for them – they are likely to need help finding material. Otherwise they are likely to get distracted by its endless possibilities.

The Internet can cause something of a dilemma for parents. On the one hand, it can be an extremely effective way to inspire enthusiasm for learning and making contact with others, but on the other, some of the information on the Net is most definitely not suitable for children. At the time of writing, the problem of restricting access to unsuitable material has yet to be solved. Although systems are available that attempt to censor what children can see, none is perfect, and all have the unfortunate side-effect of accidentally barring wanted as well as unwanted information.

The most obvious way to tackle the problem is to use 'Net babysitter' software which attempts to check web sites for inappropriate content, including sexually-explicit material, graphic violence, racism and so on. The software can look for certain words in the text at the site or can use one of the Net's own classification systems, which work very much like film ratings.

The problem with keyword searches is that they are rather unintelligent. While it is easy to get rid of most 'four-letter words', a ban on the word 'sex' for example, may make it impossible to read completely innocent sites that refer to certain English counties. Meanwhile, Net ratings are still in their early stages. There is no single standard rating system, and only a minority of sites – ironically often the ones with the most explicit content – bother to give themselves ratings. Many sites aimed at children do not do this, and unfortunately some software bars sites that are not rated. As a result, the sites that might most interest children 'disappear'. The latest web browsers are starting to take notice of ratings but, until a system is agreed upon and everyone begins to use it, ratings will remain a patchy and unreliable way to restrict access.

The situation is slightly better on the on-line services, which have a more family-oriented approach. Some services – AOL and CompuServe – offer separate account names for each family member, and these can be set up from the 'master account' so that certain features of the service are unavailable. Access to the Internet can also be controlled from the master account.

One problem is that these controls are set up using a password system, and enterprising youngsters can look over their parents' shoulders so they can 'borrow' their password later. For some children, being left in a special children's web site is not enough, and it is usually very easy to escape and follow links that lead to more adult content.

In practice, the best way to avoid inappropriate information is to rely on active forms of parenting. Finding a balance between effective concern and intrusive paranoia can be difficult here, and the whole subject needs to be handled with tact. Useful possibilities include moving the PC to a living room, where you can watch what children are using it for.

One problem that is particularly severe on the Web is the prevalence of manipulative advertising aimed specifically at children. Some 'kids' sites' are really thinly disguised corporate attempts to 'sell' to youngsters. It is useful to review these sites in the same way that you would check for information of a more explicitly inappropriate nature. Parents who would like more advice should try the NCH Action for Children web site at *www.nchafc.org.uk*

Other sources of help and support

A useful resource for parents is the Parents Information Network (PIN). This offers a range of services, including a basic introductory guide to PC buying and a selection of educational web sites.

For home schooling, BT and Anglia Media run an Internet-based service called AngliaCampus. For an annual subscription of about £50 children can get expert on-line help with homework, remedial lessons in reading and writing and information on languages, sport and study skills. The service currently covers ages 5 to 18.

Adult learning and entertainment

Adults too can benefit from continuing study. The Open University remains the most effective way to study to degree level at home, but so far it has not taken significant advantage of computers or the Internet in presenting its courses. While a small number of Internet-based 'distance learning' programmes are available, these are experimental and most often based in the US.

For adults the most useful tools for home learning are still educational multimedia packages. Most of these fall firmly into the 'edutainment' category, and cover subjects as diverse as history, science, the great works of art and literature, astrology, and so on. The wider range of titles and the fact that some are available at 'budget' prices (typically around £10) makes this a much more fertile source of software than edutainment for children.

In the mid-1990s slick design, high prices and relatively shallow content gave early edutainment titles a less than glowing reputation. The market has now matured, however, and titles are more likely to be informative as well as entertaining. As with all software, the quality is variable, so where possible it can be worth asking to see a CD-ROM before buying it.

Entertainment

In many homes the computer is beginning to compete with the TV as a tool for relaxing. By 2005 it's likely that current TV systems will have begun to merge with the Internet – which will be offering wireless satellite delivery of information. When this happens computers, TVs and hi-fis may begin to amalgamate into a single all-purpose home-entertainment system. For now, though, there remain applications for which a computer is essential.

The Internet

Increasing numbers of people are using the Internet – and especially the more popular on-line services that offer live chat – as an alternative to television and nights out. The Internet's great strength from a social point of view is that it makes it very easy to find and communicate with people with similar interests. It can also simplify social arrangements. Sending out a party invitation to 50 people using email is much quicker, cheaper and more convenient than using the post or the telephone, assuming all your guests have email.

In terms of hobbies, information on the Web and the various Internet newsgroups and mailing lists provides an enviably comprehensive collection of useful information and knowledgeable people – although the latter can sometimes seem more argumentative in groups than 'real life' friends are.

CASE HISTORY: Sian

Sian started using America OnLine with a free introductory offer in spring 1997.

'The software is very easy to use and mostly fun. It is a great way to meet new people. I found that a chap in my area had started up a sports club. The local sports centre wasn't being used much on Friday nights, so they let people use the facilities for a pound. He collects the money, and we all meet up for a laugh and a good time, and some swimming, tennis or badminton.

'There's also a website called Yell that lists all the films in all the cinemas up and down the country. If you want to know what's on in the West End, or elsewhere for that matter, it's no trouble at all to find out. Railtrack has a full timetable on the Web and some of the bus and coach companies have lists of services. You can even order wine. It can take you a while to find these things, but once you do they can make life a lot easier.

'The downsides? I have to say that being female I get a lot of unwelcome attention, some of it of a sleazy nature. And yes, it can be an expensive way to waste time if I'm bored. I've known people who've had bills of more than £400 a quarter! So even though you start by thinking that the £10 a month you pay AOL doesn't sound like much, you have to watch those phone bills or you'll be in trouble.

'I think these on-line services are probably better for people who don't use the Internet seriously. It's for the fun of it really. I suppose it's just that much more social than flopping down in front of the TV in the evening – at least you're talking to people, even if it is only through a keyboard.'

Games

Games are an extremely popular reason for buying a home computer. While not many people have the resources to spend more than £1,000 on something that is only used for entertainment, those that do seem to be unusually keen. They are not only happy to invest £30 to £40 for each new game when it appears, but also to add the latest game-specific hardware to their PC when it becomes available.

Computer games fall into five main groups.

Shoot-em-ups place a player into an electronic virtual world where he or she (usually he – these games are most popular with adolescent boys) is expected to explore the surroundings and dispatch the 'baddies' in any number of graphically violent ways. The effect is very similar to that of an animated cartoon, and relies on a combination of quick thinking, fast reflexes and occasional strategic planning on the part of the player.

Games such as *Quake* and *Doom* are the best-known examples of the tasteless end of the genre, although much milder and relatively innocuous examples such as *Descent* are also popular. Some are tied in to popular films. Lucas Arts, a division of the media empire run by George Lucas, maker of the *Star Wars* films, has done well with a range of *Star Wars*-related games.

In general, shoot-em-ups are ideal for anyone who wants a quick adrenaline rush without having to think too hard. While the graphics used in games improve every year, and the strategic challenges become more complex, the basic premise never changes. Some gamers revel in the familiarity this offers, while others find it dull.

Adventures work at a much slower pace. These build atmosphere with more carefully crafted computer-designed artwork than the relatively crude graphics of shoot-em-ups. The premise of a virtual world is the same, but players are expected to pick up and use a much wider range of items, and typically have much longer to think about their moves. Many adventures are a very elaborate setting for some logic puzzles of varying degrees of difficulty, and it is fair to say that some are much better designed than others.

Adventures can be divided into rough sub-genres. Among the most highly rated adventures are *Myst* and *Riven*, its much more complex and visually impressive sequel, and the *Zork* series of games. *Riven,* in particular, offers astounding graphics and a fascinating imaginary world to explore, although some of the puzzles are ferociously difficult and may leave many people stumped.

Sims (short for simulations), also known as god-games, offer a more complicated gaming experience. In these the player is in charge of developing a virtual environment – which can be anything from a theme park, to a hospital, to a whole civilisation – and is expected to make decisions about how to make the environment prosper. Bad decisions lead to failure, and to make the games more interesting some also offer a number of disaster scenarios.

The end result is somewhere between a war game (where the enemy can be fate, or relentless economic forces, or neighbouring civilisations) and a management simulation. (Some academic management courses use sims to prepare their students for the challenges of running a real business.) The original ground-breaking sim was called *SimCity*, which is still available in a number of updated and modified forms, and is perennially popular with players. Examples of this kind of game are always available, and always near the top of the best-seller lists.

In a **flight sim** the player is behind the controls of an aeroplane with a simulated landscape which he or she can fly over – or crash into. The player learns to take off, fly, perform aerobatics and land, often at simulations of real airports. In many flight sims there are no enemies to kill and no weapons to experiment with. However, some flight sims offer a more military-minded slant, and include accurate simulations of real military aircraft, complete with navigation and weapon-control systems, in a variety of battle settings.

Flight sims can be frustrating for beginners because keeping a plane from colliding with the ground can often be more difficult than it seems. However, this is a specialist genre, and more lackadaisical gamers may find that the persistence required to master it demands more commitment than they are prepared to give.

The most popular flight sim is Microsoft's *Flight Simulator*. This offers a range of civil aircraft simulations, from an old biplane to a business jet, and is upgraded regularly. The game comes with information about the navigation techniques used by real aircraft, as well as very detailed scenery.

Related to flight sims are **driving sims**. These are similar, except that they take place behind the steering-wheel of a car that (usually) stays on the ground. Typically these include some element of racing, based either on a realistic simulation of a Formula One track or in a completely imaginary fantasy world.

Other simulations cover a range of games. Pool, snooker, various card games, and Monopoly and Scrabble are all now available in computer-ready form. Perennially popular examples include football games, where players can manage teams and/or play the game directly on the screen, car racing and rallying.

Networks and tournaments

Enthusiastic gamers, particularly those interested in shoot-em-ups, can expand their experience by playing games 'live' with other players. Many shoot-em-ups offer a multiplayer option, which either pits players in teams against various computer-generated enemies or against each other. These add a whole new dimension to the experience – so much so that many of these games are now banned on the networks used by large businesses, because employees find the experience addictive.

Multiplayer options can work over a simple link or a local area network if the computers are physically close to each other, over a direct modem-to-modem connection via a telephone line in the case of two-player games, or over the Internet. (The latter can be slow. However, some Internet service providers even go so far as to offer dedicated 'servers' - large computers dedicated to one particular task – for certain very popular games, so that their customers can play against each other.) Games that offer this option invariably include instructions on how to set it up. BT offers a service called Wireplay which is aimed specifically at gamers and is now completely free, except for local-rate call charges. Gamers can play others in the UK using a special fast network, or over the Internet via a Wireplay connection (an existing Internet connection is not required). More details are available from the web site at *www.wireplay.co.uk*

A related feature of the gamer's world are tournaments where players can compete with each other directly – often face to face, or at least in the same room. These are advertised in gaming magazines, on the Internet, and on bulletin boards.

Finding and choosing games

Full-price computer games are not cheap. Fortunately, there are a number of low-cost options for the aspiring gamer on a budget. The shelf-life of a modern game is rarely more than six months to a year, after which time the game is either forgotten or reappears on a budget compilation – a CD with a collection of popular games – or as a 'white label'. The latter is a repackaged game in a less impressive box sold at a much more reasonable price – usually comparable to or even less than a music CD.

The other option for gamers is to investigate a local exchange store which buys games second-hand for a fraction of their original price and sells them on. Even with the mark up, this can be a good way to get more recent games at a more realistic price.

As for completely new games, the endless torrent of new releases makes it impossible to keep up with the latest and best without reading any of the monthly gaming titles. These usually have the word 'Gamer' in the title to distinguish them from other computer magazines, and are devoted to in-depth previews, reviews and retrospectives about the various current games.

Game consoles

Why buy a PC when a game console is a cheaper option? Consoles can sometimes (but not always) provide better animation and graphics than a computer, and can also be much easier to use.

The advantage of computers, however, is that they can be used for other things. And computer games can be cheaper than console titles. In the end though, this is very much a matter of personal choice. For anyone who uses a computer solely for games, the question is largely one of cost and convenience. For those who wish to have a more general-purpose tool in the home, the computer is usually the more sensible, if also the more expensive, option.

Other options

Computers are now regularly used to listen to music and even to watch TV. The speakers available with most computers are hardly true hi-fi, but they can compete favourably with the cheaper mini and micro systems sold in the high-street hi-fi stores. As a result, computers are now often used to play music where previously a small portable CD-player or other system would have done the same job.

When it comes to images the situation is more complex. Some people are quite happy to watch TV and video on their computer's monitor. This is unlikely to become more than a minority interest. TV tuner cards that allow live TV signals from a conventional aerial to appear on a computer screen are improving rapidly, and a number of systems are widely advertised for less than £100. In fact, it is now possible to buy a system that can 'capture' live video to hard disk for less than £300. The size of hard disk required makes this an unlikely replacement for the home video system, but it does allow anyone with a moderate disposable income to set up a small video editing facility for use with a portable camcorder.

In general, the computer world has yet to decide on a workable video format, although DVD (Digital Video Disk – also known as Digital Versatile Disk) shows signs of becoming an affordable standard – albeit with the disadvantage that disks purchased abroad may not work on UK players because of deliberate copyright restrictions. For now, though, it is prudent to wait before buying a video playback system until the situation has settled.

Creativity tools

Perhaps the most entertaining other uses of computers are the creative ones. For the first time beginners can experiment with art, animation and music without spending a fortune on specialist tools. The software available in all of these fields ranges from basic tools for dabblers to advanced packages that can also be used professionally. What makes the technology so interesting is that astounding results can often be achieved with very little effort.

In terms of sound and music, software is available to teach basic piano keyboard skills and sight-reading, or to make it easy for anyone to put together very professional-sounding examples of modern dance music. While this 'music-by-numbers' approach may worry purists, it can be an excellent way to get beginners started and provides plenty of continuing satisfaction where more challenging traditional methods can appear too difficult to master.

For art, it is possible to buy a graphics tablet and some software for not much more than the cost of a collection of high-quality acrylic paints, an easel and a pad of artist's paper. While this approach is rather more expensive than starting with a 6B pencil and a rubber, it can help beginners overcome their fears about making mistakes. Some beginner's software also includes features that make it easy to create very impressive results with some simple experimentation. For example, Fractal Design's Dabbler has a range of 'filters' that can modify an existing image in various ways. While not art in the conventional sense, this can still lead someone with a good eye for shapes, colours and textures to create results that are very satisfying and impossible to do any other way. Similarly, 'world creation packages', such as Metacreations' Bryce, can produce images of realistic virtual landscapes with an astonishing degree of detail that would previously have required years of traditional art training.

All of these options can make it easier for beginners to investigate their potential creative talents. In a handful of cases this has even led to people developing interesting new career opportunities for themselves.

A music collection?

The arrival of a number of new, efficient ways of storing music inside a computer (for example, the MP3 system) and the relatively huge disk capacities available in modern machines mean that some people are now storing complete music collections inside their computer – often inside a laptop, which can then replace a number of tapes and CDs when on the move.

While it's possible to convert existing tracks from existing CDs to the MP3 format, it's also easy to copy completely new music from the Internet. A number of web sites, such as MP3.COM (*www.mp3.com*) offer music created by amateurs and available for free. The owners of the site make no editorial choices, and so the quality is variable. However, the best music compares well with commercial recordings, and the system as a whole offers a creative outlet to anyone who makes music that is unlikely to be released in the usual way.

Currently, it takes a long time to copy an MP3-format song to a computer. However, as Internet speeds improve and hard-disk capacities increase, it's likely that separate hardware players will eventually become much less common than they are now. Instead, computers and laptops will be used to store complete music collections.

Let the buyer beware!

There are many good reasons to be wary of buying a home computer. The most obvious is cost. At more than £1,000 for a full system, a computer is a major investment. It is useful to look realistically at the benefits this outlay will bring, and also to be aware of 'hidden' costs such as upgrades and support.

The question of upgrades is a particularly difficult one. Business computers are most often bought as a package that fulfils a specific need. The need is unlikely to change over the life of the machine, and – unless the business expands or changes significantly – the package as a whole can be expected to offer more than five years of sterling service before becoming obsolete.

The situation is different in the home. To give of its best a home computer needs a steady diet of new software titles. This is not only expensive – far more expensive than creating a videotape or CD collection – but much more demanding of the hardware. Where a video recorder or CD player can be expected to last perhaps five years, it may be as little as six to twelve months before a particular computer is heading towards obsolescence, as the latest software titles demand more and more from its performance. The only options then are either to forgo the more interesting software releases, or to spend even more money on an expensive upgrade.

Manufacturers seem indifferent to the chaos that this can cause in the home market. One notorious example occurred in January 1997. With minimal warning Intel released a completely new kind of processor chip – the MMX range – which compromised the value and usefulness of Pentium-based computers bought in the run up to Christmas. While it took some time for MMX-ready software to appear in the shops, the confidence of many new computer owners was dented.

If you are thinking of buying a computer for home use remember that a computer is not so much a one-off purchase as an ongoing investment. Like cars, computers cost a lot to run. Taking out a long-term loan or a hire-purchase scheme can be particularly foolhardy in this respect, as you will need to find further money for upgrades long before you have paid off the original amount.

Learning the lessons

When buying a computer for use at home you could save yourself some grief by following these four steps:

1. **Learn the basics**. At the very least it's useful to be able to compare different processor chips and memory sizes, to know what Windows is, and to understand what a hard disk does.
2. **Always get a package price**. Multimedia is now standard on all home PCs, and it is reasonable to expect a computer system to include a printer as well. If any free software is included, check it carefully to see how useful it really is.
3. **Shop around**. Some high-street stores sell systems at an astonishing mark-up – as much as 100 per cent in some cases, compared to certain smaller retailers. A thorough survey of comparable machines in the various computer magazines should make it clear what the average price of a given system is. Cheaper is not necessarily better, but in the computer trade more expensive is not necessarily better either. To facilitate your choice it can help to consider technical after-sales support and location as well as price.
4. **Support, support, support** This is critical. As with business purchases, customers looking to buy a computer for home use can learn a lot about a retailer's approach to support from the helpfulness of the sales staff. Helpfulness should not be confused with professional charm, but should combine a thorough knowledge of the options available, a willingness to demonstrate their differences, and an awareness of new developments. Ideally support should be local. Telephone support is perhaps better suited to those who are no longer complete beginners.

Retail vs mail-order

While there are no hard and fast rules about the difference between buying over the counter or by mail-order, retail sales can often be a better choice for first-time buyers. The advantages are purely practical – the computer can be taken home immediately, and if there are any problems it can also be returned to the shop. Stores that don't offer this kind of over-the-counter support should be thought of as having more in common with the mail-order suppliers.

Mail-order is perhaps better for more experienced computer users who already know something about what they are getting for their money. It is **very** important to compare prices and specifications thoroughly when buying by mail-order, and to talk to sales staff – again to get an idea of the company's approach to sales. Trained salespeople will always try to 'close' a sale by asking 'So would you like to place an order?' as soon as they can. It can be useful to time how long each sales person takes to get to this phrase, as a rough guide to how much more concerned they are with selling you something than with deciding what is best for you.

The biggest advantage of mail-order is that there is no pressure involved. Buyers can pick and choose between different companies and different specifications in their own time, without any feeling of obligation. This can be harder to do in a retail setting, where sales staff can use the time they spend demonstrating a system to pressure a buyer into a purchase. The main disadvantage is a lack of hands-on experience with the computer. Sometimes the extras – mouse, keyboard and especially the monitor – can say a lot about the internal build and general quality of a machine. Many of these questions are commented on routinely in magazine comparative reviews. As with all computer buying, a little research can go a long way. For more details about mail-order buying see pages 159–60.

Chapter 8

Job-specific software and computer utilities

All the software we have discussed so far has been aimed at home or general-purpose business use, but your computer can also help you with your work itself. Job-specific software is not as widely available as the common business–related packages. It is usually written by professional users for other professional users in the same trade. They tend to work independently of the large software manufacturers and often sell their products as **shareware** – a 'try-before-you-buy' system discussed in Chapter 9. Many of these programs are advertised in specific trade journals.

CASE HISTORY: Ted

Ted Smith runs a small electronic design consultancy.

'Computerising some aspects of my trade has freed up a lot of my time. First, we can model circuitry mathematically without having to build it. There are a lot of calculations involved in design, and now the computer does them. So we have time to experiment with different ideas and approaches when attacking a problem. We can also answer "what-if?" questions such as checking for the effect of component tolerances.

'Second, the computer helps with circuit board layouts. This used to be very time-consuming. You have to lay the components out within a certain area and then work out where to make the connections. It's a tough job to do by hand, and there used to be a lot of trial and error involved. There was no guarantee we'd got it right either. The computer does it all for us automatically. It also prints out the track pattern, and we can use that as the master artwork for the circuit boards. On some projects we've cut development times by 75 per cent.

'I found the software in a shareware catalogue. Off-the-shelf products tend to be expensive. The shareware was much cheaper, and I've been in touch with the author with suggestions that he's included in new versions. If there are any problems I can call him up and ask him about them. Of course not all shareware authors live in the UK, so I've been lucky there. There is also a level of personal contact you wouldn't get with a larger company.'

Software can also be used for non-technical jobs, and more and more trades of every kind are taking advantage of the possibilities that computers offer. Whatever kind of work you do, there is a good chance you will be able to find software to help you do it more effectively.

CASE HISTORY: Delia

Delia Shepherd breeds toy dogs known as affenpinschers. She uses a computer to keep track of pedigrees and also to watch out for possible genetic defects.

'I used to draw the dogs' family trees by hand, but now I get the computer to do it. They're not just for fun. A very small number of dogs are believed to suffer from a rare recessive gene which can cause them problems. The computer helps me keep track of which dogs are likely to have the defect, and I keep that in mind when arranging matings.

'The software isn't particularly hard to use. It's advertised in the popular dog-breeding magazines and is fairly affordable. I don't know much about computers and I'm not really interested in learning. In fact I don't know how any of it works at all. A friend set it up for me and showed me how to use it.'

Computer-aided design

Some work-specific products are popular and widely available. Although they started out as tools for particular trades, they are now almost as common as the ubiquitous business office suites.

Computer-aided design (CAD) is one of the largest of these practical applications. At its simplest CAD offers an electronic replacement for the drawing board. Plans can be created and printed out without the tedious and time-consuming business of drawing them by hand, and changes can be made on screen without leaving a trail of untidy and distracting correction marks.

An architect, for example, using a CAD system can create perspective drawings from any position and is able to shade materials (the technical word is *render*) in different ways, so that images can seem almost real.

CASE HISTORY: William and Martha

William and Martha Philips, who design and install kitchens, use a CAD program to help with floor layouts and three-dimensional visualisations.

'We started off with a simple package designed for architects that gave us a top-down or side-on view of the working area. It was like a drawing board, but on the screen. We could draw in different units, experiment with positioning, and then show a client the various possibilities. The greatest advantage was the speed with which we could move things around. If someone said, "No, I want the washing machine there", we could pick it up, move it and shuffle everything around to suit. That's what makes CAD so much better than a drawing board. Once we'd got the layout settled, we'd use that and the side elevations as the basis for the final plans. The computer did these too.

'At the moment we're experimenting with a system that enables us to do three-dimensional visualisations of a finished kitchen. The pictures are in colour, and have the right textures – wooden areas appear woody and so on. We can show night and day views by changing how the scene is lit. We can even move around inside a view to try all the different perspectives, including impossible ones such as looking down from the ceiling!

'It's very impressive, but it's also very time-consuming; it takes ages to create a new design. We have a library of units – or rather, pictures of units – inside the computer and we can slot these into a view without having to redesign them from scratch. Even then, telling the computer exactly where every last thing has to go can take ages.

'CAD is very demanding: we have a powerful machine – fast processor, lots of memory, a big screen – and you couldn't do what we do with less. The 2-D stuff is fine on just about any machine, but if you start working in three dimensions you need something that can really move.'

Early CAD software was geared very much towards the professional user. This meant it was powerful but also difficult to master. A variety of much simpler CAD packages are now available which are designed for specific tasks, for example, garden design. These can vary in quality, but at their best make the CAD process much more straightforward and accessible than the older CAD packages.

Image manipulation

While CAD is used for plans and diagrams, image–manipulation software works with photographs, illustrations and other images. This is a rapidly growing field, which is now encompassing some of the work previously reserved for professional photographic studios, and can be used to help with advertising and promotion.

CASE HISTORY: Lyle

Lyle Kennet used a combination of image manipulation and desktop publishing to produce a brochure and price list for his software sales company.

'We used to use a photographer for the photos, and I'd hire a design shop to do the layout. This year I thought I'd have a go myself. I took the photos at home on the dining-room table – I used a sheet for a backdrop – and had them developed on to CD-ROM. You can get this done in the high street now. It costs about £30 for a roll of film and around £10 for the blank CD, which can hold hundreds of snaps. You can keep adding to it, so it's like a photo album on a disk.

'I'm no expert, and the photos weren't actually that great, but I ran them through the Adobe Photoshop package to sharpen them up and bring out the colours. I also added some interesting background effects.

'I used a standard DTP package to lay out the photos and text. It took about two days to do the double-page spread. I sent it to the printer on a data cartridge, and we got the price lists back soon after.

'I based the design on what we'd used in the past. The logo was already in the computer, and the rest just slotted in around it. It's not quite as slick as a designer could do, but it does the job. It took me about four days, doing it in my spare time. I think I saved myself something like £2,000. It will be even quicker next time, and I can re-use some parts when I do it again.'

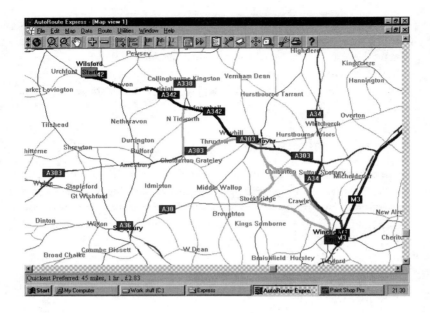

Route planners

Route planners are automated maps. You specify a start and a destination, and the computer works out the best way between the two points. The possible criteria for 'best' include the fastest, cheapest or shortest route, and the computer can combine all of these to create a route based on your personal preferences, for example avoiding motorway routes. Typical speed and fuel consumption figures are used to give an estimate of journey time and fuel cost.

CASE HISTORY: Melanie

Melanie Scott is a sales rep with a major cosmetics company and she uses a route planner to help her manage her time efficiently.

'When I started I used to sit there with a map trying to work out the best way to visit all our customers. Now I get the computer to do it for me. On average I think it's saved me between half an hour and an hour a day when I'm on the road, and I can work out my expenses in advance.'

Route planners have proved invaluable for haulage firms, courier companies and sales forces, as they make it possible to estimate costs and delivery times accurately and to work out the most time- and cost-efficient ways to move people and products around from place to place.

Project management tools

These are used to keep track of large projects. Project management (PM) consists of planning, communicating and managing, and PM tools help with the first two of these.

CASE HISTORY: John

John Adams runs an architect's practice and has been using a project-management software package for three years.

'The architect's job is not just to design the building so it fits the setting and doesn't fall down. We're also responsible for overseeing construction as a whole. This involves keeping track of information, resources, raw materials and people to make sure the project is finished on time and within budget.

'The most useful PM tool is the Gantt chart, which shows a breakdown of the project in terms of what is due to happen when. With the software we use we can track resource usage as part of each Gantt line, so that we keep abreast of costs. It also shows where we are, as opposed to where we should be. If the project starts to slip, the software warns us, and we can take action.

'We use critical path calculations to work out which parts of the project matter the most. This helps us identify key tasks that we can't afford to have running late. The next stage is to assign the tasks to people and that's when the different charts come in useful. It's a good way to give everyone an overview and to show where they fit in. They can then take the information away and use it with their own teams. Since using the software we've been a lot more organised about the work that we do, and it's been a great help to the practice.'

Computer utilities

As well as tools to help you with specific jobs there are also more general computer utilities which make your computer work better, faster and more efficiently. They are available to help with most aspects of computer use. If you are a beginner you can usually get by without them, but more confident users find them useful.

Screensavers

These are entertaining, if largely useless, decorative programs which blank out the screen if you stop working on your computer for longer than a set time. On older machines there was the possibility that a picture on the screen could burn into the phosphor if left for too long. Screensavers were developed to prevent this. After a period of inactivity the picture on the screen changes to something with some movement. As soon as the user presses a key or moves the mouse the old screen is restored, and work can continue.

Over the years screensavers have developed into something of an art form. A screensaver called 'After Dark' started the trend with a famously surreal scene of flying toasters, complete with wings, and included options such as a fish tank with convincingly animated fish and ferns. This led to increasingly ornate animated cartoon sequences, some with full musical backing, and various film and TV tie-ins. Meanwhile on the Internet screensavers are being used as part of huge collaborative computing projects. For example the SETI@home screensaver uses the relatively slow processing power of home computers to check for radio messages from alien civilisations. Users copy information to their PC, process it while their PC would otherwise be idle, and then send the results back when complete.

Unless you enjoy the sheer whimsy of these products and have no objection to spending money on random entertainment, you can ignore most screensavers. Modern monitors are much less prone to burn-in, and newer software such as Windows comes with a simple but effective screensaver of its own. The only good practical reason for using a screensaver is that some offer a measure of security if you need to leave your machine unattended for a time.

Disk doublers

When computers had much less storage space a popular accessory was the disk doubler. By compacting the information into a smaller space this could give you up to twice as much free space using your existing hardware.

However, disk doublers have several disadvantages: very occasionally information would simply be lost; compatibility problems with certain kinds of software were also reported; and speed was another problem, because compacting and restoring information every time the disk is accessed slows work down considerably.

In general, disk-doubler software is not necessary any more for desktop work. Storage hardware is now so cheap that there is no reason to settle for a small disk and augment it artificially, when for a few tens of pounds more you can buy all the storage space you need.

For users of portable computers, however, disk doublers can be a useful option. Storage areas on portables are much smaller, and it is much more expensive to buy larger sizes for a portable than for a desktop. If you have a lot of software installed you could easily find yourself running out of space, and a disk doubler can solve this problem.

Some computers come with free disk-doubling software. All PCs that use the MS-DOS system (most of them, in other words) have an option called Doublespace which is a simple disk doubler. If you need this option you should ask your dealer to set it up for you before you buy the machine.

Extending memory

Apple computer-users can purchase a useful product called RAM Doubler. This works exactly like a disk doubler, except it doubles memory space rather than storage space. RAM Doubler slows the computer down by a few per cent, but otherwise it is a very good way of expanding what your machine is capable of without spending money on real memory. (PC owners who use the Windows operating system have the equivalent of a RAM Doubler in the form of the **virtual memory manager** that is part of the control panel.)

Memory managers

IBM-compatible PCs use memory in a notoriously inefficient way. The original design for the PC set an upper limit of 640Kbytes on how much memory could be used. At the time it was felt that this would be enough for any user. A few years later, however, it was clear that this was in fact a major limitation of the design.

As a result two different schemes – extended memory and expanded memory – were devised to break through the limit. Neither of these works particularly efficiently and both slow the whole computer down.

A related problem is that some software – especially **software drivers**, which are small programs that control hardware extras such as soundcards and CD-ROM drives – need to use certain sections of memory. When a PC is fitted with a large selection of extras, these sections can become very crowded and there is not enough room for other software. As a result the computer will flash an 'out of memory' error message on the screen, even though there is plenty of free memory inside the machine. Memory managers solve this problem by arranging the drivers so they take up as little room as possible.

All IBM-compatible PCs are now supplied with a free program called MemMaker which offers basic memory management. This program has its limitations, and if you have tried it and are still having problems, you will need a commercial memory manager. One such is QEMM from QuarterDeck which is designed to solve memory-related problems. Very occasionally it runs into compatibility problems with some kinds of software but, on the whole, it does the job well.

PCs and software that use the new Windows 95 or Windows 98 system are much less prone to these kinds of complications. Windows 95 can – in theory – be set up to make the best possible use of all the available memory whatever the application, and can also run older games with full control over how the memory should be set up for each one. In practice, Windows 95/98 isn't perfect, but it is a huge improvement on the convoluted and confused system that earlier PC users had to contend with.

Uninstallers

Another useful utility is the uninstaller. When you install new software, new information is copied to various parts of your machine. Removing this information later can be very time-consuming if done manually. Windows 95/98 seems to be particularly clumsy in this respect – often the process used to remove software simply appears not to work correctly, and a manual clean-up is required to finish the job properly.

The best uninstallers keep a list of the type and location of new information added by a software package. You can then uninstall the software with a single command. A less useful type tries to guess where information is kept. These will often ask you first before they delete anything. Unfortunately, even experts can be confused about what is and is not relevant to a given piece of software.

In general, if your set up is fairly fixed and you do not spend a lot of time trying out new software, then you will not need to worry about using an uninstaller. If you plan to add to your computer throughout its life, however, then it can be well worth investing in one of these simple and useful tools.

System checkers

Some products claim to offer PC support 'out of the box'. They look at your computer and your applications, check out the whole system, warn you of any problems and sort them out for you automatically.

These can be very appealing to beginners. Unfortunately, in practice few of the current crop work as well as advertised and many are useless. Although they offer help for popular software, this often applies to versions of software that are no longer current. The troubleshooting features are also limited. If you want support you will need to learn how to do it yourself or pay an expert to do it for you.

Compression and decompression software

When archiving or transferring information from one computer to another it can be useful to compact software and data so they take up less space. This is a two-way process. First, compression software is used to perform the compaction. This squeezes the information into a smaller space, but also renders it temporarily unreadable. To restore it to its original form decompression software reverses the process. Shareware (discussed more fully in the next chapter) is often supplied in compressed form, as this is the only way that a complete package can be made to fit on to a single floppy disk. Compression and decompression tools such as PKZip and PKUnzip are the most popular, and both are available as low-cost shareware.

General-purpose 'tool kits'

These include a collection of useful tools, such as Norton's Utilities, to help you manage your computer more efficiently. Many of these have been rendered redundant by the newer operating systems (Windows for the PC, and Mac O/S for Apple machines). If you use an older operating system, however, they can make your machine easier to use – rather like the computer equivalent of a Swiss army knife. A good example of a typical tool they include is the undelete utility, which recovers information if you accidentally delete it. Another useful option is a graphic display of the way that information is arranged on your computer's hard disk. This makes it easier to find what you are looking for and also to copy and move information from one place to another.

Backup software

The backup process (described on pages 144–7) can be simplified with suitable backup software. Examples are sometimes supplied for free with backup hardware, but even these can often be improved upon. The best backup software keeps track of changed information for you automatically, works around a proven and reliable backup scheme, and can handle a number of different backup hardware options.

Chapter 9

Choosing the right software

It is important to avoid buying software without trying it out first unless you have absolutely no alternative. A 'try before you buy' approach can save time, temper and money in the long run. To a large extent, the software you choose determines whether you will be happy with your computer.

Training courses can be a good way to try out software before buying it (these are discussed in more detail in Chapter 13). Another alternative is to visit a dealer. This can present some problems, however, as many dealers and high-street stores will have neither the time nor the inclination to demonstrate a software package in detail. In itself, this is useful as it can show you which dealers are prepared to be helpful. A dealer who is interested enough to discuss and demonstrate your software options is preferable to someone who resorts to high-pressure sales talk.

Magazine reviews can be another useful guide. Many magazines run multiple tests where different products are compared with each other. Even if you do not understand them fully, you will get some idea of how well one piece of software rates against another. The best reviews include usability and productivity ratings, and use independent testers in work-related situations. These give an excellent indication of how easy it is to use a piece of software, and also how easy it is to get useful work done with it (the two are not always related).

Free offers

Free copies of trial software are often given away with computer magazines. Sometimes the software is fully functional, but not the latest version: a special offer inside the magazine lets you buy the current version at a reduced price. Alternatively, the software is a trial version which is limited in some way; it may be designed to work for a certain number of days, or a set number of times.

Older trial versions are an excellent way to try out software. As software dates far more slowly than hardware, you may find that an old version does everything you want it to. Unfortunately, manuals are not usually supplied with the software, although they may be available for a small charge from the manufacturer. Paying the extra also renders you eligible for free help from the manufacturer.

Limited-use trial versions allow you to try software for nothing. There are no notable drawbacks to this approach, and if you buy the full version it may be possible to keep the work you created using the limited one.

A variation of the trial version is the **encrypted** demonstration. This contains both a demonstration copy of the software that you can try out in the normal way, and a full working version which can be used only with a special access code. To obtain this code you telephone the manufacturers with your credit card details and make a payment, they give you the code over the telephone and agree to send any manuals and other extras you need.

Be wary of this kind of offer. You may be tempted to make an impulse purchase. Test the software *thoroughly* before buying to be sure it really does meet your needs. You will pay the full recommended price for software bought this way, whereas by shopping around you can often get a sizeable discount on software.

Demonstration versions and money-back guarantees

Some business software vendors offer a 'no-quibble, money-back guarantee'. You can try their software for a limited period (usually 30 days) and if you return it you get a full refund. This kind of approach gives you the relaxed opportunity to try out competing products. Always ask if this kind of deal is on offer before you buy software.

Shareware

Shareware (often known, slightly inaccurately, as **public domain** software) is explicitly provided on a try-before-you-buy basis. The software is available for a nominal amount and comes with a legal agreement which states that it may be used for an evaluation period – typically 30 days – without payment. Once this time has elapsed the software must be either **registered** – you do this by sending a cheque to the author – or removed from your computer.

Most shareware is produced by independent software writers who work from home and do not have access to the development resources of a large company. The quality of such software can vary. The best shareware packages can compete with professional products costing many times the price, and for those on a very tight budget can be a cost-effective alternative to mainstream products. The worst examples are badly designed, hard to use and unreliable. Some professional products are also badly designed, hard to use and unreliable, but they are, as a rule, at least partially usable. Unfortunately this is not always the case with shareware.

Many shareware authors add incentives when users pay for their work. These include copies of a 'full' version of the software with useful extra features, or perhaps a properly printed and bound manual. (Most shareware documentation is supplied as text on a floppy disk.) There may be some kind of irritating regular message or warning that you are using an unregistered copy. Registered versions will not have this.

Some authors take a more extreme approach and release shareware which is all but crippled. For example, an accounts package may allow a maximum of 100 entries, or word-processing software will only work with very small documents. Limitations like these can be irritating, but even a hamstrung version of a package will still give users an idea of whether the package suits their needs.

Many shareware authors are in the US, and payment is often specified in US dollars. It is rare for an author to accept foreign currency or credit cards. Registration can be made difficult if the address given in the documentation is no longer the author's current address. Some authors have tackled this problem by setting up national dealerships which collect registration fees.

There are three main sources of shareware: bulletin boards, the Internet (see Appendix VIII) and public shareware libraries. The Internet is now the most popular source, simply because the range of available shareware is huge – almost every shareware product that has ever been available can be found there. Collections such as

Shareware.com (*www.shareware.com*) include search facilities so that shareware for a specific task and specific kind of computer system can easily be found. Many magazines now include a small selection of popular shareware copied from the Internet on their monthly free cover disks.

Bulletin boards and shareware libraries have been eclipsed by the rise of the Net as a medium for shareware distribution, but still offer a valuable resource for anyone who wants to investigate what kinds of shareware are available, but does not want or need a full Internet connection. Libraries act as clearing houses, cataloguing and supplying shareware for the cost of a small copying fee. Apart from shareware, they now also provide a range of information copied from the Internet and supplied as CD-ROMs. One example is the *Libris Brittaniae* series sold by most libraries, which offers summaries of information and shareware relevant to electronics, maths, scientific developments, and so on. The same information is available on the Net, but buying it on CD-ROM is often more convenient than having to find it one self. Note that the content of these CD-ROMs is rather less rigorous and more patchy than that available from textbooks and more formal sources. In spite of this, some of these products offer a fascinating, if perhaps slightly eccentric, overview of a field, and can be of interest to serious students and dabblers alike.

Freeware

A handful of software titles are freeware. As the name suggests they can be used for free. The author maintains the copyright, but the software can be legally copied and used by anyone. (Strictly speaking, only freeware should be called public domain software, as only freeware is genuinely free of copyright charges and hence truly in the public domain. However, the words are traditionally applied to shareware as well.)

Freeware tends to be written by hobbyists or enthusiasts and is unlikely to offer much to the less experienced user. For example, the POVRAY2 computer graphics package can produce very impressive photo-realistic images and animations, but demands a high degree of technical knowledge.

Custom software

Unless your needs are very unusual, you should be able to find a software package off the shelf or a standard package that can be adapted to suit your requirements.

If you cannot find one, you have the option of commissioning a programmer to create some custom software. However, this is not to be undertaken lightly. It is an expensive option: a good programmer can charge in excess of £1,000 a week. It can also be a lengthy option. You may be lucky and come across a programmer who gets the job done in time, but this often proves impossible for any number of reasons, and so it is wise to allow yourself a generous schedule and an equally generous budget.

Software writing is still as much an art as a science, and for many reasons a project can go over time and over budget. It is advisable to negotiate a fixed-rate contract, with an initial payment, a stage payment when the first version is completed and a final payment when everything has been tested thoroughly. The final stage – known as 'bug fixing' – will take the longest. Getting a piece of software 90 per cent right is comparatively easy; getting it 99.9 per cent right sorts out the professionals from the cowboys.

To find a programmer, look in *Yellow Pages* and the classified ads of computer magazines. Your local training and enterprise council (TEC) or business centre may also be able to make suggestions. Follow the same criteria you would use to find a consultant (see Chapter 2). Previous experience is particularly important here. The most appropriate programmer for a project will have done one or more very similar jobs in the recent past and will be able to offer references.

Deciding what you want

Choose your software first and then find the hardware. This rule of thumb bears repetition. It is far more important to choose the right software than the right hardware as most reasonably priced hardware today can handle anything needed to run an office. If you work on this principle you are almost certain to get a smooth-running, efficient system that does what you want it to.

When buying a software package, watch for the following:

Ease of use Does the package do what you want in a simple and straightforward way, or do you have to work around its quirks before you get results?

Features Be wary of packages that claim to do everything. Some office-oriented software packages now come with so many options that a number of the features remain unused. Sometimes a cheap and basic package can be much better value – and prove more useful in everyday terms – than a more upmarket product.

A spreadsheet, for example, is a good general–purpose tool for financial analysis, but if you want something to help with your accounts it may not be the ideal purchase.

Productivity How much more easily and quickly will the software help you get your work done? (This is not quite the same as ease of use.) Some packages are tricky and slow to set up, but once up and running are speedy and efficient. Others are easy to understand, but can seem laboured once you have mastered the basics and are feeling more confident.

The best software includes shortcuts and automation features for commonly repeated tasks. It also has on-line help – a brief summary of the manual within the program itself.

Hardware requirements How much hard disk space does the package take up? How much memory does it need? How fast is it? Here again, modern software packages can be very demanding. A full installation of Microsoft's Office Professional system – a popular package which includes a word processor, spreadsheet, business presentation generator and database – can take up over 60Mb of storage space. Competing packages from other major software companies make comparable demands. If you plan to install a number of applications, you will need to be sure that you can afford the hardware to cope with this.

Operating system requirements Within the hardware specification you will find a reference to an operating system. Operating systems are a special kind of software that run your computer. (For further details on operating systems see Appendix III.)

The last two points are particularly important, as they will dictate what kind of hardware you should buy. Together they give you a detailed hardware specification to shop for.

Software buying tips

When buying software you should be very careful to make sure that it does what you want it to – in practice, as well as in theory. The most widely advertised business packages are **office suites** which include a word processor, a spreadsheet, a database, a business presentation package and also extras such as a personal information manager, or a home accounts program. These may seem appealing at first sight, especially as they are often sold at a discount, but they may not do exactly what you want. If all you want is some simple accounting tools to help with income tax and VAT, and a way of keeping track of your business contacts, you may well get better value from simpler and more specialised software.

CASE HISTORY: Richard

Richard Kent discovered that office suites are not always as useful as they can appear to be.

'I work as a computer and music journalist, and it was becoming obvious that I was losing work because I didn't have a PC. It took me six months of research to find the system I wanted at an affordable price. By then prices had come down as well, which helped.

'I found an office suite package advertised for £175, excluding VAT. This seemed like a very good price, so I phoned the dealer and got him to confirm. He told me it was a "competitive upgrade". I said I didn't even have a PC, never mind any competitive PC software. He told me not to worry – that was all sorted. I gave him my credit cards details and ordered the software.

'It arrived a couple of days later. I installed it, and for a long time was very happy. The word processor was much better than anything I was used to, the computer was very fast, and the organiser was – and still is – a godsend.

'But nine months on, I'm beginning to wonder if I got over-excited. The package also included a business presentation creator, a spreadsheet and a database. I deleted all three of these a couple of weeks after I got the package, and I still haven't used them yet. I may reinstall the spreadsheet to do my tax – but then again, I may not.

'I think these packages are designed for medium-sized businesses and corporate users. They are good packages – there's no doubt about that – but for a single person working at home they're not really necessary. I could have done with more help organising my tax returns and my invoices, neither of which I'm very good at, but they didn't help at all there. I'm sure they could, but I can't be bothered to set them up. And it would be easier to buy a proper package for exactly those jobs from somewhere else.

'In general I'd warn people to be cautious of software advertising – especially "free" software. You may be lucky and get exactly what you need, but also you may not. I was lucky in that I got a good deal and didn't really waste any money. If you need a word processor, buy a word processor – and don't get a whole suite unless it's only slightly more expensive, or you know what you are getting, and it really is what you want.'

Upgrade deals

Richard's story illustrates another useful buying tip – the 'upgrade' deal. Some software is quoted with three prices. The first is the official retail price. The second is the 'competitive upgrade' price. This applies if you have a competing software product from another manufacturer; you trade in your old software and get new software in return.

Some dealers will supply you with free software which qualifies for the upgrade deal, so you can buy from them at the reduced rate. The third is the 'version upgrade'. If you already own an older copy of the software, you can get a new copy – with improved features – by paying this price. The numbers and letters after the name of the software are important if you decide on this price level. For example, Word Pro v2.0 means you are buying version 2.0 of the Word Pro program (sometimes the 'v' is left out). The higher the number, the newer the software (thus WordPerfect 6.0 is newer than WordPerfect 5.1). Version numbers are usually included in advertisements.

By shopping around you can pick up one of these older versions at a bargain price and use it as the basis for an upgrade deal. Often you will pay less for the old version plus an upgrade than for the new package. You may find that the older version does the job you want and you will not need to upgrade.

Vouchers

With some upgrade deals, however, you may not get the software immediately. Instead, you will be given or sent a voucher which you then pass on to the manufacturer, sometimes with proof of ownership of relevant older or competing software. The software will arrive through the post. This can be irksome if you need to get on with some work quickly.

Before ordering an upgrade of any kind, check to see if there are any vouchers involved, and if so, what the time scale will be. If you are going to have to wait for three weeks you may want to reconsider your purchase or factor this delay into your schedule.

Bundles

Another way to get cheap software is to accept a bundle that comes with your computer when you buy it. Many larger hardware dealers include an office suite as a bundle. If you do not want it, you can delete it or choose not to install it, but unless the software is what you want anyway you should be wary of allowing a bundle deal to sway your decision about where to buy.

In practice, some bundles are not quite as good value as they appear.

CASE HISTORY: Ralph

Ralph Harris, a wine and spirits wholesaler, discovered this for himself – but managed not to waste his money.

'I'd been thinking of computerising my operation for a while, and I was asking advice from a friend. After months of checking I'd found a likely-looking deal in a magazine and I wanted to know what he thought. The deal included accounts software for free and a good price for the hardware. There were some other bits and pieces thrown in – a route planner, a couple of games, that kind of thing.

'I was surprised how dismissive he was when I told him about the deal. He told me that most of the software would be pretty useless and that offer deals were put together to shift the software by giving it away.

'All the same, I decided to buy the whole lot. The price was so good that I could add some good software later.

'In fact he was right. The accounts package was terrible, and the games wouldn't even work on my machine. It turned out to have something to do with the way the memory was set up. I phoned the dealer, and he told me I needed something called a memory manager. As I'm not much bothered about games, I decided to leave it.

'But I must say the route planner has been a great toy and very helpful with deliveries. So it wasn't all completely wasted.'

OFFICE SUITES

Many computers are supplied with an 'office suite', either as part of the package or as an optional extra offered at a discount compared to the prices usually charged in computer stores. As shown in Chapter 1, these suites include a complete set of business tools – a word processor, spreadsheet, address book and, typically, extras such as a presentation manager and a database.

Microsoft Office has become the standard for office suites. Many documents are now prepared using the Word word processor; for formatted text Word has become a *de facto* standard. The latest version of Office, known as Office 2000, makes it possible to exchange documents using the HTML Internet standard, as well as using Microsoft's own proprietary system. This helps to make Office documents easier to share with people who don't use Office.

The most sophisticated version of Office is aimed at businesses which need a system where employees can make sales and track contacts on different computers that have been networked together. As well as providing all the usual appointment-management, email and other groupware facilities, it enables sales to be made and tracked automatically on the Internet, and managers can see summaries of business activity at any time.

Lotus Corporation (now part of IBM) offers its **Smartsuite** series in competition. The latest 'Millennium' edition of Smartsuite includes the same general set of tools as Office 2000, but without the most recent Internet-oriented sophistication. Older versions of

Disks and manuals

If you do decide that a bundle is right for you, check that the disks and manuals are included.

Having a copy of the software on your hard disk is not enough. If something goes wrong and your hard disk loses the programs you have lost your software. You can of course make safety copies of your own, but this can be extremely time-consuming. With manufacturer-supplied master disks this problem can be avoided. The software can be reinstalled and work can continue as before (assuming that your information has also been backed up regularly). The same applies to the manuals. Although modern software often includes a help feature,

Smartsuite are sometimes given away free by magazines, and these can be worth looking out for by anyone on a tight budget, or who simply wants a free high-quality word processor. The Millennium edition comes with IBM's ViaVoice speech-recognition system built in (see pages 53–4).

Corel Corporation's **WordPerfect Suite** is not as widely available. A completely free version is available for users of the Linux system (see Appendix XIII). Otherwise, WordPerfect Suite is perhaps most notable for its inclusion of the WordPerfect word processor, which many users find preferable to Microsoft's Word.

Even when supplied 'free', a full office suite may not be a good all-round business solution. For typical home users even the simplest version of Office is likely to be overkill in terms of both price and facilities. Suites use a lot of computer power and storage space, and offer many features which are often left unused or even undiscovered. When they are bought commercially, prices are relatively high.

Microsoft Works is a much cheaper option, and provides simplified versions of the usual address book, word processor and spreadsheet combination. A similar simplified product that is worth considering is **Claris Works.** While these lack the many complex options available in their professional counterparts, they are easier to learn, easier to use and much cheaper. Most home and small business users will find them perfectly adequate.

this can be sketchy. Access to printed manuals is essential for beginners and for reference.

Most dealers are willing to supply disks and manuals for an extra charge – a typical price might be around £80 for a full set of manuals and disks. Even with this extra cost you may find a bundle can save you money.

Chapter 10

Choosing the right hardware

From the outside one computer looks very much like another. So why are some computers so much more expensive than others? How can you find the one that best meets your needs?

Several factors influence the selling price of a computer. Some, such as performance, can be measured objectively. Others, such as brand image, offer more elusive (some would say illusory) benefits. But to a beginner or a professional user support stands out as being particularly important.

Features to look out for

The following factors will affect the cost of a computer:

Speed A computer's price is directly related to how quickly it can perform a task. Most office work does not require the fastest machines available; an 'average' machine will be sufficient and the best value for money.

Space for your information There is a limit to the amount of information a computer can store. As a rough guide the more your computer costs, the greater the limit. The limit depends on what you want the computer to do. The whole of this book, for example, takes up less than 1/400th of the total storage space available on the computer on which it was originally written and would take up less than 1/10000th of the space available in a modern machine. Unless you need to keep track of huge amounts of information, have to deal with thousands of clients' records or want to use your computer to work directly with sound or video, then the space available in almost any modern machine will fit your needs.

Room to grow Most computers can be upgraded to offer new facilities and better performance. This is easier to do on some machines than on others. Computer technology is improving all the time, and extras designed for the latest machines may not work with older ones.

Deciding whether or not you will need to upgrade can be difficult. Many new features are bought for fun rather than for good business reasons. Fortunately, you should be able to upgrade any modern machine with ease. Older computers are more problematic, and you should assume that you will not be able to upgrade them. (This is something of a simplification, as often you will be able to add extras – but not as cheaply or easily as you could with a modern machine. In some cases you may end up spending more than a new machine would cost.)

Build quality Some computers are built more solidly than others. The details are slight and most of them will not be obvious unless you open up the case and look inside. However, these differences can affect long-term reliability and also the ease with which you can upgrade. Buying from a good dealer should ensure that your machine is solid enough for your needs.

Brand image In theory you should get a better-quality product and better support from a large and established manufacturer than a smaller one. But a computer made by a large company with a famous name will cost more than one made by a small-scale start-up business. The reasons for this are partly historical. Larger computer manufacturers traditionally sold to big businesses, which could afford to pay higher prices. Over the last few years this has changed, but some of the big-name brands – such as Compaq, Dell and IBM – still carry a price premium. Brand image can be a red herring for the unwary buyer. Unless you are impressed by the products and support service of a big-name manufacturer, there is no good reason to go for the extra expense. A big name does not automatically guarantee you a better computer and may sometimes mean you are paying a lot for some fancy lettering on the case. However, it is more likely that a larger manufacturer will remain in business for the lifetime of the computer. And some of the larger companies, notably Dell and Gateway, do make an effort to provide high-quality support.

Support The important question to ask here is 'What happens if my computer goes wrong?' You might expect the quality of after-sales service to be reflected in the price. This is not always true. Many buyers have found that they get better service from a small, locally based retailer who also sells hardware at a reasonable price. Small companies are sometimes run by enthusiasts who take the time to build up a good working relationship with their customers. A large company will often treat its customers more impersonally.

It is advisable to find out about a dealer's support service *before* a problem occurs rather than after. Although there are no guarantees of support, you can check a dealer's attitude to support by asking a few questions. Someone who is enthusiastic and helpful will give you much better support and in the long term could prove a much better supplier. Good support is vital. It is well worth paying a little extra to be sure of support. Some dealers will take the long-term view and provide you with help and advice in the hope that you will buy from them in the future. Others will take your money and send out the goods, but will not offer any more service. However, if you have access to expert help from elsewhere and therefore do not have to rely fully on the dealer, then you can sometimes get bargains from these latter dealers.

What's inside the box?

By choosing your software first and making a note of the specifications required by that software you are on the way to ensuring that you get a system that will fit your needs.

However, some basic computer knowledge can also be useful. Here is a short introduction to the inside of a computer (more detailed explanations are included in the Appendices, especially Appendix IX).

A computer consists of a main system unit with attached extras such as the keyboard, screen and printer. Inside the main system unit are the parts of the computer that do the actual work. They include:

A motherboard This is the heart of the computer. It holds the processor chip that does the calculations, and also the RAM (random access memory) that the processor uses. The processor does all the work, rather like the engine in a car, and the memory works rather like a desk in an office − it is used as a work area, where information can be held temporarily while being worked on.

Hard disk drive (often shortened to **hard drive**, or **hard disk**) This provides fast-access, longer-term storage and is equivalent to a filing cabinet. Information held in the computer's memory is lost when it is turned off, so it has to be saved to the hard disk beforehand. It is loaded from the hard disk when it needs to be used again.

Floppy disk drive This is used to get information into and out of the computer. Software is often supplied as one or more **floppy disks** – small plastic wafers with a metal catch that protects a thin disk of magnetised plastic. The plastic holds the information and the rigid case protects it from finger prints and other hazards.

Memory, hard disk and floppy disk capacities are all measured in **megabytes** (Mb). One megabyte is roughly equivalent to one million letters – including spaces and punctuation marks. You will also come across **kilobyte** (Kb – one-thousandth of a megabyte) and **gigabyte** (Gb – one thousand megabytes, occasionally shortened to 'gig') units of information capacity. The text of this book – which is approximately 70,000 words – takes up roughly 700Kb. A long letter might take up 3Kb. A large piece of software will need around 40Mb. Typical capacities are between 32Mb and 128Mb for a computer's main memory, 1.44Mb for a floppy disk drive, and 9Gb and upwards for a hard disk drive. Floppy disk drive capacities are more or less standard across all machines but the other figures can vary. Hard disk drive capacities are increasing rapidly. By 2000 the standard hard disk size is likely to be at least 12Gb. Meanwhile, floppy disks are slowly being superseded by a number of other systems – for further information see pages 215.

Extras are either internal and plug straight into **expansion slots** on the motherboard, or external, plugging into **serial and parallel ports** on the back of the machine. Expansion slots provide a direct connection to the computer's internals and allow you to add extra features, such as sound and graphics, by plugging them straight in. Most computers include blanking plates at the back to hide the slots when not in use.

Serial and parallel ports are connectors on the back of the computer and are used to get information into and out of the machine in a less direct way. The printer is usually connected to the parallel port, and the mouse (a small palm-shaped pointing device that is rolled around the desk) is connected to the serial port. (Parallel and serial refer to the way the information flows – either in big chunks or spread out along a single wire.) Modern computers are also supplied with **USB ports** which are designed as a replacement for both serial and parallel ports, and work much more quickly.

Common extras today include:

Soundcard, which allows your computer to record and play back sounds and music. Often a small pair of loudspeakers will come with a soundcard. Less often you will also be supplied with a microphone.

CD-ROM or DVD drive, with which, in combination with a soundcard, the computer can play ordinary music CDs. More importantly, it can also access information and software that is now also being supplied on a special kind of CD known as a CD-ROM. Examples include the *Oxford English Dictionary*, some encyclopedias, games and even some business software. CD-ROMs have become popular with manufacturers because they are a good way to supply a lot of information (over 650Mb or 5Gb for DVD) on a single small piece of plastic. They are also ideal for the new breed of multimedia applications which combine text, sound and video. (Since 1999 some computers have become available with DVD drives instead of CD-ROM drives – see pages 214–5.)

Modem, which is used to transfer information along the telephone line to another computer. Most modems can also send and receive faxes and work as an auto-dialler.

Scanner, which transfers images from paper to your computer. You can take a photograph and scan it across to the computer screen. Once it has been scanned, you can manipulate the images using photo-editing software such as Adobe's Photoshop.

IBM or Apple?

There are two kinds of computer that are widely available and they are sold in slightly different ways. Your choice will depend on the software you want to use. Businesses tend to use the common **IBM-compatible standard** (also known as a PC). Such machines are designed and built by a huge range of manufacturers and are available from all kinds of outlets, ranging from high-street stores to specialist dealers. The word 'compatible' – 'clone' is sometimes used to mean the same thing – means that all these machines are designed to work to the same specification. Hardware and software that work on one modern machine will work on all of them. (Note that this applies only to new designs. Old software will usually work in new machines, but the reverse is not true.) It is easy to exchange information between different brand names and models.

Users with creative or artistic interests tend to favour computers made by Apple. Apple used to control the production and distribution of its machines very strictly. They were made only by Apple itself and sold by a strictly regulated chain of dealerships. This changed in early 1995. Apple is now licensing its technology to one or two other companies and Apple machines are available through many of the same outlets that sell PCs.

In general, Apple machines are much more popular with their users and inspire an almost religious devotion unmatched by other systems. Perhaps this is because Apple-compatible systems – both hardware and software – seem much more colourful and 'human' than their IBM counterparts. Apple hardware also tends to be more appealing aesthetically. However, the IBM market has the advantage of scale. Competition is very fierce within the PC market, and prices can and do fall spectacularly.

For home or light business use there is very little to choose between the two lines. The same kinds of software are widely available on both machines, and it is a case of trying out each brand to see which feels the most comfortable and easy to use.

For more serious and professional use, the markets diverge significantly. Apple machines are used more for applications such as design, and book and magazine publishing. Both the hardware and the software tend to be geared towards these areas of use. IBM machines are used for everything else. Equivalent 'creative' software is available, but powerful IBM machines tend to be used more for business-oriented applications. Prices diverge at this level too, with Apple machines becoming approximately half as expensive again as equivalently powerful IBM models – although this does not become a factor until the very top-line models in each range are compared. Apple machines tend to hold their resale value.

How much can you expect to pay?

Even with the pace of technological development, computer prices have stabilised into price bands, from second-hand 'antique' to showroom-new. (Note that these are prices for the main hardware only – the main system unit, the keyboard, the screen and an operating system. You will need to allow for software, support, maintenance and other extras such as a printer before you can estimate the total system price.)

Vintage – between £50 and £100

These machines are more or less obsolete and are only available second-hand. They cannot be upgraded to offer new features, they work very slowly and many cannot work with modern software at all. For tasks such as basic word processing, however, they can fit the bill perfectly. Many are still being used successfully ten years after they were purchased.

Dated – between £100 and £250

Although almost obsolete, these machines are still viable for light-duty work such as letter-writing and basic accounts. They are significantly more powerful than vintage machines, but not powerful enough to work with the very latest software. There are severe restrictions on how easily they can be upgraded so they should be bought on a 'what you see is what you get' basis, rather than with an eye to future possibilities. Many of these machines are still used in offices today, although they are now available only on the second-hand market.

Recent – between £250 and £500

These machines are at the trailing edge of recent developments and are still available new. They can be upgraded but there will be limits to what they can do. They will work with the latest software, albeit very slowly. They offer a good deal for medium-duty work such as simple spreadsheets and payroll calculations for a small company.

Because Apple has such a tight grip on its market, Apple computers do not appear in this price bracket. When older models become obsolete Apple simply replaces them with newer and more powerful designs. Only very rarely are these older machines sold off as 'bargains'.

Entry level – between £500 and £750

These are the cheapest of the modern machines. They will work with all the latest software. It is possible, but not certain, that you will be able to upgrade them to work with the very latest extras.

Although much faster and more powerful than older machines, they may appear slow when compared to more expensive models. However, this speed difference will only become apparent when you attempt more demanding work. More modest applications will hardly show any difference at all.

Established – between £750 and £1,000

These offer the best price/performance ratio of any computer design. They provide enough speed and power to cope with recent software and can easily be upgraded. If you expect your needs to increase over the next couple of years, you should consider an established machine.

Advanced – between £1,000 and £2,000

These offer more performance than the established designs and are intended for users who require speed. Typical applications include professional-quality DTP, financial analysis and graphic design.

There is often some overlap between this category and the leading edge, which means that some of these advanced machines may use the latest technology. For reasons given below these should be treated with suspicion. If in doubt, ask your retailer how long a particular design has been available. If it is less than 18 months, you are almost certainly dealing with a leading-edge machine and all the comments below will apply.

Leading edge – between £1,500 and £10,000

These machines are the very best that are available. However, as with software it is a good idea never to buy a completely new design. In the industry the leading edge of technology is sometimes known as the 'bleeding edge' because it can cause users so much heartache. Competition between manufacturers is fierce, and there is a lot of pressure on the industry to keep ahead of the market with new and faster designs. Products are often released before they have been fully tested. If you are using a computer to maintain a business, you cannot afford to be in a position where your computer works only occasionally, gives wrong results or deletes work without notice.

This level of computer is also far too powerful for everyday use. In an everyday office environment most of that power will be wasted. Leading-edge systems are designed for demanding applications such as sound and video editing, architectural visualisation and software development.

Desktop vs portable

You have one more choice to make when deciding on a specification, and that is whether or not to buy a portable computer. The advantages of a portable are obvious – you can use it anywhere, you can keep your important information with you all the time, and you can even use it to keep in touch with a larger computer at home or at the office.

There are disadvantages too: cost and security. Portables tend to be much more expensive than a desktop machine with a similar specification; you can pay £6,000 for a top-of-the-range model, although prices for reasonably powerful machines start at around £1,000. As for ensuring the security of your information, you can install password protection on your portable, but anyone who is computer-literate can work around most password systems fairly quickly.

Battery life and weight are two further considerations. Only the very best portables offer more than a few hours of useful working time, so their range in the field is limited. Some portables are quite heavy: the shirt-pocket computer that can replace a desktop machine has not quite arrived yet.

Some people like the freedom of a portable, and if you can see yourself writing letters in bed before breakfast then a portable will be perfect for you. But for most ordinary office tasks a desktop machine will be cheaper, safer and easier to maintain and to use. (See Appendix VII for more details on portables.)

Obsolete bargains

You will often see computers advertised for less than £500. Many of them are machines that are now obsolete and being sold off as bargains. Depending on what you want from your computer these can offer good value. However, modern machines can be upgraded to make them more powerful and are therefore a better investment in the long run, as their effective working life is extended and they can be made to work with more modern and powerful software tools. This will not apply to an obsolete machine. It will be harder to upgrade, will not work with modern software and, eventually, it may even need to be sold or thrown away completely.

However, in practice this may not be a problem. For simple, undemanding tasks a cheap obsolete machine may be perfect, as long as you buy it knowing its limitations. If you cannot envisage your computer needs expanding significantly in the near future, then an older machine can be a good buy. Bear in mind that if it is very old you should check for the availability of consumables in the same way that you would for a second-hand machine.

Upgrades

All recent computers can be upgraded to take advantage of new technology as it becomes more widely available. If you buy a reasonably priced computer – costing around £1,000 or so – you will almost certainly find you have a range of upgrade options to choose from.

When starting out, however, it is prudent to ignore these until you are familiar with your machine and have got the most you can out of it. If you have an older machine you may find yourself under pressure from trade magazines (perhaps even from friends) to bring it up to more modern standards. Think long and hard before you do. If your computer serves all your current needs, there is no reason for you to upgrade. You should only start to think about this seriously if you feel that your machine is annoyingly sluggish at times, or if some new software arrives which could be useful to you but will not work on your machine.

Deciding whether to buy a high-specification model or a low-specification one that can be upgraded later can be a bit like playing the futures market on the Stock Exchange. In general, it can be worth buying a slightly more powerful machine than you need. For office work, however, it is unlikely that a working system will need to be updated more than once every few years at most. This corresponds to the time it takes a generation of computers to move down from the leading edge to obsolescence. It also corresponds to the four-year writing-down period for capital tax allowances. It is not usually advantageous to get a cheap machine with a view to upgrading later.

The situation is slightly different for home computers that are used for playing games as well as for work. Surprisingly, perhaps, games are much more demanding of computer power than most office applications. You will find that a computer used for games has a much shorter active life and will also need to be upgraded regularly. If games are a serious interest then consider buying the very best computer you can afford.

Buying step by step

By choosing your software first, you have already decided on the hardware to make it work. Most software comes with a minimum, or a typical, hardware specification which is mentioned somewhere on the packaging or in the manual. You can quote this directly to a dealer, even if you do not understand what the words mean. Where possible, choose a 'typical' or 'recommended' rather than a 'minimum' specification, as these will give you the extra power to work comfortably. By following the specifications you will get a computer that does what you want, rather than one the industry wants to sell you. What you choose depends on your requirements. If you foresee your needs expanding, choose a better and more powerful machine than the software specification suggests. If you are looking for a system for basic office work that you can install and forget, ignore the high–pressure sales techniques and follow the specifications.

Once you have a rough specification, you can start contacting a few dealers. The best place to look first is in your local *Yellow Pages*. Quote the specification you need, explain which software you will be using, mention that you are a beginner and will need good support, and see what kind of response you get. If you find someone sympathetic and helpful, ask if they can do a package deal which includes all the software you want.

In any conversation with a dealer, note down the time and date, the name of the person to whom you spoke, and any prices you are quoted. You can leave any further details, such as warranties and extras, for a later call. Make a list of the dealers who seem knowledgeable and approachable, together with their best quoted prices. If you find a dealer who responds positively on the telephone, it is worth making a visit to see how you are treated in person. Do not be surprised if you find yourself in a shoddy-looking shop instead of a stylish showroom; it is the level of enthusiasm, interest and professionalism which is important.

Your next step is to repeat the exercise with dealers from further afield. You will find these advertised in any computer magazine.

Buying long-distance has its drawbacks, but finding out the going rate for hardware on a nationwide basis can sometimes give you a good negotiating position with your local dealer.

The advantage of buying from a larger company – such as Dell or Gateway – is that they are more likely to be financially stable and less likely to disappear overnight. The disadvantage is that they will often charge you more for their services.

Smaller dealers will usually offer slightly better prices. Some machines are assembled in garages and bedrooms, advertised in the low-cost trade weeklies and sold by mail-order. Others are built by huge companies with multi-million-pound turnovers. Both kinds of dealer use the same sets of parts, which are bought in bulk from wholesale electronic design companies in South-East Asia. The only thing that distinguishes these wares is the level of support the dealers can offer you, and the care and attention the manufacturers give to assembling their machines.

Advertising ploys

Smaller dealers sometimes quote rock-bottom prices and it is not until you read the small print that you discover that the system is incomplete – a keyboard, screen and mouse are extra. Another tactic is to sell the operating system (Windows) as an 'optional' extra. This can add around £70 to the quoted price. To get around this you should ask if the price you have been quoted includes everything you need to run your software right away. Then, just to be sure, check if there are any 'extras' you need. As usual you should make a note of the replies.

Another marketing tactic is to pepper a specification with emotive words such as 'fast', 'powerful' and 'huge'. Often such words are used to confuse the unwary and hide the fact that the system is no better – and sometimes significantly worse – than average. The more of these words you find within a specification list, the less likely it is that you are dealing with someone you can trust.

Your shortlist

By now you should have a shortlist of dealers. You still need to sort out support, maintenance and (perhaps) insurance for your purchase, and you will also need to think about security and protecting your information. These will be discussed in the following chapters.

Chapter 11

Insuring and protecting your computer

Before you buy your computer, you need to be sure that you are protected from the various things that can go wrong. Computers can and do break down. They can also be stolen or damaged. Sometimes the problems are easy to fix and no harm is done apart from a few hours' delay. At other times the results can be catastrophic, with months or even years of work obliterated in seconds. How can you protect yourself? And what other dangers do you need to take into account?

Warranties

As a first step, it is essential to make sure you get a warranty with your computer. The simplest is the **back to base warranty**. Under this scheme your computer will be repaired, and defective parts will be replaced if, and only if, you send the computer back to the retailer. You pay the cost of this initial delivery, although the retailer usually pays for the return of your machine.

This is the standard minimum warranty you will be offered. It has very serious limitations if you are planning to rely on your machine for business purposes. First, the warranty is worth nothing unless you can return the machine to where you bought it. If your retailer is not local you can expect to pay between £10 and £15 for a next-day delivery using a courier service.

Second and far more important, this kind of warranty does not usually guarantee how quickly your machine will be repaired. If it needs to be sent back to the manufacturer it may take weeks. If you rely on your computer on a daily basis this kind of delay can be extremely inconvenient.

Reputable dealers may be willing to provide you with a temporary machine while the repairs are being done. This is a useful option to have, but bear in mind that when your computer goes back to the manufacturer, so does all the information – including the software – you keep on it. Even if you keep safety copies of your work, recreating your working environment on a new machine can take anything from an evening to a few days.

A variation on the back to base warranty is known as **collect and return**. Although popular once, it is now becoming increasingly rare. With this warranty you do not have to pay carriage costs. This is a slightly better option, but all the same caveats apply.

Far more useful is the **on-site warranty**. Under this scheme your supplier contracts to send an engineer to you when something goes wrong. Unfortunately, it is still no guarantee that your computer will be repaired immediately.

On-site warranties vary greatly. Sometimes they are available as an optional extra when you buy a machine. You may even get one year's free on-site service as part of the initial purchase deal, and another year or two for an extra fee. However the deal is arranged, check the small print of the service contract. Watch out for the following:

Call-out time and repair time A warranty that guarantees that your computer will be looked at within eight hours of your call is worth much more to you than one that states that it will be looked at within five working days. Very few companies will guarantee a repair time, but this is obviously a highly desirable feature if you come across one.

Charges What exactly does the warranty cover – parts, labour, both or neither? Is there an excess charge for the first part of any costs?

Company reputation Many dealers subcontract their warranties to independent support firms; some of these are reliable and professional, others are cowboys. Try to get the telephone number of the support company from your dealer. Then telephone the support company and ask about their charges, call-out times and references from customers. The quality, tone and efficiency of the answers will indicate the kind of support you can expect. If you like the way the company works, take the opportunity to ask about their services. You may even want to think about taking out a longer-term contract.

Company stability The worst possible situation to find yourself in is with a warranty contract from a company that has gone out of business. This does happen, and the results vary from the inconvenient to the disastrous. You could ask the company directly about its financial stability. Someone in a professional and stable company will understand the need for your question and should be able to reassure you immediately.

Experience and references Does the company know what it is doing? Some firms have been known to claim to maintain certain types of computer, when in fact they have no experience of them at all. If in doubt, ask for references. Experienced and professional companies will be able to provide you with references.

Resources Ask about the company's 'back-room' technical resources and repair facilities. Does it subcontract the work?

Contract Is it possible to see a standard contract in advance? If not – be very wary.

Location The company should be within easy travelling distance or have a local office.

Quality control Is the company certified as complying with the ISO 9000 or older BS5750 quality-control standards? Or is it applying for certification? These impressive-sounding titles guarantee the existence of quality-control procedures, but offer no further assurance that work really is done to high standards. In practice, the certification system seems to be open to potential abuse, and some quality-control professionals are unhappy with the loopholes that exist. It is likely that these standards will be changed soon. In the meantime it is wiser to judge a company's reliability on the other criteria mentioned here.

Service contracts

In many cases now, PCs are being sold with additional service contracts which extend the existing warranty for an additional period, typically an extra year or two. The value of these is problematic, and depends on the reliability of the hardware in question – something that is obviously unknown to most buyers.

Factors to consider when deciding whether or not to pay for an extended warranty include:

Disruption caused by failure If a non-working PC will cause major problems for your business, then the value of the peace of mind offered by a service contract increases. Conversely, a machine occasionally used at home is unlikely to need such a high level of service.

Contract details As with standard warranties, it is important to check exactly what you are paying for. For a business, the only extra warranty worth considering seriously is an on-site one. As before, it is essential to check the call-out time and turn-around time you can expect if something does go wrong.

Repair vs replacement For a business using a number of PCs, it may actually be cheaper to buy a spare machine than to take out a service contract for all of them. It is relatively straightforward to transfer information and settings to an identical machine. (Usually all that needs to be done is to take the hard disk from the dead machine and fit it into the new one – something that should take an experienced technician two hours at the very most.)

Contract repair vs one-off repairs It can be worth checking alternative local sources of repair and comparing prices for piece-work with a full formal service contract. A good way to do this is to get a list of prices for standard operations, such as replacing a hard disk, a motherboard, a processor chip, and so on. Very serious faults can usually be fixed quickly by simply replacing a dead part with a new one, and this makes the potential costs easy to estimate. Sporadic faults are more problematic, harder to guesstimate, and much less predictable.

Insurance

An increasingly popular option for some businesses is to take out insurance. This pays for the cost of any repairs and may also help indemnify your business against problems caused by the loss of your computer.

Your existing household insurance may cover your equipment and public liability if you work from home in a small way. But you must tell your insurer that you work from home, or you could find that your cover is invalid. Your insurer is also likely to insist on a special policy once your business equipment rises above a certain value, if your work involves people visiting your home, or if the risk of fire or theft is increased (because you store flammable materials, for example).

Several companies now offer policies specially for people who work at home. Some of these provide you with the equivalent of a maintenance contract – some insurance policies compare favourably with maintenance arrangements, and you should investigate both to give yourself the widest range of options. Others are fully comprehensive policies which cover you against damage by water, fire, theft, and may even include extra funds which allow you to hire a machine while your original computer is being repaired. A number of policies also include options which cover the costs of 're-instating' data, which can mean recompiling it from the original sources, or paying someone else to do this for you.

Some will even cover you for 'consequential loss', although this is usually an expensive option. This means that if you lose work because your computer is out of action, you will be reimbursed for some or all of your financial losses.

As with any insurance policy, it is a good idea to read the small print to see what conditions you have to fulfil for the policy to be valid. You will normally be charged an excess – typically £50 – if you make any claim. Some policies also stipulate certain security arrangements you need to take to minimise your risks. These vary from making sure that data is safe, by keeping safety copies and checking for viruses, to making your premises as theft-proof as possible – perhaps bolting your computer to your desk. If you work in an 'unsafe' environment, expect to pay extra. Most British policies cover the use of notebook computers in the UK, but if you travel abroad a lot you will usually be asked to pay a higher premium. A useful source of more detailed information about insurance is the free booklet *Insurance Advice for Small Businesses*, available from the Association of British Insurers (see Addresses).

Backups

Even without insurance, you can take steps to make sure that your information is as safe as possible. This is *vital*, especially for business use.

Your first step is to *save your work regularly* on the computer's hard disk. If something happens it will still be there when you turn on the machine again. Some software has an **auto-save feature** which does this automatically.

Once your information is on disk, you need to make copies and keep them somewhere safe. These are known as backups, and are a time-consuming but essential chore.

CASE HISTORY: Simon

Simon Jones is a computer consultant.

'Half of the phone calls I get are from people who have accidentally lost some work on their computer and want me to try to get it back for them. I try, sometimes I succeed, but often I don't. The users may have deleted what they want by mistake, had a faulty hard disk or had their machine stolen. In all these cases their most urgent need is for the data which is now unavailable for whatever reason. If they had taken regular backups this problem would simply not exist.

'I try to drum into them the value of taking regular backups of work. It may seem time-consuming and silly at the time but it will save heartache and bad temper in the long run.'

Floppy disks are ideal for low-volume work. You can simply copy the information from the computer to a floppy disk. 50Mb is about the maximum you can comfortably archive on floppy disks. (This is how the backup copies of this book were maintained – the text fits on to a single 1.44Mb high-density disk.) Most computers come with a free backup utility that packs the information more tightly on to each disk and also automates the process across multiple disks. As a rough guide, you can expect to spend about 20 minutes archiving 50Mb of information. Newer LS120 drives (see page 215) can fit nearly ten times as much information on a single disk, but are also relatively slow.

For higher-volume work, the cheapest options are the various **tape cassette** systems now available. These can store varying amounts of information – 1Gb, 3.2Gb and 4Gb are typical sizes. The units are fairly cheap – around about £200 for a 4Gb system. They are slow but, unlike a floppy disk-based system, you can leave them running overnight unattended. The cassettes themselves are also cheap – around £20 for a 4Gb cassette.

Tape cassettes do not have a reputation for reliability. Where possible you should verify information after you have backed it up to confirm that it has been recorded accurately. Backup software is usually supplied with the tape streamer. You should make sure that it includes a 'verify' option.

Many cassette systems offer a 'compressed' option which attempts to squeeze even more information on to a tape – for example, a 4Gb tape can hold around 8Gb of compressed information. Where possible use the uncompressed option, again because it is more reliable.

DAT (digital audio tape) systems are more reliable, but also much more expensive. At the time of writing DAT systems cost around £800, and offer 24Gb of storage – ample for most situations. The system also uses tape cartridges, but these are much smaller – around half the size of an audio cassette – and much more robust. A DAT system is recommended if you need a 'bullet-proof' backup system. DAT backups are also very much faster than other tape systems. An 8Gb backup can be done in as little as 20 minutes, as opposed to an hour or more.

Tape-based systems suffer from the disadvantage of being linear – the information is arranged in order along the tape. If you want to restore some information that is at the end of the tape, you have to wait for the tape to wind to the right position. A tape system is recommended if you do full backups of everything on a regular basis, which you should do at least once a month, ideally once a week. It is also possible to do incremental backups. These only backup the information that has changed since the last full backup. This should be done daily.

Tape backup systems also suffer from more subtle drawbacks. Tape wear can be a problem if you use the system regularly, and this can lead to wasted time if you regularly have to back up the backups to prevent information loss. Another problem is print-through – information tends to leach to adjacent loops of tape when the tape is tightly wound. In large organisations which maintain huge tape archives, these are regularly unwound and retensioned to minimise this problem.

One final backup option is CD-R – you create a CD with your own information written on it. These special writable CDs are as reliable and robust as any other CD and offer a high capacity – around 650Mb.

Disk blanks cost around £1 – much less in bulk. At around £200 this is now a very affordable option, and also offers the additional advantage of allowing users to create their own music CDs for use in the car or on the hi-fi.

Other systems

A number of other products are very affordable and work very much like floppy disks, but have greater storage capacities. The most popular are the Iomega **Zip** and **Jaz** drives and the **Syquest EZ** drive range. These are discussed in more detail in Appendix II.

Software backups

As well as keeping your information safe, it is a very good idea to make safety copies of the software you use. If it was supplied on floppy disks, you should make copies and never use the originals. You will need between 50 and 100 floppy disks to make a backup of a typical full set of business software. Although it is a tedious chore, the advantages of this single task outweigh the disadvantages. If your hard disk loses its information and your software originals have become defective, you will have to buy the software again – even if it is one disk out of ten that is at fault. Making safety copies can save you time and temper later.

Storing backups

All backup copies should be stored somewhere safe and secure. The ideal is a fire-proof safe, or perhaps – if the information is sensitive as well as valuable – a bank safety-deposit box. A cheaper option is simply to keep safety copies somewhere off the premises – perhaps at home, or at a friend's or relative's house. If your business is burgled or burns down, your safety copies are intact.

As a further aid to security you may want to encrypt your work before you back it up. This will make your information look like gibberish – even to the trained eye – and can give you near-perfect security. The most secure encryption software available today is a shareware package called PGP (see page 85). PGP is available from most shareware libraries. It is slightly awkward to use, but provides near-perfect security.

Uninterruptible power supplies

While the UK National Grid is usually solid and reliable, under extreme conditions, or in remote rural areas, the power supply to your computer can become erratic and this can cause problems. In extreme cases a lightning strike or other power surge can actually damage your hardware.

A **UPS (Uninterruptible Power Supply)** solves these problems. It smoothes out fluctuations in the mains power level so that your computer always receives clean, steady power. UPS units also offer a short-term backup power source. In the event of a power cut your computer will remain on for a few minutes; this will allow you to shut down the system in a controlled way without losing any work.

Although UPSs are not cheap – prices range from a couple of hundred pounds to thousands for 'industrial-strength' models – they are recommended if you use your computer for 'mission critical' applications.

If you use a modem, another useful extra is the **line surge protector**. Every year a handful of computers are frazzled by lightning strikes coming in directly over a telephone line. (The risk may seem negligible, but one insurance company reported over 20 lightning-based claims a year.) BT wall sockets include basic surge protection but are not designed to cope with a direct strike. Fitting a surge protector can ensure that your computer stands a good chance of surviving a strike.

Chip coolers

A very useful – and recommended – hardware protection device is the **chip cooler**. This is a small metal radiator (known as a **heat sink**) that clips on to the computer's main processor chip and conducts heat away before it can do any damage. More recent examples include a built-in fan to cool the chip even further. Chip coolers come as standard on Pentium II and Pentium III computers, and some hard disks and graphics cards now run so hot that they also require them. AMD processors are typically not supplied with a chip cooler, although they do benefit substantially in terms of longer working life from having one fitted.

Viruses

Computer viruses come in two types. Most are simple, small programs that hide among useful information and copy themselves into your computer. They can then copy themselves onto any floppy disks or even home-recorded CDs that you make. If you swap information with a colleague or friend, his or her computer will also be 'infected'. Software copied from the Internet can also include this kind of virus.

A different kind of virus is the *macro virus*. This takes advantage of the automation features in an office suite – most often Microsoft's Office, as this is the most widely used suite. A good example is the Melissa virus which infected many Internet users in 1999. This copied itself by searching through a user's address book in Outlook Express and then creating a new set of email messages, which it then sent out automatically. Recipients found an official-looking email in their inbox. When they read it, the process started again.

Many viruses are harmless. Some are little more than elaborate practical jokes. However many can be very destructive. The worst a macro virus is capable of is wiping all the information on a hard disk, or bringing a company's mail system to a standstill until it is eliminated. Non-macro viruses can be even more destructive. The CIH/Chernobyl virus, which activates itself on 26 April every year (the anniversary of Chernobyl – some variants activate on the 26th of every month) not only wipes all the information on the hard disk but also attempts to wipe the computer's BIOS as well (see pages 183–4). If it succeeds, the only way to restart the computer is to have a new motherboard fitted. Without special tools it is impossible to check whether or not your computer is infected or to do anything about it. Fortunately these tools are readily available, easy to use and affordable.

It is possible to protect yourself from viruses by following a few simple rules. Never swap information with anyone unless you have to. When exchanging information electronically, text, graphics, sound and video clips are all virus-free. However, formatted documents (for example those prepared using Microsoft Word) and software sent electronically may not be virus-free. If someone sends you software 'attached' to an email, DO NOT start the software without first checking it for a virus.

If you need to work with other people's floppy disks, **anti-virus software** is recommended. This removes existing viruses and keeps new viruses out of your machine. Anti-virus packages respond only to viruses that have already been isolated and analysed. New viruses are being created all the time. Many packages now include a subscription option that will keep you safe from the latest examples.

Computer security systems

If you work with other people, you may need to make sure that your private information remains private. Short of encrypting information (for example, using the PGP system mentioned earlier), there is very little you can do to prevent a computer expert from gaining access to your computer. Desktop computers simply are not secure, and most security systems have loopholes.

On PCs, the most secure option you have is to use a **BIOS password** which you type in when the machine is starting up. This can only be changed by opening the case and short-circuiting or removing the battery on the main computer board. There is no easier way to change it if you forget it. Unfortunately not all PCs have this option. Check with your dealer if security is important to you.

For less secure applications, you can use a **screensaver password**. Most screensavers include a password feature which locks your machine so it cannot be accessed if you leave your desk. (A BIOS password offers protection only while the machine is starting up. Once it is running there is nothing to prevent anyone getting access to your records.) Password protection is perhaps the most useful feature of a screensaver. The protection can easily be 'hacked' by an expert, but it will deter casual users from trying to access your machine.

Many networks include reliable security features, most of which are password-based. If you forget your password, your network supervisor will be able to create a new one for you.

All password systems can be fallible if the password is obvious, or obviously visible. Never use a password that can be guessed easily such as the names of friends, children or spouses, or words associated with your hobbies. PIN numbers are another bad choice. The best passwords are nonsense combinations of words and letters which are all but unguessable.

Avoid typing in your password if anyone is standing close by. Never write a password down, but if you have to, don't keep it anywhere near the computer itself. It is traditional in some businesses to keep passwords on sticky notes under the desk or in a drawer or as a note in an address book. Avoid all of these options. Finally, make sure you change your password regularly – at least once a month, preferably once a week, perhaps even once a day if security is very important to you.

Some security systems are hardware-based. The most common of these is the **floppy disk lock**, a disk-sized square of plastic that can be locked into the floppy disk slot with a key. Disk locks are a good way to avoid viruses and unauthorised copying of software, but they will not protect you against unauthorised access to your computer.

Many insurance companies will ask you to improve security before they will agree to give you a policy. They will consider loss-of-earnings policies for home and business users, but may start to insist you secure your premises. The theft losses have been quite staggering. Some insurers used to do a flat rate, but now are including location-based payments. Premiums can vary by as much as 400 per cent between safe and high-risk areas.

Computer theft

Preventive measures

A senior crime prevention officer with first-hand experience of computer crime advises on how to prevent it.

'I'd look for a good standard of security generally. The first step is to keep the burglars out. That means curtains and blinds to hide the equipment so it can't be seen from outside, as well as good locks.

'Internal security is important. Who's doing the cleaning, for example. If it's contracted out, who are the contractors using? Are they secure, or are they likely to leave the key with someone? Laptops are another problem. Some thieves just walk in in broad daylight and help themselves to anything that isn't watched or secured.

'Once the burglar is in the building the alarm system means he needs to work fast. We [the police] can get to an alarm in under ten minutes, but it's important that the keyholder is on hand to let us in – sometimes this can take an hour or more, by which time it's too late to do anything. If the criminals can get in without an alarm, they'll spend all night taking things apart. Now that lock-down plates are common, some gangs are taking computers apart and just stealing the chips.

'Property marking is another useful deterrent. It makes it harder to resell things. Big organisations such as health and education authorities are going down the route of overtly marking everything very clearly. It's easy to change the case on a PC so it's not so important there, but with Macs it's harder and marking is more of a deterrent.

'For software and work, backups are essential. I've known some businesses that folded when they lost everything because they didn't protect their work. Boxed sets with the original packaging are very appealing to thieves. They can be sold at car boot sales, so I'd suggest people take the software out of the nice boxes and throw them away.

'If you take serial and model numbers, get rid of attractive packaging, anchor the hardware, reinforce the doors, put in an alarm and make regular backups you're as safe as you can be. But we still like to go to individual premises, so I'd suggest people call in their crime prevention officer – the advice is free – preferably before it happens.'

CASE HISTORY: Josh

Josh Brown is director of a desktop publishing bureau. He has been a victim of computer crime several times.

'It started in 1993. We got in one morning and all our Macs had gone – over £75,000 worth of equipment vanished overnight. It was a complete and utter disaster. The thieves took all our backup systems as well as the main machines. Most people had left backup cartridges in their drives, so we lost the lot.

'That almost killed the business. We lost a lot of work, a lot of goodwill, and it took a long time before our insurers came up with a cheque. Fortunately, we were covered for consequential losses. Otherwise that would have been it.

'We took advice from our insurers when we replaced the machines. As a result we put stronger locks on the doors and fitted an alarm system. But these gangs are professional, and three months later we were hit again. They broke in through the first-floor windows, ignored the alarm and took everything again. However, by then we were keeping backups and had taken to leaving them somewhere safe each night.

'Now we have bars on the windows, all the locks and the doors have been specially strengthened, and our Macs have been bolted to the desks with lockdown plates. I looked at having the desks reinforced as well, but it turned out to be too expensive.

'We've had no problems since, but it's been a complete pain to live with. Maintenance takes forever now, as we have to pull the machines apart on the spot before we can take them anywhere. And of course you can't just pick up a computer and move it now. You have to unbolt it first. Everyone hates it, and I don't blame them. But it's either that or the risk of losing everything all over again.'

Chapter 12

Buying a computer – the small print

The bulk of the cost of your computer system will come from your initial investment in hardware and software. By telephoning around and asking for quotes you should already have an idea of what these are likely to be, but there are other costs you also need to consider. The most important ones are:

Electricity How much power will your computer draw? Exact figures depend on the make and model involved, but typically you can expect the following:

Computer unit	200W
Monitor	80W
Laser printer	70W
Total	350W

This is roughly equivalent to keeping six 60W lightbulbs lit. A rough calculation shows that this adds between £10 and £15 a quarter to your bill, assuming an average use of around six hours a day.

Consumables If you are considering a laser printer, make sure you find out how many pages it prints before it needs new supplies. Then estimate how many pages you are likely to print. To get a realistic idea of how many you will print, double this number – at least. This allows for mistakes and misprints. Also check consumable costs. Although ink-jet printers are cheaper, if you are printing in bulk the laser is typically one-third the cost of the ink-jet (comparing ink with toner). (See Appendix II for more details on printers.)

You will also need to budget for floppy disks to keep safety copies of your work and your software. Floppy disks can be expensive. It is cheaper to buy in bulk (100 or more) direct from specialist dealers, many of whom advertise in computer magazines. Buying disks in twos and threes from high-street computer, stationery and business stores is not cost-effective. For small quantities the high-street discount chains, such as Argos, offer a much better deal. Buying by the hundred may seem excessive, but it is easy to use this many by keeping regular backups. If you have arranged to make regular backups using some other medium, allow for these in your final budget.

Maintenance, training and support costs How much is your maintenance cover going to cost? How much do you expect to pay for support? At the very least, you should allow for the purchase of books and magazines to help you get the best from your investment. At the other end of the scale you may opt for access to a full technical support line and a few training courses. These costs should be included in your budget before you buy.

Insurance Are you going to insure your machine? Will your policy cover you for a replacement if it is damaged or stolen, or will you also insure yourself against loss of business if your computer becomes unavailable for any reason? You need to decide on just how vital your computer will be to your business, and how much you can afford to be without it – as well as how much you can afford to pay to cover yourself against this.

VAT and delivery charges The prices of most computer equipment are quoted without VAT, so allow for this in your cash flow if you are VAT-registered, or simply write off the extra if you are not. You will probably also have to pay for the delivery of your system. This can add another £20 to the quoted price.

Telephone charges If you are buying any on-line services, allow for their charges, and also for increased telephone-line use. Bills of over £100 a month are not unheard of but can usually be avoided with careful planning.

First, since 1997 there has been a price war between BT and Cable and Wireless, and a small number of other telecommunications companies, so it is worth investigating their special offers.

Second, try to use the service during off-peak hours. It is possible to set up a system where the computer sends and receives mail and picks up news automatically during the early hours of the morning. Unless you need access to mail immediately, it's worth waiting till after the 6pm watershed.

And third, if you are expecting to spend a lot of time on–line, make sure you get the fastest modem you can. This can halve your costs and is well worth the small extra initial outlay.

Do not underestimate the cost of consumables and other extras.

CASE HISTORY: Colin

Colin Taylor runs a poster and card shop. He tried to expand his business to offer desktop publishing and design services.

'Doing the work was the easy part. We were getting plenty of casual trade from local businesses. The problem was, it was costing much more to run than I thought. After about six months it became obvious just how expensive our laser printer was. For starters we were getting through reams and reams of paper. What you get on the screen always looks slightly different when printed out. Some clients were very fussy, and it was taking ten or twelve printouts before they were happy.

'But it was the other costs that really surprised me. We were getting through a toner cartridge – at £100 a time – every few months. And after a year the drum needed replacing. I worked out that after two years we'd paid out more for the extras than the printer itself. Another big expense was backups. Desktop publishing needs lots of space, and a cheap backup system wasn't enough. We invested in an external tape drive and started to run a proper backup and archiving system. It's worth it for the business because customers can come back to us for minor changes. We can put a new date on a poster without starting from scratch.

'And then there's security. We're insured against theft, and that's not cheap. We can't afford a loss-of-business policy – they're just too expensive – so we're only insured on the basis of like-for-like. If we lose the machines, we get new ones.

'By the time you add it all up, we're spending well over £1,000 a year on extras. If I was starting again I'd look more closely at the price of extras before committing myself. With printers in particular it's worth finding out how much the consumables cost and how many pages they're good for.'

Renting or buying?

You have three options:

- an outright purchase
- purchasing with a loan or other finance
- renting.

Each of these options will affect your cash flow and tax position.

Buying a computer can represent a sizeable investment for a small business and buying one outright can jeopardise cash flow. However, you can claim this money back against tax as a 'writing-down allowance'. Currently this means the cost is spread over four years. After four years your computer is assumed to be worth nothing (unless you sell it) and you have claimed your initial outlay back against tax.

Computers can also be classified as 'short-life goods' with a separate writing-down allowance. If you sell your computer, you are allowed to offset the loss against tax, instead of being taxed on the income from the sale. Because computer equipment depreciates so quickly this can make a significant difference to your tax liability, to the extent that the sale of an obsolete computer at nominal cost can sometimes be very worthwhile indeed.

Purchasing with finance can be a better deal, at least as far as short-term cash flow goes. You will usually need to put up some of the money yourself – banks and loan companies are not keen on 100 per cent loans, unless you are borrowing a lot less than you can afford – but you will be able to spread the cost over a much longer period. If the computer brings in extra work and improved profits, this can be an excellent investment.

Interest payments are also tax-deductible, so in effect you have the loan 'for free'. The capital value of the computer is depreciated in the usual way, and on top of this you simply add the interest from any payments you are making.

Renting is similar, with one important difference. *All* payments are immediately deductible as a direct business expense. Many renting schemes provide the option of buying the machine outright at the end of a set period – usually three or four years. The sums charged are nominal and at the end of the rental period it is highly possible that the computer is still adequate for your needs. An outright purchase can be a sensible option at this point. Rental payments have been written off against tax, so with a single modest payment you can purchase the computer. This final payment can also be claimed as a capital allowance.

One disadvantage of renting is that it can be much more expensive. It is advisable to avoid short-term rentals unless you need the equipment desperately. Most business rental schemes work out significantly more expensive than an equivalent loan repayment system. However, the rental scheme covers you against equipment failure and other problems, and when you include these extra factors in the equation a renting deal can become more appealing.

As ever, you should read the small print in the rental contract to check the nature of the support that is offered. If it meets your needs and is still cheaper than an equivalent outright purchase, then renting is more advantageous for you than buying.

Renting seems to have become a fairly rare option. Computer magazines occasionally carry advertisements for rental computers and a small number of high-street stores currently operate rental schemes.

While renting hardware may be a good idea, renting software usually is not. Over the course of a few years you may end up paying two or three times more to rent software than to buy it outright. Some package deals include software at a good price, and some companies ask for extra payment for software. In the latter case, it is worth shopping around to compare the price of buying the software.

Painless buying in detail

Now is the time to talk to each retailer in turn and check the other services they offer, particularly technical support, warranties, money-back guarantees, delivery charges and delivery times. Confirm the quoted price. Make sure you get a price that includes VAT.

If you are buying everything, including the software and a printer, from one supplier it can be worth trying to negotiate a lower price for the package. If the retailer is local and you can collect the goods in person, it can also be worth negotiating a price for cash. Some retailers, especially the smaller ones, prefer to take cash as it avoids cheque charges.

Don't be afraid to haggle! If your retailer refuses to reduce the price, try asking for essential extras (such as a couple of packets of floppy disks or a printer cable) to be thrown in for free. These are often low-margin items for retailers and they can comfortably afford to give them away in small quantities. At worst you will get a refusal. At best you can save yourself some money.

Smaller retailers may well ask you what the best price you heard elsewhere was. Some would rather have your business, even with wafer-thin margins, than lose your custom to a competitor. It is important to be honest here, because if you quote an unrealistic price the next question will often be '...And did they say they had them in stock and ready to go?'

Be wary of high-pressure 'special offer' deals. Some larger retailers will attempt to use sale techniques to close a sale, by implying that the offer will only be available for a limited period. Although very, very occasionally you may miss a genuine bargain, the general trend in the computer trade is for more power at a lower price – even six months can make a big difference. Unless you really want to order right away and have already decided on a particular retailer, then it is prudent to deflect the salesmanship and say that you will think about it.

If you are a complete beginner, ask whether you will be sent any instructions on how to connect up your system before you place an order. A typical PC comes with five or six different items that need to be linked together, and it is not always obvious how this should be done. More thoughtful dealers include an instruction sheet or will be happy to talk you through the process over the phone. Remember to ask about this before you commit yourself to buying, as this kind of small extra can save you a lot of time later.

Confirm your order in writing, either through the post or by faxing it. For those buying by mail-order many magazines offer pre-printed order forms that you can cut out and fill in, and then send or fax to your retailer as appropriate. *It is important to keep a copy of this document*, which is your proof that you purchased an item via the magazine. If your supplier goes out of business before your order is fulfilled and the magazine subscribes to the MOPS (Mail Order Protection Scheme) the magazine is then liable under MOPS to make up your losses (see box overleaf).

If you need to have your order fulfilled quickly and have already discussed this with the retailer, make a note to that effect across the order – the suggested wording is 'to be delivered on (insert date here) as discussed with (insert salesperson's name here). Time is of the essence in this contract.' If there are any problems and delivery is delayed this wording gives you the option of cancelling the contract.

> **JUST WHAT CAN YOU EXPECT FROM MOPS?**
>
> In theory MOPS should protect you if a retailer ceases trading. In practice, however, most magazines limit themselves to a fairly low ceiling on compensation payments: £30,000 for any given retailer, and up to £100,000 in any given year.
>
> Realistically, therefore, MOPS is best thought of as a last resort. Your first line of attack should always be to take up the claim with the company's receiver, and then with your credit card company. If you are paying for your purchase with a loan or with extended credit you may also find that you are insured against non-delivery of the goods. The details will be in the small print of your agreement. If this is the case you will also need to register a claim with your loan or credit supplier.
>
> MOPS awards are *discretionary*, which means that there is no legal and binding obligation on the part of the magazine to pay you more than it thinks is reasonable. A large computer retailer may receive hundreds of orders a day, and may be trading on the verge of bankruptcy for weeks, or even months. A payout of a few tens of thousands of pounds will not amount to much if it has to be split between thousands of buyers. Although you may be lucky, especially if you are dealing with a small retailer, the harsh truth is that it is unwise to expect more from MOPS than a token compensation payment.

The preferred method of payment is by credit card. If the retailer goes out of business the credit card company is liable for your loss as long as the cash price of the individual item you are buying is more than £100. There are exceptions to this rule: corporate credit cards and purchases made by anyone other than the named card-holder will not be covered by the credit card company. Transactions made from companies registered overseas should also be covered. In general, this method of payment should give you effective protection against a supplier going out of business or not fulfilling your order for any other reason.

If paying by credit card, make sure that you will not be charged until the goods are despatched. It is not unheard of for companies to take an order for goods that are out of stock, take the money immediately and then fulfil the order a month or two later when the goods arrive in their warehouse.

Also check whether a credit-card surcharge will be added to your bill. Many smaller suppliers (and even a few larger ones) do this to offset the commission they have to pay the card company for each card-based transaction. Make sure you know where your supplier stands on this before telling it your card number.

Most retailers also now accept debit cards (for example Switch, Delta). These give you *no protection at all*. Beware – some retailers will try to surcharge on these as well. Debit cards are not liable to the same surcharges as credit cards, they do not offer you the same degree of protection and they cost the retailer a fixed transaction fee, exactly like a normal cheque. If you have to pay by debit card (and this is not recommended unless you have no other option) make sure that you get an assurance that a credit surcharge will not be added to the bill. You may need to argue this point strongly. If your retailer insists on applying the surcharge, go elsewhere.

If your retailer is local, you may prefer to pay by cash and pick up the goods yourself. This could save you the delivery charge (usually not more than £20 or so) and may give you the option of negotiating a better price. Not all retailers accept personal calls, and not all prefer cash sales.

If you decide to collect the goods yourself, ask if you can see your system working before you take it away. Apart from peace of mind, this also gives you a chance to see for yourself how to connect up the different parts of your computer. For a beginner this can be a major confidence booster. It is also a chance to ask the support staff any simple technical questions.

Unfortunately only smaller retailers are able to provide this level of personal service. Some, although not all, larger companies tend to keep their sales and delivery teams well apart from their engineering and support staff. If you are dealing with one of these it is far more likely that you will be presented with a stack of boxes.

If you run a medium-sized business it can be worth trying to pay on account – 30-day terms are often possible if you can supply trading references. This offers all the usual advantages of improved cash flow, but these have to be offset against the amount of work you need to do to set up an account in the first place. If you are likely to be using a single retailer for most of your computer equipment purchases it can be advantageous to arrange an account facility.

When the goods are delivered write 'Goods not yet inspected' on the consignment note. This improves your legal standing if you need to return the goods for any reason. Inspect your order as soon as possible and, if you have any queries, contact the salesperson responsible for your order immediately. Follow this up with written confirmation of any defects or missing items as soon as you can.

Teething troubles

Not all costs are financial. You will also have to spend some time setting your system up once it has arrived and dealing with any teething troubles that arise.

Even for a small, single-user computer system, you should allow at least a day after the machine arrives for checking and general setting-up. This should give you enough time to become familiar with the system and work out how all the parts link together. If you are a relative newcomer, allow at least a week before you think about using the system professionally. This gives you time to make mistakes without worrying about the consequences. It also gives you a chance to get to grips with the software.

The best way to avoid problems is to choose your dealer wisely. A good dealer will be more likely to sell you a machine that has been fully set up and less likely to misbehave. *Skimping on good support is a false economy*. By the time you have allowed for your time, a cheap system can prove to be far more expensive than one with excellent support that costs that bit extra.

Even the best dealer will sometimes make a mistake and you may be left with a system that does not function properly. At this point the time you have put into looking for good support will pay off. If your computer does not work, double-check all the connections. If everything is as it should be, call the technical support number and explain what the problem is. The Sale of Goods Act 1979 (as amended) covers your contract with the supplier. It is the supplier's responsibility to provide a product that is of satisfactory quality and fit for the purpose for which it is purchased. If the product does not work properly, you may reject the product and claim your money back (but only if you reject it within a few weeks of purchase) or at least claim that the supplier should put the problems right at his or her cost. Always confirm any complaint in writing and keep a copy.

When telephoning, make a note of the name and position of the person to whom you spoke. This gives you a chance to establish a personal contact inside the company. Explain the problem, make a careful note of any solutions the person suggests and then try them out. You will have a much better case if you do this as soon as you can. If, after a week or so of trying, your computer is not functioning properly, consider taking the matter up with the company director(s) and – if necessary – ask for a full refund.

Chapter 13

Finding effective support

The majority of computer problems are minor and easy to put right: for example, you lose your last few minutes' work. Every once in a while, however, something serious goes wrong.

Problems fall into three categories: user errors, software problems and hardware problems.

User errors

These happen when you try to do something your software was not designed to do. Often the software simply does not work the way you think it should. (This is a very common problem.) Most user errors are caused by insufficient training or bad software design. There is very little you can do about bad software design, other than choosing your software carefully. Good training and support can prepare you to deal with further problems. If you are a complete beginner training and support are *essential*. Very little software is clear and simple enough for a novice to pick up on the spot. Training can help you find and use all the features your software can offer you (according to one estimate, most users are familiar with around 20 per cent of the features in a typical office word-processing package).

Software problems

Unfortunately, software is not infallible. In fact, by the reliability standards of any other trade, some software is really rather poor. Even the best programs are about as reliable as an old car on a frosty morning. Most of the time they work well, but occasionally they will do something unexpected or refuse to work at all. ·

Software problems – known colourfully as **bugs** – take various forms from the obvious (your computer stops responding – this is known as a crash, and the computer is said to have hung), to the extremely subtle (information starts to disappear for no good reason). There is very little you can do to protect yourself from bugs.

To date, the software industry has managed to survive without proper consumer resistance to its bad reliability record. If washing machines, cars and video recorders were sold with the same reliability problems the public outcry would be deafening. The unprofessional attitude to quality control of some of the major companies stems from the industry's roots in the hobbyist movement of the 1970s. Hobbyists – and this includes many computer professionals, who started out as hobbyists – are happy to work around problems, but consumers should not have to. A number of individuals and companies have taken legal action against software providers, but these are usually settled out of court in great secrecy. If the details were made more widely available it is likely that more actions would follow.

If you have software that does not work properly or causes serious problems, you should complain in the same way you would with any other product. If more consumers take action the industry will be forced to sit up and take notice, and the quality of its products will improve. Companies do respond to direct action. In late 1994 the Intel Corporation, which makes computer chips for most IBM-compatible computers, climbed down from what many felt was the high-handed position it had taken with regard to a defect in one of its chips. Intel denied there were problems, but then apologised after a month of vociferous complaints and threats of legal action from angry consumers and went on to offer a free lifetime replacement to anyone who bought a computer with a defective chip. Similar action by software users could revolutionise the industry.

In the meantime, you can expect regular problems with many common software packages. Some features will not work as advertised, others will cause error messages to appear on the screen, and very occasionally you will find software that crashes your computer. Increasing familiarity with the software will confirm that these kinds of problems are not a result of user error. But until consumers start to demand an acceptable standard of performance from the software manufacturers, problems such as these will remain a fact of life.

You should make sure that you register your software when you buy it. This necessitates filling in a short questionnaire that comes with the package and sending it to the manufacturer. Most software is regularly updated, with combinations of fixes for problems and new features. If you register you are more likely to be informed of these updates when they become available. Sometimes you may even be eligible for free updates.

Setup and installation problems

Before you can use your computer both the hardware and the software have to be fully installed. This is one area which can cause problems for beginners, and if not done correctly it can affect the performance of the whole system. If you have bought the system from a dealer, the dealer should do this for you. A scrupulous dealer will make sure that everything has been installed correctly. However, not all dealers bother and as a result you may get a computer that appears to work, but which may not have the full range of options available. You can avoid these kinds of problems by choosing your dealer carefully.

Hardware problems

Hardware problems are rare. Most computer hardware works reliably most of the time, and you are unlikely to come across hardware problems if your system has been set up properly. When they do occur, however, they are serious and can render your computer useless.

Typical hardware problems include:

No power You turn on the power switch, and nothing happens.

No hard disk The power comes on, but the hard disk does not work, or it appears to work, but all the information has disappeared.

No picture The computer whirrs and beeps, but nothing appears on the screen.

No keyboard and/or mouse The computer does not respond when you type or when you move the mouse. This can often be a software problem, but if you turn your computer off and on again and the symptoms remain it is a hardware problem. Also check all cables and plugs. Is everything plugged in properly? Are any of the connecting cables loose? Is there anything lying on the mouse?

Computer doesn't start properly This can have a variety of causes. Sometimes it means a hard disk has 'crashed' and all the information on it has disappeared. A less heart-stopping possibility is that the computer has a flat battery. Both PCs and Macs have small batteries inside which maintain important settings. If the battery goes flat these settings disappear and the computer does not function. Changing the battery and resetting the machine are jobs for a professional.

Hardware problems require expert attention, and it is at this point that support is most needed and any warranties, insurance policies and maintenance contracts you have taken out will prove their worth.

CASE HISTORY: Andrew

Andrew Thomas, an independent computer consultant, is familiar with computer crises of all kinds.

'The most common problem I deal with is rogue software. I train all my clients to use the tools effectively, but I still have to field complaints from them when the software bombs or misbehaves. I warn clients in advance about the problems they'll meet. Each package has its own quirks, and I've started avoiding some of the less reliable ones because it's not worth my time trying to explain to clients what the problems are. Some of the bigger packages can do a hell of a lot, but if they're not totally reliable, they can be more trouble than they're worth.

'Occasionally I'll have to deal with a big hardware failure. It's not something I can guarantee against, so I make sure that there's always a proper warranty or support policy involved. But I'm often called in to pick up the pieces afterwards. In one case a newsagent lost all his information when his hard disk failed. It literally disintegrated. I opened the case up at home and all that was left was some fine dust and a few small pieces. He was covered by a warranty and had a replacement fitted the next day. But he couldn't get the safety copies of his work back on to it.

'In his case it was easy to sort out, and everyone got their papers as usual the next day. Sometimes it's not quite so easy. But if you keep backups of your information and have a good support or insurance policy then you're pretty much bomb-proof no matter what happens.'

Training

Good training minimises your software support requirements, helps you to make effective use of your software and builds your confidence.

It will also help you avoid bad habits. Many packages allow you to get the same result in different ways. Training can help you find the way that works best for you. It can also show you useful tricks, such as how to undo your last action if you make a mistake.

There are two kinds of computer training. The first relates to specific software. This will teach you how to do specific tasks – lay out a page in a word processor, check the spelling of the text, and so on – for a certain product.

The second and perhaps more useful option is one that offers general computer literacy. This teaches you the skills you need to use any commonly available piece of software. It is a much broader level of training, and one that can help you become more self-reliant in the way that you use computers.

Sources of training include:

- manufacturers' training programmes
- independent training programmes
- dealers
- college or night school
- books and videos.

Training programmes run by software manufacturers tend to be expensive. You get extra support and a guarantee that the training will get the best out of the software you have. But this level of support tends to be corporate in both approach and cost and is not suitable unless you run a medium-sized business and have cash to spare.

Manufacturers usually use external training companies. Sometimes these companies go through a certification process which guarantees a certain level of competence, both in the subject and in training ability in general. This should – in theory – improve your chances of being taught properly. In practice, training can be a personal thing, and you need to find a training environment in which you feel comfortable. A beginner's first steps in computer literacy can be nerve-wracking, and it is important to find training that can support you through this phase.

Independent trainers vary considerably. At one end of the scale there are the smaller consultancy and training services which offer affordable and friendly help for anyone starting out. At the other end there are larger training companies who are geared more towards corporate accounts and charge accordingly. There is no lack of training options available – as always the *Yellow Pages* is a good place to start – and after some initial enquiries you should be able to find someone who is offering their services at the level you require.

Getting training and help from a dealer can be much more problematic. Only the larger explicitly business–oriented dealers offer this level of service, and even then they may simply recommend a local training service with which they have good links. Unless you are getting a package as an all–inclusive service from a consultant, you will often be better off doing the research yourself and finding a source of training that suits you, rather than your dealer.

Training at college or evening classes has its advantages. You will get a chance to practise in a relatively unpressured environment and may be given access to computer equipment outside class hours. This can be an excellent place to start if you know nothing at all about computers and want to learn the basics. Many colleges run classes in business-related computing which can give you practical experience of business software. Attending one of these before you buy your system can give you some insight and knowledge to enable you to make a wiser purchase. You may even be able to ask your tutor for help or free buying advice.

The only disadvantage of college courses is that the content is often determined by the software the college supports. Larger training organisations cover most of the software options that are available, and college courses can sometimes, although not always, be more limited in their scope. You may find that you learn to use software that turns out not to be right for you. Fortunately the basic skills you gain can usually be transferred to another package.

Some office-skills teaching organisations offer basic courses in various word-processing programs. These tend to teach very much by rote, rather than giving you the wider background you need to be truly computer–literate. But if you are not worried about using your computer to do anything other than certain kinds of work you may find them a good choice.

Finally, some people find the do-it-yourself approach appealing. There is no lack of books, magazine features and videos offering help and guidance in computer techniques. Working from the printed page or television screen enables you to go at your own pace and to make mistakes without feeling self-conscious, but the usefulness of these training materials varies hugely and if you get stuck you have no one to ask for help.

Your best approach to choosing training materials is to browse as thoroughly as you can. You may find that some styles are distracting. Many computer books are written with a humorous edge, which suits some people; others prefer a no–nonsense style. (Books for the computer user are discussed in more detail on pages 316–17.)

CASE HISTORY: Beth

Beth Waites ran through most of the available training options when she was starting her carpet-cleaning and house-valeting business. Her experience shows that expensive training is not always the best.

'We'd budgeted for a good computer for the bookkeeping and promotional work, and I knew I needed help to get started. We bought a budget machine on the advice of a friend, so we didn't expect much in the way of help from the dealer. It was obvious I was going to have look elsewhere.

'I started with a magazine feature on business training. But that looked too heavy for me. And the prices were outrageous. There was no way that I was going to pay £1,000 for a week away, even if it was in a plush venue. The subject matter didn't suit either. I wanted to know how to design flyers and leaflets and make our correspondence look professional, and wasn't fussed about pivot points in spreadsheets or graphical trend analysis. I leave that kind of thing to our accountant.

'I tried the local college, and that looked promising. The courses looked right, but I had missed the start of the next one and didn't have a year to spare waiting for the one after. But I talked to the course tutor, and he let me on anyway. By then I'd missed the basics, so after the first couple of classes I felt like giving up. But the tutor suggested a couple of books, so I went out and got those and started working through them at home.

'Now, this worked. They were done as tutorials, so I could start at the beginning and work my way through. Every so often I'd get stuck and I'd ask the tutor to help me out at the next class. Between us we managed to cover everything I wanted to know, and I definitely feel I've mastered the basics now.

'I didn't try videos. I've always preferred to talk to a real human being. Books are cheaper and tell you just as much, but without the pictures. If I was doing it again I'd follow the same route – books and maybe magazines, together with evening classes. It worked for me and I'm not exactly Einstein when it comes to these things, so I think anyone should be able to do it.'

Note that Microsoft, Novell and a range of other companies offer 'formal qualifications' in the use and maintenance of their products. Proficiency is tested by examination and based on an established curriculum. The full range of qualifications available is covered in detail in *The Which? Guide to Computers for Small Businesses.* For anyone who wants to become proficient in these products these qualifications are worth considering. Apart from computer basics, the curriculum includes practical network installation and maintenance skills.

Unfortunately, suitable courses teaching the information required to attain certification are very expensive. This puts them out of the reach of most small businesses and home users. Cheaper home study courses are also available, although even these rarely cost less than £600. Larger businesses, or those that are very profitable, may find that training a member of staff as an 'on–site consultant' can be a good investment.

When it comes to videos, your choices are more limited. If at all possible you should ask for a demonstration or sample video to get some idea of each company's approach to the subject. Ideally you should also be able to look at videos on approval, although for obvious reasons most video sources are unwilling to allow this. Avoid gimmicky videos. It is all very well having famous names on a training video, but you are paying for information and educational content and should assess it on that basis. Video training is advertised in most of the computer magazines.

Software support

Unlike training, software support is more of a continuing investment. Ideally, if you have sorted out your training needs properly, then you will be left needing minimal support. This is the best possible – and often cheapest – position to be in. In practice of course, you may come across situations that you haven't been prepared for, and this is where support becomes essential.

Like training, software support is available from a number of sources, including:

- manufacturers' support lines
- independent telephone support services
- consultants and friends and colleagues
- dealers
- computer clubs
- on–line services.

Manufacturers' support schemes

If you buy software from one of the big names (Microsoft, Lotus, Novell and so on) then you will be eligible for access to their help lines. Unfortunately, this is not always as useful as it sounds.

Some manufacturers now charge for technical support, so you will not be able to get help and advice unless you pay in advance. Others offer free support for a 'running-in' period – usually 90 days – and charge after that. Check the details when you buy software. Free initial support is definitely worth taking up but a paid-up scheme that ties you to any one manufacturer is *not* a good deal. Manufacturers' own-brand support schemes tend to be expensive and will not always offer you the service you need. Sometimes one manufacturer will blame another for the problems you are experiencing. If you contact the other manufacturer it may point the finger back. From a support point of view you are left floundering. It is worth remembering too that technical support lines of major software manufacturers can get very busy, and you could be kept on hold. While free services are worth taking up, paid support contracts from any one manufacturer are best avoided.

Independent support services

A much better solution is to use one of the independent technical support lines. These cover all the standard packages. They can help with problems that you may have getting different software packages to work with each other.

There are two kinds of support schemes. The first gives you a premium rate telephone number. When you need support, you call the number. You can call as often as you like, for as long as you like, but remember that you pay by the minute for this kind of help. In general, such support schemes are recommended if you simply need occasional help with occasional problems and are confident with your computer. If you have sorted out your training, you may find that this is all the help you need and it will also provide you with a cost-effective way to get access to professional help when you are unable to work out what to do on your own.

The other option is the flat-rate scheme. This can be expensive – perhaps £100 for a year's support – but you will be able to ask all the questions you need and will also have the benefit of support for a wide range of industry-standard software. This circumvents the 'It's not us – it's some other software' problem that besets some manufacturers' support facilities. These schemes are advertised in computer magazines and may also become available from other sources in the future, for example BT now offers a computer support line.

Some schemes offer a sliding scale, whereby you get access to better support by paying more per year. Training is a better way to spend your money than on this kind of open-ended support. A recent development is combined support and insurance services. These can be very good value, although it is prudent to check in the usual way that both the insurance and the support facilities are up to par.

The managing director of a large company that provides a variety of PC support services, including support lines for a number of monthly computer magazine titles, explains what the services include.

'We find that 80 per cent of problems are manual related. People simply haven't read the manual or had the training they need. But we're not here to train people, just to solve specific problems.

'We work according to very definite guidelines. We're open 24 hours a day, 365 days a year. Our busiest day last year was Boxing Day – it's when everyone is trying their new kit out – and we were ready for that. We guarantee to answer the phone within six rings, which means we always keep an adequate level of cover.

'When people phone us they're usually irate and frustrated, so the first thing our staff are trained to do is to calm them down. If you've got a problem you don't want to be messed around with tone phones, you want a real person to talk to right away. Our staff are taught to identify the problem. This isn't always what the caller thinks it is. If a printer isn't working it may just be that it's not switched on, so our staff will check all the options.

'If we can't solve it right away, we guarantee to call people back within ten minutes. We have a database of problems that we can refer to which has all the common problems and their solutions. If that doesn't help we keep copies of all the software we support so we can call up the real live version and try things for ourselves.

'I'd suggest to anyone looking for phone support that they check response time, the number of packages that are supported and whether support is available all the time.'

Consultants and other help

If you have arranged for an all-in-one deal with a consultant, then your consultant should be your first port of call when you need support. You may also be able to call up a consultant and ask for help with a specific problem. Some consultants are unwilling to do this unless the problem is major and is likely to require a large amount of time to put right.

As with buying, a good source of help is from friends and colleagues. It is very rare to come across problems that have never occurred before, and you will often find other people have encountered and perhaps dealt with your difficulty already.

Informal support from dealers

You may, if you are lucky, be able to find a dealer who can answer your questions for free. Some dealers see this as part of the service they offer, others as an unwarranted intrusion on their time. If you have chosen your dealer prudently you should be able to get a basic level of help. It is unrealistic to assume that your dealer should know everything about every possible piece of software, but for hardware-related problems a call to your dealer should be your first choice.

Computer clubs

Local computer clubs tend to be the domain of hobbyists and this does not suit everyone who is in need of support. However, they can be a good source of useful advice and information.

There is also a national support group: the PC Users' Group (PC-UG). It offers support on a more or less non-profit basis and takes a keen interest in keeping users happy. It also offers buying support (although it does not advise on hardware) as well as a range of other services. The PC-UG also prints a monthly newsletter, *Connectivity*, and runs regular training courses and conferences in London. It can also supply information about training organisations. Membership fees are very reasonable.

On-line services

Some on-line services, such as CompuServe and the Internet, include areas where you can ask for computer advice. The advice is free as it

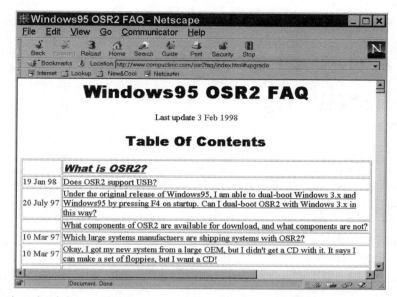

The Web includes many FAQ documents available on-line. The example here shows a tiny section of the Windows 95 OSR2 FAQ. The full document contains nearly 100 questions about buying, installing and using OSR2, with detailed answers for each of them.

comes from other users. (Parts of this book were written with the help of complete strangers on the Internet who were able to provide detailed technical information.) If you already have an on-line connection, or are considering one, then you should investigate this kind of support. However, you need a certain basic level of technical literacy to start to make use of the system, or at least access to someone who can set up a connection for you, and there are no guarantees that you will get an answer to your problem. In practice you usually do, especially for the more commonly asked questions.

Another on-line resource is the FAQ (Frequently Asked Questions) document (see example above). This is exactly what it claims to be – a list of common questions, with useful answers. FAQs are maintained on an informal, volunteer basis and there is no guarantee that the information is correct, although technical FAQs are usually maintained by experts and mistakes are soon corrected. FAQs are regularly posted to newsgroups on the Internet. (For more about on-line resources see Chapter 6 and Appendix VIII.)

Appendix I

A beginner's guide to hardware

What follows is a guide to specifications, which will help you understand computer advertising and compare like for like. Readers who are not interested in technicalities can skip this section and simply quote the recommended hardware specification of their chosen software. If you are interested in games or multimedia titles, then use these as your base specifications, as these applications will need more powerful hardware than business applications.

Many advertisements for computers are little more than a list of technical specifications, which mean less than nothing to many people. Since 1993 any new Apple or IBM-compatible computer has been more than powerful enough for basic business use. If this is all you need a computer for, you are spoiled for choice.

Like cars, however, computers come in economy and performance versions. Performance computers go faster, and – surprisingly, perhaps – are better suited to play than work. Computer games and leisure products tend to put much higher demands on machines than basic business software.

Most of the information in this Appendix applies to IBM-compatible machines. These are often sold on the basis of a specification, rather than as a brand name. The fact that a computer is made by IBM, Dell, Gateway or any other supplier tells you very little about its performance – although it may offer some hints about build quality and support – and marketing titles such as 'Premier' or 'Executive' are simply window-dressing. What matters is what is inside the box, and it is now traditional to list a certain basic set of specifications so that buyers can see what they are getting.

The situation is slightly different with Apple machines, because these are sold more as commodities. The number of Apple suppliers is much smaller, and the market is much less competitive. For the sake of comparison, however, some of the basics – processor type and speed, memory and hard disk size and so on – are often quoted anyway. The two ranges are not strictly comparable, and you should still take the time to sit down and try out each kind of machine for yourself before you buy. However, you can use this section and the one that follows to understand specifications for either kind of machine.

The processor

This is the technical name for the main chip at the heart of your computer. This chip does most of the work and its speed and power largely determine the capabilities of the machine as a whole. The rest of the hardware exists to get information into and out of this chip.

The chips themselves are sold as square ceramic slabs with hundreds of tiny pins, or as large, long 'modules' that plug into a thin slot. The top surface is printed with the chip model number. The underside contains the pins arranged around a sliver of processed silicon which is visible in the centre through a glass window. This sliver does the work. The chip is in fact a tiny circuit board, with microscopic circuit elements etched into place using a variety of chemical processes.

The most important thing about a processor is its model identifier, which can be a number (e.g. 68040), a name (Pentium), or a cryptic combination of letters and digits (604e). Associated with the code is an optional modifier (e.g. MMX) and a speed rating with the letters 'MHz' after it (e.g. 200MHz). The modifier tells you the sub-class of the chip. Sub-classes differ slightly in efficiency and the features they offer – some older chips were deliberately hobbled for marketing reasons, while others offer extra facilities. For example, Pentium MMX chips are slightly faster than older Pentium chips, and also offer extra features that make certain kinds of software work much more quickly and efficiently – especially that which works with sound and video.

The model code, modifier and speed rating tell you everything there is to know about a chip and give you a very good foundation for assessing the power of the computer as a whole.

Processors used in PCs

One company – Intel – has been associated with the IBM-compatible product line from the beginning. As machines have become more powerful, each development has become synonymous with one particular kind of Intel chip. So a computer built around a Pentium chip is simply known as 'a Pentium'. A complete list of Intel chips is shown in the table opposite.

All processor chips use the standard speed rating system. This is measured in MHz (MegaHertz – millions of ticks a second) and this indicates the 'heart rate' of the machine, also known as the clock speed.

The higher the speed rating, the faster the chip works. Each chip model is available in a range of speeds. For example, 'Pentium III' series chips are available in speeds from 500MHz to 1000MHz (also known as 1GHz – 'one thousand megahertz'). Older Pentium II chips covered the range 233MHz to 450MHz.

Chip speed is similar to engine capacity in a car. A two-litre model will be faster than a one-litre design, but never twice as fast. The same applies to computer chips: a computer built around a 200MHz chip will not run twice as fast as one based on a 100MHz chip, but it will run noticeably faster.

Since 1995 Intel has been facing increasingly stiff competition from various other chip manufacturers, notably Cyrix and AMD. These offer chips which work as well as, and in some cases even better, than Intel's own designs, but cost significantly less. While Intel has tried to create a strong brand image for itself with an 'Intel Inside' marketing campaign, this has not worked as well as hoped, and the market is now much more open to computers built around other chips than it was at the start of the 1990s. This is good news for consumers, as prices are being driven down steadily while performance improves by leaps and bounds.

As a buyer, there is usually no compelling reason to go for an Intel-based PC. For most applications computers built around competing chips are well worth considering, and in some cases can offer a significant cost saving.

Overdrive processors

On many IBM models you can change your processor chip to another one of the same family that goes faster. So, for example, you can change a Pentium II 333 chip to a Pentium II 450 chip simply by taking out the old one, changing a few settings on the motherboard, and plugging in the new one. However, there are limits to how far you can take this process. These depend on the motherboard that the chip plugs into.

An 'overdrive' processor works in the same way, but is designed to work around those limits. In general though, these chips are not good value. For a relatively small extra investment it is possible to fit a much faster chip and a new updated motherboard. This will improve performance far more dramatically, and as an added bonus you may be able to sell your old processor and motherboard to recover some of the extra cost. The disadvantage of taking this route is that it makes the upgrade more complicated.

Apple processors

The processors used in Apple computers are made by Motorola. Motorola has developed its chips in a much more straightforward way than Intel, and the chips used in Apple computers are not available in the same bewildering variety of speed and performance options. A list of Motorola chips is shown below. Motorola and Intel chips are not strictly comparable, but the table does offer a guideline when trying to assess equivalent performance.

Model designation		Performance rating
Intel	Motorola	
8088/8086	68000	Vintage*
80186		(never made available to the public)
80286	68020	Vintage*
386 series	68030LC	Vintage*
486 series	68040 series	Very dated*
Pentium	601	Dated*
Pentium Pro	n/a	(for specialist applications only)*
Pentium MMX	603e	Recent*
Pentium II	604e & G3	Entry level
Pentium III	750	Established
Merced/IA-64	G4	Next-generation, leading edge available 2000

* Now only available second-hand

179

And the rest?

Cyrix and AMD have produced their own chips which compete with Intel chips head-on. They have their own distinct advantages and disadvantages.

Pentium chips are now no longer available. They had competition from the Cyrix 6x86 and the AMD K5, both of which were significantly cheaper and apparently faster overall. However, the latter were slightly slower at tasks that required intensive numerical calculations. Because of this they remained a relatively obscure option, ignored by major manufacturers.

Pentium MMX chips are also no longer available. They had competition from the AMD K6 range and the Cyrix M2 (confusingly, also known as the 6x86MX). Both these chips appeared to offer slightly better performance at a lower price, and were used by major manufacturers instead of the Pentium MMX range.

Pentium II chips now have competition from the AMD K6, especially the most recent K6-III. This is only slightly less powerful than a Pentium II but costs very much less, and is to be offered by many manufacturers up until the middle of 2000. Cyrix withdrew from the market in 1999, and so there are no more competing Cyrix chips to consider.

Pentium III chips have competition from the AMD K7 (now known as Athlon), which in some ways is a faster and better processor, although it lacks the Pentium III's enhanced KNI features (see page 243). Again, the K7/Athlon is significantly cheaper than the Pentium III.

Xeon Pentium II and **Xeon Pentium III** chips are advanced versions designed for corporate computers. They are very expensive, and so are likely to be out of the reach of home users. They are usually only sold as part of a general very-high-performance computer package. Business users should note that they often offer exceptionally poor value for money, and sometimes also surprisingly poor relative performance. It may be possible to make a huge saving by accepting the slight performance degradation offered by conventional Pentium II and Pentium III models, in return for paying perhaps a quarter as much.

One advantage of the Xeon range is that these chips are designed to work together in **multi-processor systems**, which dole out all the work among a number of computer chips – typically between two and eight – instead of making a single chip do it all. This requires a significant technical overhead, which means that a multi-processor system will not usually be as fast as might be hoped. (For example, two processors are likely to be only 1.5 times as fast as one, at best.) This approach is only suitable for situations where money is no object and very high performance is required.

Making sense of the pattern

While the huge number of chip names and numbers can seem bewildering, it is possible to sketch out a simple map which shows how the different options relate to each other. Different chips are aimed at different kinds of users. The names and numbers have changed, but the underlying pattern has remained very similar since the early 1990s.

Year	Undemanding	Standard (Intel)	Standard (AMD)	Advanced (intel)	Professional
1992	386 16MHz	386 20MHz	–	386+387 33MHz	–
1995	486SX 25MHz	486DX/2 66MHz	K5 50MHz	486DX/4 120MHz	–
1997	Pentium 120 MHz	Pentium 166MHz	K6 200MHz	Pentium MMX 200MHz	Pentium Pro 200MHz
1998	Celeron 266 MHz	Pentium II 300MHz	K6-III 300MHz	Pentium II 350MHz	Xeon Pentium II 350MHz
2000	Pentium II 400MHz	Pentium III 500MHz	K7/Athlon 750MHz	Pentium III 750 MHz	Xeon Pentium III 750 MHz or IA-64 1GHz

Undemanding work includes basic word processing, simple office work, email, web browsing and other Internet use. Games will run very slowly. These models use a crippled version of the day's standard technology. This makes only a slight difference while they are being used, but it will significantly depress second-hand prices.

Standard models are the average computers of the day. They can do all the work that an undemanding model can, but slightly faster. They can also be used for games. In general, they offer the best value for money, although shopping around among different dealers will show that there can be a price spread of as much as £500 between similarly specified computers in this category.

Advanced models are for those who want a 'performance' computer. They are ideal for getting the best from the lastest games and for anyone who needs to do demanding work, such as computer animation or graphic design. Typically costing some 50 per cent to 100 per cent more than the standard models, they are aimed at people who want the best possible performance and are happy to pay a price premium for this.

Professional These models are aimed at medium to large businesses, and are typically too expensive for the general public. Where domestic computer chips typically cost manufacturers between £50 and £400, these chips can cost thousands. They are most often sold in server computers, which are designed to be used by an entire department or company.

The future

Not only does the industry move fast, but developments are speeding up. At the time of writing, the Pentium II range is about to become obsolete, replaced for most applications by the Pentium III. Based on previous form, it's likely that a 'crippled' version of the Pentium III will appear some time in 2000 in an attempt to forestall AMD's K7/Athlon. However, because the K7/Athlon is such a powerful and fast processor chip – tests have shown that it is anything up to one third as fast again as a Pentium III with the same MHz rating – it remains to be seen exactly how Intel will choose to respond.

In the longer term, Intel plans to release a completely new range of chips in 2000. Codenamed 'Merced', or 'IA-64'(Intel Architecture 64-bit) these promise to offer a huge leap in performance over existing chip designs, giving users speed and power that a decade ago would have been the preserve of million-pound supercomputer systems. These chips are expected to be priced initially to suit the professional part of the market, and so will have no impact on domestic and small business computers. However, it's likely that cheaper versions will start to appear some time in 2001, and they may well become the new standard by 2002, especially if competition from AMD serves to push prices downwards. Microsoft is preparing a special version of its Windows system – to be known as Windows 64 – to make full use of the chip's new features.

Apple, meanwhile, is readying its G4 processor for launch some time in 2000. This may offer a slightly poorer level of performance than the IA-64 chips, but at a much more reasonable price. Given Apple's newly found strength in the market, this could result in Apple machines being much more popular than they are currently. (Note that Apple processors tend to run slightly slower than Intel models. For example, a 400MHz 704 is perhaps equivalent to a 550MHz Pentium III for certain kinds of work. However, because the two chips work differently it is extremely hard to make accurate comparisons of like with like.)

Motherboard

After the processor chip, the motherboard is the second most important component in an IBM-compatible computer. (Apple computers use proprietary motherboard designs which means there is less variation, and differences are much less important to purchasers.) For IBM-compatibles, the choice of motherboard determines the following:

- Maximum possible memory
- Maximum possible processor speed (e.g. 450MHz)
- Memory type (SDRAM)
- Compatibility with non-Intel processors (not all boards will work with AMD and Cyrix chips)
- Number and type of 'expansion slots' for extras that fit inside the case
- Built-in extras, such as sound cards and graphics cards
- Number and type of connections for external extras
- Hard disk connection system (EIDE, Ultra DMA/33 or /66, occasionally SCSI)
- General operating efficiency (more modern boards are faster and more efficient than older designs)
- The ability to use more than one processor chip at once (known as SMP – Symmetric Multi Processing).

However, an increasingly bewildering and acronym-laden range of motherboard options are now available. Below are some of the terms you may come across in advertising material in the mainstream computer press:

BIOS – Basic Input Output System. This is a special piece of software burned on to the motherboard that makes it unnecessary for the rest of the computer to know exactly how to go about getting information to and from a hard disk drive, a printer, and so on. They are made by many different companies. Popular examples include Award, AMI and Phoenix. Apart from minor technical differences, one BIOS is much like another, and usually there is no advantage to having any particular one.

'Form factor' Computer industry jargon for 'shape and mechanical dimensions'. For motherboards, two main types are available – AT and ATX. These specify the physical size of the board and where the screw holes are placed. When upgrading a motherboard you will have to make sure you buy one of the same type, otherwise it will not fit into the existing case.

Speed As with processor chips, motherboards are now being supplied with a speed rating in MHz. This indicates the speed at which the board can move information around. The current standard is 100MHz, although 133MHz boards are sometimes available. AMD's K7 processor uses a 200MHz system, which makes it work significantly faster than existing designs. It is important not to confuse motherboard speeds with processor chip speeds. Where two numbers are shown, the slower will be the motherboard's specification.

Chipset This is a code that specifies what kind of chips surround the processor on the motherboard. While the main processor chip does most of the useful calculations, these other chips connect the processor to the outside world – for example collecting information from the keyboard and mouse, sending information to and from the hard disk, and so on. At the time of writing, LX and TX chipsets are slightly dated, while newer BX and ZX chipsets work marginally more efficiently. Most chipsets are made by Intel, but some, such as the VIA and 'PC Chips' sets, are available from competitors. Unfortunately, chipset designations follow no rhyme or reason, and the only way to keep track of which ones perform better is to attempt to interpret reviewers' comments in the various PC magazines.

Socket type This is the physical socket into which the processor is fitted. 'Socket 7' is the older standard once used for Pentiums but now co-opted by AMD for its K6 range. 'Slot 1' is used for the Pentium II, Pentium III and certain Celeron chips. Some Celeron chips also use a 'PGA' (Pin Grid Array) socket. From a buyer's point of view, the technical differences between these different standards are negligible. It is, however, essential to know what kind of socket is used in a PC if you wish to upgrade the processor.

Extra features Points to look for include:
USB (Universal Serial Bus – see page 195)
AGP (Advanced Graphics Port – see page 198)
Ultra DMA/33/66 or (see page 188).

Main memory

A computer's memory is rather like desk space in an office. The more you have, the easier it is to have all kinds of documents and other information scattered around without having to look things up in a filing system. If you have too little memory, then applications will either not work at all or will slow down dramatically as the computer continually swaps information between the main memory and the hard disk.

Like hard disk space, memory sizes are measured in Mbs. On modern PCs and Apple computers, a minimum size, adequate for most work, is 32Mb. Because memory is so cheap now, it is more common to find 64Mb or 128Mb as standard. This is possibly overkill for many users, but in practice it makes a minimal difference to the price of a PC, and the extra breathing space it adds is very useful. Web browsing on the Internet can be particularly demanding of memory, so 64Mb should be considered a minimum for anyone who plans to do this regularly; 64Mb will also appear to speed up a computer that is regularly used with lots of different software working at once (for example a word processor, spreadsheet, web browser, diary, email software, and so on).

On almost all computers, extra memory can be added at a later date. This is a cheap and simple operation that more experienced users can do themselves. At the time of writing, an extra 64Mb costs around £50. When adding memory, it is essential to know which type to buy. EDO (Extended Data Output) RAM is used on older, slower computers. It is supplied as SIMMs (Single In-line Memory Modules). More recent machines uses SDRAM (Synchronous Dynamic RAM), which is sometimes also labelled 'PC100 SDRAM'. This is much faster than EDO RAM and is supplied as DIMMs (Dual In-line Memory Modules).

As we go to press, two new memory technologies are planned. 'Rambus' memory (also known as 'DRDRAM' – Direct Rambus Dynamic Random Access Memory) appears to perform very poorly and is very expensive compared to existing memory types. However, it is being pushed by Intel, which means that it is likely to appear in at least some designs. DDR (Double Data Rate) SDRAM is a 'next-generation' version of SDRAM that – very simply – works twice as fast. It is more affordable, but is currently being marketed by a smaller collection of companies.

Cache memory

This is super-fast memory used as a convenient and speedy notepad by the processor chip. Older Pentium computers had 256Kb (Mb) of cache memory on the motherboard. Currently this is still true for any computers that use the Socket 7 system, especially the AMD K6 series.

All Pentium II and Pentium III processor chips feature a similar amount of cache memory built into the same case as the chip itself. Xeon-range chips justify their price by offering more cache – either 256K, 1Mb or 2Mb. In practice, though, more than 512K of cache seems to have a minimal effect on the working speed of a chip. The original Celeron 'A' range lacked any cache at all, which led to very poor performance; the newer, updated Celeron series offers 128Kb or 256Kb. Motherboards for all these chips do not include any cache at all.

The hard disk drive

This is the computer's filing space. Although a typical hard disk unit may be roughly the size of a thick paperback, it will have enough room for more than 400 copies of the text of this book.

Hard disk capacities are measured in megabytes (Mbs) where 1Mb is the space needed to store one million letters or other characters. The more Mbs, the more room the computer has for software, records and other information. A gigabyte (Gb) is 1,000 Mbs, and multi-gigabyte drives (which are large enough to store long snatches of sound and video) are now becoming common. Disk sizes of 10Gb and upwards are now standard. These offer plenty of space for all but the most demanding users. If you are buying a new computer do not buy less than 9Gb. The difference in price between this and larger sizes of hard disk is now so small that there is very little reason to settle for less than 9Gb unless your budget is very tight indeed.

Apple computers offer similar-sized hard disks to PCs. Both Apple and PC computers used for multimedia work, such as audio and video editing, need very much higher disk capacities: 20Gb is a reasonable minimum for anyone who does this kind of work professionally, although 40Gb or more is not unreasonable for video projects. Disks of this size will usually have to be ordered and fitted specially.

Note also that on some PCs, the BIOS cannot handle disk sizes above 9Gb. Even if you buy and fit a larger disk, the motherboard will only be able to use 9Gb of it. Some disks are sold with special 'disk mapping' software pre-installed on them to fix this problem. This approach can slow down the disk, however, and certain kinds of problems may cause the software to be lost, rendering the disk useless. A better approach is to make sure that your PC's BIOS can work with larger disks directly.

Hard disk types

Size apart, not all hard disks are the same. Different systems have evolved to connect the disk to the motherboard and transfer information as quickly as possible. These fall into two main families – SCSI (Small Computer Systems Interface – pronounced 'scuzzy') and IDE (Integrated Drive Electronics). Both of these have evolved a number of sub-types.

In general IDE is used for undemanding work, while SCSI is preferred for high-performance applications. SCSI disk drives tend to be slightly faster, and they also transfer information more efficiently; very fast SCSI drives can be very expensive indeed.

Both SCSI and IDE can be used to connect other devices to a computer. IDE is limited to two items on the same cable (although most computers offer two cable connectors, making for a maximum of up to four items) and is never used outside a computer's case. SCSI, on the other hand, can be used with up to 16 different items, some of which may be outside the computer. Compatible options include scanners, CD-ROM drives, CD writers, external hard disks and even music synthesizers. SCSI is available in a dizzying range of variations (nine at the time of writing) which differ according to speed, the number of items that can be used, the maximum length of all the connections together, and so on. Full technical details are outside the scope of this book, but an Internet search for the words 'SCSI primer' or 'SCSI basics' should list all the most recent relevant facts.

IDE is a much simpler system. The current standard for IDE disks is known as 'Ultra DMA/33', sometimes shortened to just 'Ultra DMA'. A new standard known as 'Ultra DMA/66' is being tested but seems to offer only a marginal speed improvement in practice. Older standards, such as the original 'IDE' and 'EIDE', will be available on second-hand machines.

A recent trend in hard-disk design is to speed up the rate at which the hard-disk drive rotates. Inside each is a collection of platters, rather like a pile of flat plates. The speed at which this spins has a direct effect on the speed at which the disk can move information as a whole. The original standard speed was 5,400rpm. Some drives now offer 7,200rpm, and a few offer 10,020rpm. The latter tend to become very hot in use, and may need to be cooled with an extra fan.

Another recent trend is to add cache memory to some IDE designs. This works rather like cache memory on the motherboard, and can appear to improve the apparent speed of a disk. A minimum cache size is 512Kb, but some high-performance drives offer as much as 2Mb.

Floppy disk drive

This is a slot at the front of the computer that takes plastic wafers known as **floppy disks** (usually shortened to floppies), which are now rigid not flexible. The information is stored on a thin disk of magnetically sensitive plastic. The tough outer casing protects the sensitive surface from fingerprints, dust and other damage which might destroy the information.

All modern machines include one 3.5-inch 1.44Mb floppy disk drive. This means that you can use two kinds of floppy disk with them – high-density 1.44Mb disks, and older, double-density 720Kb disks which hold half as much information (now no longer available). Either will work in the same slot.

The 3.5-inch floppy disk is a venerable old standard but is now technically obsolete. Unfortunately, no single new standard has emerged as a replacement. However, some computers are now sold with LS120 drives instead of floppy disks. These work with existing floppy disks, but can also use new LS120 disks which can store up to 120Mb of information (see page 215).

Some antique machines use a different kind of floppy disk. These are 5.25 inches across and protect the inner disk with a much thinner floppy plastic sheath. They hold less information (a maximum of 360Kb) and take up more space. Unless you buy a computer with a dual-format disk drive (and these are very rare) or with one of each kind of disk drive (also rare, and now usually available only to order) you will not be able to use either kind of disk in your machine. The two systems are mechanically incompatible.

Some software is still sold on 5.25-inch disks, although these are now all but obsolete. It is moderately straightforward to upgrade from one kind of disk to another, although this will not be possible on very old machines.

Monitor/screen

Monitor is just another word for screen − the part of your computer that displays information while you work. The monitor is one of the most important parts of your computer system. It is essential to choose a model that does not cause eyestrain.

To some extent specifications are something of a sideline with monitors. *Never buy a monitor without checking display quality first.* This will tell you far more about whether or not you can live with it on a daily basis than any number of facts and figures. However, specifications can be useful. Various factors in the specification to watch for include:

MPRII, TCO-95 and TCO-99 certification ensure that as little stray radiation as possible is released.

TCO-95/99 are the most stringent specifications. These two standards are virtually identical, and a monitor certified to either will produce minimal stray radiation.

Power-saving features NUTEK, Energy Star and VESA DPMS (Display Power Management Signalling) are all energy-saving options. They will switch a monitor to low-power 'standby' operation after a period of inactivity. Although they are unlikely to make a huge difference to your electricity bill, these features are worth having and using for environmental reasons.

Dot pitch is the size of each dot on the screen. The smaller the dot size, the sharper and clearer the image. Some monitor manufacturers use a 0.30mm dot pitch. Avoid these. Aim for at most a 0.28mm pitch – the current standard. If you can afford it, a monitor with a 0.26mm pitch will give an even crisper image.

Scan rate tells you how rapidly the screen flickers. Typically one or two numbers are shown. The 'horizontal scan rate', typically shown in kHz (kilohertz) is related to the fineness of the image. The more important measure is vertical scan rate, which is shown in Hz (Hertz) – in this case flickers per second. Anything below 72Hz tends to cause eyestrain. One essential point to check is whether this scan rate is interlaced or not. A non-interlaced monitor gives you a solid picture. Interlacing effectively halves the scan rate, so a 60Hz interlaced monitor will flicker 30 times a second. Most people find this unbearable, even for short periods. Avoid interlaced monitors if you can. It is worth noting that many PCs are sold with the scan rate set to 60Hz, even if the hardware can do better. When buying a PC check if this can be altered, and if so ask the dealer to set it as high as it can go.

Screen size Monitors are available in a range of sizes. Like television screens, they are based on the size of the picture tube measured diagonally from corner to corner. Not all of this may be available. For example, a 21-inch monitor may have a visible diagonal of just under 20 inches. Most PCs are now sold with 15-inch monitors; 14-inch models are now something of a penny-pinching option, while 17-inch and larger models are becoming increasingly popular as prices for these models fall sharply. A high-quality 21-inch monitor now costs just over £1,000 although cheaper models which may have a slightly limited range of screen resolutions are available for around £750. Screen size, resolution (see below) and scan rate are intimately related. For details see the table opposite.

Resolution tells you how much detail the screen can show. The more dots there are available, the finer the image becomes. A good minimum to watch for is the SVGA standard, which is 640 dots across and 480 dots vertically. Each dot can be one of 256 colours. This is enough to reproduce photographs with some semblance of realism. Other

Standard resolutions and the necessary monitor sizes

CRT monitor size	LCD monitor size	Comfortable resolution*	Cramped resolution*	Comfortable flicker	Possible uses
14in	12.1in	640 × 480	800 × 600	72Hz	Letter-writing, accounts, spreadsheets (with difficulty)
15in	13.3in	800 × 600	1,024 × 768	75Hz	Spreadsheets, simple desktop publishing
17in	14.4in	1,024 × 768	1,280 × 1,024	82Hz	Image editing and retouching, large spreadsheets
21in	18in	1,280 × 1,024	1,600 × 1,200	85Hz	Multiple applications at once, very advanced word processing, huge spreadsheets
22in	N/A	1,600 × 1,200	1,800 × 1,440	90Hz	Advanced commercial design and publishing

*resolution is measured in the number of lights across and down

standard sizes are 800 x 600 and 1024 x 768, 1280 x 1024 and 1600 x 1400. You will need a larger monitor to make use of these.

The number of available colours also varies. The minimum is 256 and is best avoided; 64,000 and 16.7 million are the other common options. Almost all modern machines are capable of displaying 16.7 million colours at once on the monitor they are sold with. If you need this degree of detail with a larger working area, check to make sure that your computer's graphics card will be able to offer 16.7 million colours at higher resolutions on a larger monitor.

For those who find conventional displays hard to work with, solid-state displays are an expensive but worthwhile option. These take the form of a flat panel based on the same technology used in laptop computers. They offer a maximum of 64,000 colours at a resolution of 1024 x 768 or less and cost between two and three times as much as an equivalent CRT monitor. They may prove to be the displays of the future.

At the time of writing, plasma displays are starting to become available. These are thin, flat panels that can be hung on a wall. Physically they typically offer a 40-inch diagonal and are designed to be viewed from a distance instead of close-up. The maximum possible resolution at the moment is 1,280 x 1,024. They are currently very expensive indeed – between £5,000 and £10,000. Current designs also consume a lot of power, and can sometimes run hot enough to cause minor burns if touched. All this puts them out of reach for home users; they are, however, of interest to businesses, where they are popular for presentations.

Keyboard

On IBM-compatibles, the 102-key keyboard is the standard. This includes extra keys for numbers on the right-hand side and also arrow keys which are used for moving around the screen. Some keyboards feel much more pleasant to use than others. Some people prefer more of a spongy bounce, others a definite 'clack'. This is a matter of personal taste. Try a keyboard before buying it, especially if you are a touch typist. 'Cherry' keyboards made by the Cherry company, are often offered as an optional extra. These are built to a higher standard than budget keyboards. If possible, buy a *weighted* keyboard; these include a metal weight that makes them less likely to slide around the desk as you type.

Keyboard fashions come and go. The 'ergonomic' designs of the mid-1990s are still available, although less popular now than they once were. These models attempt to place the keys in a more accessible position than the standard flat design. As with keyboard 'feel', this is very much a matter of personal taste.

Wireless keyboards do away with connecting cables, replacing them with a local radio link. They can be used at a distance (perhaps while playing a game with the computer plugged into the TV), on one's lap while reclining, or simply as a way to help avoid the snarl of cables that typically builds up behind a PC. Compatible wireless mice are often also available. *Internet* keyboards offer extra keys for Internet browsing. These help make certain operations easier and quicker. Although they are gimmicks to some extent, dedicated Internet users may find them helpful.

Cases (IBM only)

IBM-compatible machines are sold in a standard range of case styles; these do not affect the performance of your computer in any way. A big case does not mean a fast and powerful computer, but it does mean you have more room to add extras.

Cases are now divided into two types – AT (also known as 'baby AT') and ATX. These do exactly the same job, and look identical from the outside, but are designed to be used with the two sizes of motherboards that are now available. If buying a new PC, the ATX option is the better one. ATX systems are better designed, are easier to take apart and put together, and are less prone to annoying problems (for example, memory chips that are almost inaccessible because they are hidden behind an unfortunately positioned power supply).

Apart from this basic distinction, cases come in different sizes. Besides taking up more space, larger cases have more drive bays – special areas that extras can slot into. Typically, they also have more powerful power supplies to take care of the extra load.

Drive bays are used for extras that need front-panel access – floppy-disk drives, hard disk drives, tape backup systems and CD-ROM units. Other extras slot into the expansion slots inside the computer's case.

Drive bays come in two sizes – 5.25 inch, which are suitable for 5.25-inch floppy disk drives and CD-ROM players, and 3.5 inch, which are used for 3.5-inch floppy drives and hard disk drives. When not in use they are screened off with plastic blanking plates. To install an extra you simply remove the plate, slot in the new drive, tighten a few screws and then make the connections to the rest of the computer.

Slimline cases look trim, but are only recommended if you know exactly what you want and are sure you will not need to upgrade. They typically have one of each size of drive bay.

Desktop and mini-tower cases are the most common. The desktop model sits on your desk horizontally and the monitor sits on the case. The mini-tower model stands vertically. These are designed to sit to one side of your desk or perhaps even out of sight under it. Either model will have two of each kind of drive bay as standard.

Full tower cases also stand vertically. They are used for larger computer systems and offer four or five drive bays. These cases are best left on the floor – they are too tall to be used on most desks.

Larger cases tend to have more powerful power supplies. For a typical PC anything more than 200W should be adequate, although if you plan to add a lot of extras 250W or even 300W may be required. Power supplies are available separately and can be swapped quite easily;

fitting a larger one is straightforward. However, it's usually cheaper to make sure that any case you buy has a suitably hefty power supply to start with. It's worth noting that case prices can vary significantly. Some companies in *MicroMart* magazine advertise serviceable cases for around half the price of similar examples advertised in the more mainstream computer press.

Some cases have a door which closes to hide the drive bays. Unless you are running your computer as a file server, you should avoid this design – the door only gets in the way during everyday use.

And, of course, no computer would be complete without a small array of flashing lights and numbers. These will usually include:

- a 'power-on' light
- a hard–disk activity light: this is useful – it tells you when your hard disk is working.

There will also be a handful of buttons. 'Turbo' is no longer seen on all cases, and even where it is fitted it is often not connected. (On very old computers this button was used to slow them down, because certain software refused to work properly at high speeds. However, this feature has been obsolete since 1994.) 'Reset' forces your computer to go through its start–up sequence. *Do not touch this button without a good reason.* You will lose any unsaved work. The reset button should only be used when your computer has obviously stopped working and needs to be restarted. Switching the power on and off again strains the hardware slightly (although whether or not this makes a lasting difference is debatable); use the reset button instead.

Expansion options

Extra hardware can be added to a computer in one of two ways – inside the case, where it lives permanently, or outside it using one of the connectors on the back, together with appropriate cables.

Inside the case, all motherboards offer a number of 'expansion slots'. These now come in two types – ISA (Industry Standard Architecture) and PCI (Peripheral Connect Interface). (An older standard called Vesa is now obsolete, and only appears in second–hand 486 machines. Spares and extras are no longer available for this standard.) ISA is used for slow devices such as soundcards, modems and slow network cards. PCI is used for faster devices such as high performance sound cards (graphics cards use a different system again called AGP). ISA is now being phased out, and recent PCs no longer include any ISA slots at all. Apple computers, meanwhile, have switched to a PCI-based system from a proprietary one. This means that some PC extras will now work inside an Apple machine. In the medium term the PCI system is likely to be replaced by a new design called PCI-X, which is due towards the middle of 2000. However, PCI-X is controversial, and it is not yet clear if Intel will fully support it. If not, today's PCI technology will remain as a *de facto* standard.

To install extra hardware, the relevant circuit card is simply plugged into an empty slot. Once all available slots are in use the PC is 'full'. If you have a lot of extras installed, it is important when upgrading to check that a new PC offers a similar number of suitable slots. Otherwise you may find that one or more of your extras becomes unusable, simply because there is nowhere to plug it in.

External connectors consist of five types – parallel ports, serial ports, Universal Serial Bus (USB) sockets, a system called 'Firewire' (currently standard on some Apple machines, and available as an optional extra on PCs), and infra-red links (IrDA). The first two are traditional computer connection options, which have been used for 20 years. Parallel ports are large chunky sockets typically used to connect printers. Serial ports are smaller sockets that are more often used for modems and mice.

USB has now started to become a practical option, and USB-compatible devices such as scanners and monitors are starting to become widely available. Where a single connection needs to be shared or parcelled out among a number of different devices, a 'USB hub' can be used to distribute the information from a single cable to a number of USB sockets (often four, occasionally eight). Note that USB is not a 'guaranteed' system. Using a USB cable to connect a monitor, for example, will use up most of the available connection power ('bandwidth'). USB is best used for low-bandwidth applications, such as connecting mice and keyboards, modems and sound-cards.

USB and Firewire are both attempts to overcome the rats' nest of connections that can build up at the back of a computer. They work by 'daisy-chaining' (connecting from item to item) a single cable from the PC through printers, monitors, modems, speakers and other extras. Thus, instead of multiple cables connecting the computer to individual devices, there is only one. At the time of writing only a limited number of PCs and extras work with this system, but it shows every sign of becoming a new standard in computers built from around 1999 onwards.

The IrDA system is available primarily on laptops and personal organisers, although it is also beginning to appear on desktop PCs and printers. It uses a wireless link that works rather like a TV remote control to move information from one item to another. For example, it can be used to copy a list of contact addresses from a PC to a personal organiser or vice versa. No cables are involved, although of course any devices that are to be connected have to be visible to each other and less than ten feet apart – the system will not work through walls and doors. There are plans for IrDA to start appearing in public places such as telephone boxes, airports and station waiting-rooms, where it will be used to provide a link to the Internet or some other public data network.

Some companies are experimenting with wireless systems, the most popular of which is called 'Bluetooth'. The eventual aim is to make it possible for someone to carry a laptop anywhere in a building, and have access to an Internet or network connection and all the information in base machines wherever they are. Wireless systems are not widely available yet, but this is likely to change by around 2002.

Until USB and IrDA become standard, you will continue to find connectors for monitors, keyboards and mice on the back of computers. It's almost impossible to connect them wrongly when setting up a computer for the first time. One point to be aware of is that most computers offer 'PS/2' connectors for the mouse and perhaps the keyboard. This is a very useful option for the mouse, as the PS/2 connector is linked directly to the motherboard. This has the advantage of making it possible to use both serial ports, instead of having to dedicate one to the mouse.

Graphics card

The graphics card controls what appears on the monitor. It sets the maximum number of colours that you can use, the resolution and the scan rate. New computers are sold with good basic graphics cards that are perfectly adequate for most work. However, if you plan to work with photographs, animations or a large monitor you may need to upgrade your graphics card to match. Graphics card specifications quote the amount of memory used, but in practice you are better off

SPECIFICATION CHECKLIST

Using the recommended system needed to run your software of choice as a guide, you can work out a target hardware specification based on the following:

(1) Apple or IBM
(2) processor chip
(3) memory
(4) floppy disk type
(5) hard disk size
(6) monitor and graphics card
(7) operating system software: this is included as part of the hardware, as they are almost always sold together
(8) all connectors, manuals, mouse and keyboard
(9) optional extras: (i) a printer; (ii) a CD-ROM drive or DVD drive; (iii) a sound-card and speakers; (iv) a modem; (v) a scanner; (vi) networking facilities; (vii) video cards, joysticks and other less usual extras; (viii) backup facilities.

When buying, check each of these items in turn and make sure that all have been included in your order.

Details of the hardware differences between Apple and IBM are discussed in Appendices IV and V.

checking for scan rate, maximum resolution and maximum number of colours available. Better still, ask to see a graphics card in action at its highest resolution with the maximum number of colours it can produce. This should tell you everything you need to know about the speed and clarity of the display.

All graphics cards are now **accelerated**. They are built around a special chip that takes some of the load from the main processor – so, for example, the processor can ask for a rectangle to be drawn on the screen without having to do all the calculations required to make it appear. The majority of graphics cards plug into AGP (see below) slots. (Very rarely you may come across a much slower card that plugs into an ISA or PCI slot.)

The graphics card market is beginning to divide into two: cards for home use and business cards. The former include extra features that make games appear more appealing and realistic. Cards for the business market are often designed to work with larger monitors instead. In practice, however, these distinctions are subtle, unless you are an extremely keen game player or someone who needs an unusually large monitor. For most applications the cards sold with modern machines work perfectly well. One drawback with cards enhanced for games is that as yet there is no one standard for them. As a result, some games work better with some cards than others. Until the industry can agree a single standard and stick to it, this situation will remain.

Very recent PCs use an enhanced kind of PCI connector called AGP (Advanced Graphics Port). This doubles the maximum speed at which a card can work. AGP-compatible cards are now standard on most PCs, and have contributed to making games look more detailed and realistic, as well as making it easier to use larger monitors.

Appendix II

Hardware extras and upgrades

Some hardware extras are entertainingly useless, such as a simulated sailing tiller which connects to your computer and lets you practise your navigation skills. Others, such as printers, are all but essential.

Like the other parts of your computer system, each extra has its own specification and jargon. Not all have specifications that are quoted with software. To some extent they depend on personal preference. Fortunately, most extras are relatively straightforward and do not demand the same kind of technical knowledge that computers themselves do.

Printers

If your business needs to make a good impression, it can be well worth taking the time to choose a high-quality printer. The currently available options include:

Daisy wheel These printers are now obsolete but they were popular until the early 1990s and do occasionally appear on the second-hand market. Daisy-wheel printers work by slamming metal dies against a ribbon, which then print letters on to the paper. The dies are arranged in a circle on spokes around a central support. The whole arrangement looks rather like the petals of a flower – hence the name.

Daisy-wheel printers are very slow and very loud and can only produce text – pictures, decorative borders and so on are not possible. Their only advantage is that they can produce true typewriter-quality print. With the relative affordability of good-quality laser and bubble-jet printers, however, these printers have fallen by the wayside.

This is an example of near letter quality (NLQ) mode printing
from a dot matrix printer.

This is an example of draft mode printing
from a dot matrix printer.

This is 9 point Times Roman

This is an example of Times 12 point output
on a 300 dpi laser printer.

This is an example of Times 12 point output
on a 600 dpi laser printer.

This is an example of Times 12 point output
on a 1200 dpi laser printer.

Dot matrix 9–pin These printers are the most basic models available. Because the printing system is mostly mechanical (a print head with 9 retractable pins scans across the paper and 'punches' dots on to it) these printers are slow, irritatingly loud and produce poor-quality output. However, they are cheap (a typical example might cost around £100) and have negligible running costs. Apart from paper and minimal electricity consumption, the only extra costs are inked ribbons. These need to be replaced once or twice a year and cost under £10.

These printers are now almost obsolete, and are usually used where quality of print is less important than reliability, low running costs and the ability to produce multiple carbon copies – for example, invoice printing for garages. Although most printers offer a 'near letter quality' (NLQ) mode which provides sharper letters, the print quality is noticeably rough when compared with a good typewriter.

Only the simplest block and line graphics are possible with these printers; photographic images are not. The machines can produce a range of lettering styles with appropriate software, but compared with other printers the results can look amateurish and rough.

Dot matrix 24–pin 24-pin printers offer improved print quality over 9-pin printers, but otherwise have the same advantages and drawbacks.

They cost between £150 and £500. The more expensive models are ideal for long inventory listings which are most convenient when printed on continuous paper – paper which is sold as a very long strip divided into pages by perforations – and can also accommodate wider paper than cheaper examples.

Bubble-jet/ink-jet These are now the budget printer standard, and work by electrostatically squirting tiny blobs of ink on to a sheet of paper. They are quiet, slightly faster than dot matrix printers and give reasonable results at a modest cost – typically £60 to £500. Running costs are moderate for light use. The ink is supplied in the form of cartridges, which cost between £15 and £30 to replace. Ink and re-inking equipment are available if you want to refill cartridges by hand, although this can be messy.

A bubble-jet printed page will always look slightly rough, although the print quality is significantly better than that offered by dot-matrix machines. The quality can be improved by using high-quality paper rather than photocopier paper. This makes the printers suitable for professional work, especially for sole traders working from home. For a start-up business on a tight budget a bubble-jet printer provides the best compromise between cost and print quality. With suitable software, bubble-jet printers can produce different kinds of lettering. Some printers are now specifically designed for photographs and high-quality images. These 'photo' models can produce surprisingly good results. Note, however, that the output from an ink-jet printer can be more prone to fading than a true photograph.

Colour, however, is still an expensive extra – an A4 page of colour can cost as much as 20p – and some printers can be painfully slow, taking up to an hour per page. (Black-and-white printing is very much quicker.) Print quality has improved steadily, and more expensive models can approach photographic quality when used with appropriate high-quality paper. Colour printing can be used for bar charts and other business graphics, and also for domestic and light business colour printing, such as cards, letters and advertisements. Some models can print on overhead transparency film.

As with laser printers, fineness and accuracy are specified in dots-per-inch (dpi). However, it is impossible to compare the two different kinds of printer directly in this way. The print quality of a 300dpi ink-jet is fairly rough for both text and graphics. From 600 to 720dpi is better, but still not comparable to a 300dpi laser. You need to go to 1440dpi on a bubble-jet to even begin to approach 300dpi laser quality for text, and when used with special paper this can produce moderately satisfactory renditions of colour photographs and other images.

Some ink-jet printers can print on A3 as well as A4 paper. This is useful for posters and advertisements, and can also be a way to improve print quality for very demanding work. For certain applications printing on A3 and photocopying in colour at 50 per cent to A4 can appear to produce a more detailed image than printing directly to A4.

If you are sure that an ink-jet printer is for you, it can be well worth considering one of the 'all-in-one' office units that are now available. These combine the functions of a scanner, a fax machine, an ink-jet printer and a photocopier in a box only slightly larger than the printer itself. However, it's important to give these units a fair trial run to make sure that each of the individual sections meets your needs.

Micro-dry Micro-dry printers use ink supplied on ribbons in special cassettes. These printers can print T-shirt transfers which can be ironed on to clothes, and are also the only printers that can print using metallic gold, silver, red or blue ink.

However, they are quite expensive compared to a typical ink-jet, and are also slow. Colour print quality does not seem to be quite as fine as a reasonable ink-jet, although black-and-white photographs appear to be printed more realistically.

These printers seem to be something of a curiosity, and are unlikely to be worth considering except for those few situations where their advantages become compelling.

Laser Laser printers use a tightly focused beam of light to 'paint' an image on to a special light-sensitive surface. This image is then printed to paper using a system based on photocopier technology. Laser printers give results which approach those possible with conventional typesetting and printing machinery, at a fraction of the cost. A close examination of a laser-printed page will show that the letters are slightly rough compared with work that has been professionally typeset but for many applications the differences are unimportant.

Laser printers are no longer the expensive option they once were. Prices are heading down towards £100, which makes them the first choice for anyone who requires high-quality black-and-white printing. You can pay up to £20,000 for a lightning-fast printer that can serve the printing needs of an entire office.

Running costs vary from model to model. In addition to the unit price, laser printers are expensive to run. Not only do they consume significantly more electricity than the other printer types, they also require expensive consumables. To produce a laser-printed image, very fine dust-like particles of ink (known as toner) are literally melted on to the page. The toner is supplied in the form of cartridges which need to be replaced every 5,000 pages or so. Toner cartridges can cost up to £100. However, laser printers can still work out cheaper than ink-jets in the long run, and require less maintenance. By way of comparison, a typical ink-jet cartridge costs £20 and will need to be replaced every 500 pages.

Another cost can be the replacement of the drum on which the laser writes the image. This is made of a special light-sensitive material which slowly wears out as the printer is used. Drums can cost up to £100 a time. Fortunately these need to be replaced much less frequently than toner cartridges. The latest laser designs, especially the cheaper models, attempt to minimise running costs by including drum and toner in the same unit. These all-in-one cartridge designs cost between £30 and £50 to replace. If you plan to do a lot of printing, it can be a very good idea to estimate running costs: over the course of a few years consumables can add up to three or four times the original cost of the printer.

Laser printers can handle just about any black-and-white printing task. (Colour laser printers have now come down in price, but they are still very expensive. Prices for the very cheapest 'budget' models start at around £1,500 and go up to many times this. This puts the technology out of reach of most home users, although businesses sometimes use them to check page proofs before a major colour-printing project.) As well as producing different kinds of lettering in different sizes, laser printers can also produce drawings and cartoons. Mid-range and better lasers can also produce good reproductions of black-and-white photographs.

Laser printers are specified according to how finely they can print dots on a page. A low-cost printer can create 300 dpi. This is more than adequate for most office work, although lettering produced on a 300 dpi printer does look very slightly rough when compared with professionally typeset printing, and so these printers are not recommended for photographs. The results are usable for casual dabbling and informal use, but slightly rough for professional presentations.

The next step up is 300 dpi with resolution enhancement. This process fills in the spaces between the dots with smaller dots, creating a sharper result. When buying a laser it is important to check if resolution enhancement is available, as it significantly improves print quality for little, if any, extra cost. However, these printers are still not ideal for work involving photographs.

Higher-quality printers can produce 600 dpi. This is useful for low-budget professional publishing work, as the letter quality is sharp and photographs can begin to be reproduced convincingly. Some printers are billed as having a resolution equivalent to 600 dpi. This is simply marketing speak for a 300 dpi printer with resolution enhancement.

Top-end printers can produce 1200 dpi or better. This begins to approach the results achieved using professional typesetting equipment. Lettering is pin-sharp and photographs can be reproduced realistically. However, these machines are significantly more expensive and are recommended only if your work needs the extra quality. For conventional word processing they are unnecessary.

An important laser-printer specification to watch for is speed. This is specified in pages per minute (ppm). This is the maximum rate at which the printer can feed paper through. Many lasers do not approach their quoted speeds. Low-cost laser printers can usually manage four pages per minute, which is adequate for everyday business use. More expensive and sophisticated machines offer twice or even three times this rate. These machines are usually designed for heavy-duty work in an office environment where the one printer is shared between many users on a network.

In addition to the printing hardware itself, most laser printers include a sizeable built-in computer of their own to manage the printing process. Like other computers, they need memory to be able to work effectively. Some lasers are supplied with the bare minimum needed to print a single page of A4 text. Graphics, photographs and other styles of lettering may well need more memory than this, and this will have to be bought and installed as an extra. Check with your dealer if you will need to do this, based on the kind of work you have in mind. Extra memory can add significantly to the cost of a laser printer.

Some lasers get round this problem by using the PC's own resources to do the preparatory work. This is a much cheaper and simpler option, but it can cause a PC to stutter while it 'thinks about' what will go on the page. It can also be a difficult option to use with older MS-DOS software.

Laser printers are sometimes advertised as **Postscript-compatible**. Postscript is an image-definition system that has become a world standard since it was introduced on the Apple Mac in the mid-1980s. The inclusion of Postscript offers extra facilities and makes a laser printer ideal for use with the many DTP and graphics programs that support this standard.

Dye sublimation, thermal transfer and solid ink printers are all aimed at the professional colour-printing market. They are very expensive and only of interest to businesses that need to produce very-high-quality print proofs in-house.

Modems

There are three things you should know about a modem. The most important is to check for BABT approval. This means the modem has been through a rigorous programme of testing and certification and is fully compatible with the BT network. Unapproved modems are no longer common, but they are still sometimes sold to unwitting users. While they may work well most of the time, it is illegal to connect one of these modems to a telephone line, and you are more likely to suffer from minor incompatibility problems (such as not being able to recognise the BT 'busy' signal) than if you buy a fully approved model. Unfortunately the approval process is expensive, and approved models cost slightly more than the unapproved variety. In terms of peace of mind and long-term reliability, however, the extra cost can be worth it. Approved equipment carries the green triangle mark. Unapproved equipment is marked with a red circle.

Next, check whether the modem is internal or external. To install an internal modem you will need to remove the case from your computer and slot the modem into an expansion slot. You are more likely to come across obscure problems while doing this. An external modem is a better choice if you prefer to keep things as simple as possible. You can attach this to your computer with a special cable. Any further setting up should be minimal. When buying an external model, make sure that a cable is included.

Modems work at different speeds. These directly affect your telephone bill, as the faster the modem, the more quickly it gets information. Speed is measured in baud or bps (bits per second). Often this is shown as a number – 14,400 for example. These numbers can be compared directly – so a 28,800 modem will move information twice as fast as a 14,400 modem.

If two computers have different-speed modems, the speed at which they will communicate is the highest they can both achieve (for example, a 9,600 and a 28,800 will talk at 9,600). All modems can communicate at speeds slower than their quoted rates.

Older, slower modems (14,400 or slower) are sometimes available second-hand, but these are always a false economy. The nominal cost savings possible when buying a second-hand slow modem are more than outweighed by the much larger phone bill which is likely to result. A new V.90 modem is now within the budget of most buyers, and so there is little need to compromise with a slower model.

Speed is often shown as a 'V' figure. These are industry-standard codes for different modem speeds and features. The table below lists the most common speeds and typical applications.

Speed	Code	Suggested usage
2,400	V.22bis	Completely obsolete. No longer worth considering
9,600	V.32	Also obsolete. Can be used for very occasional email, but too slow for anything more demanding.
14,400	V.32bis	Also obsolete. Can be used for very occasional email, but too slow for anything more demanding.
28,800	V.34	Superseded almost immediately by V34+,
33,600	V34+	Adequate for light use, but now superseded by V.90
57,600	V.90	The current standard, fast enough for all domestic and light business applications.

V.90 replaced two earlier incompatible systems known as X2 and K56Flex. These are still used occasionally. However, a V.90 modem should be able to work with either of them. These 57,600 modems employ special tricks to get the fastest possible connection from the ageing technology used in the public telephone system. This has important implications. First, the maximum speed is only available when the modem is receiving information – when sending information, these models work at the same speed as a 33,600 modem. As most home and small business users receive far more information than they send, this is not a drawback. Second, the top speed is only available over an interference-free telephone connection. A more realistic working speed using a typical noisy connection is around 40,000. To some extent this depends on the quality of the modem – better (although not necessarily more expensive) models will be able to approach the theoretical top speed more closely. Comparative magazine reviews are a good way to check how these fast modems fare against each other.

Some older 33,600 modems and X2 or K56Flex models were sold with a 'flash upgrade option'. If you have one of these, it can be worth visiting the manufacturer's web site to see if this option is available to you. The upgrade is very simple and consists of a piece of software which 'reprograms' the modem so that it works with the newer V.90 standard. There is no need to open the case of either the computer or the modem.

Many modems now include answering-machine features. The best can take voice messages, and perhaps receive faxes, even if the computer they are connected to is turned off. Some even include a built-in loudspeaker and microphone, so that they can be used just like an ordinary answering machine. Speech quality in these models is not as good as that from a high-quality tape unit, but for convenience and cost-effectiveness they offer very good value.

An extra line?

Because Internet use can tie up a telephone line for long periods, many home users and businesses are now adding an extra telephone line specifically for faxes and modem use. This is usually considerably cheaper than an ISDN link (see below), although of course connection speeds are rather lower.

However, note that BT sometimes uses a 'DACS box' to split one line into two when the second line is installed. This will have the effect of limiting the modem speed to around 36,000bps, no matter what kind of modem is used. BT has sometimes proved unwilling to take away the DACS box and replace it with a genuine two-line connection unless plenty of pressure is applied. (The usual argument offered is that the line is for speech use, not data use.) Anyone having a second line installed for Internet use should make sure that this question is cleared up before installation goes ahead.

ISDN

BT is now offering more demanding subscribers a choice of ISDN (Integrated Services Digital Network) options. ISDN offers two 64,000bps links which can be used simultaneously to give a 128,000bps connection. (Note that this is equivalent to making two calls at the same time, so all call charges are doubled.) In practice ISDN typically offers speeds of between 55,000bps and 60,000bps for each line. Another advantage of ISDN is that a connection is made almost immediately, within a second or so. This compares with around 30 seconds that a modem requires to set up a link with another modem.

Setting up a true ISDN link is a fairly complex process with a confusing range of options. It is, for example, possible to give permanently connected items such as fax machines their own telephone number. It is also possible to use ISDN as the basis of a PABX phone network for a business, while also using it to connect a network of computers to the Internet. Setting up systems like these requires special skills, and only a handful of dealers are equipped to offer this level of expertise. BT offers a number of complex pricing options which need to be analysed carefully to see which will suit any individual or business best. Depending on usage, some of these will be cheaper, and others more expensive than BT's widely publicised Home Highway option (see below).

To make ISDN more accessible BT has introduced two schemes it calls Home Highway and Business Highway. These repackage the ISDN line as two sockets, each of which can be used either as a conventional phone line or as an Internet connection. It is still possible to use the two lines simultaneously to create a 128,000bps connection. Or the two lines can both be used for voice traffic at the same time.

Both Home and Business Highway pricing in the UK remains scandalous. Currently the line rental is £40 a month, although this does include a call allowance. Calls are charged at the usual rate. This has had the unfortunate effect of making ISDN much less popular in the UK than it might be otherwise. In comparison, many European countries offer ISDN as a standard replacement to an existing phone line, with no increase in the amount paid for either installation or use.

New installations

Modems and even ISDN are old technologies. They are being superseded by the Internet which has become one of the most important ways to move information from place to place. A number of experimental systems are currently being tested which offer much faster and more convenient connections. Some of these are likely to be introduced commercially before the end of the century.

Cable modems use the cable television network to supply very fast connections to the Internet — between ten and a hundred times faster than the fastest speeds available over a telephone line. In some cases they allow computers to be connected to the Internet permanently. Availability depends on the individual cable companies, which means that the service is only available in certain parts of the country. If you live in a cable TV area it is worth enquiring about the present and future availability of Internet services from your cable company.

Satellite links are a good choice for more serious Internet users who live in an area not covered by the cable TV companies — particularly remote rural locations. Hughes-Olivetti supplies a system called DirecPC which uses a satellite dish to receive information at speeds of up to 400,000 bps — nearly seven times faster than a 57,600 modem. DirecPC cannot send information to the Internet in this way — that part of the connection is handled by an ordinary modem. At the time of writing the dish itself costs over £1,000 to install, and a number of subscription schemes are available which depend on the quantity and time of day at which information is received. Although expensive, it can offer better value than ISDN for some users.

A number of custom satellite systems are due for launch around the turn of century, including one in which Bill Gates of Microsoft has invested heavily. In theory, these will provide a new global network which will be available for mobile telephone, Internet and perhaps also television transmissions. If they work successfully they will render many existing systems obsolete, and offer true high-speed wireless Internet connections almost anywhere in the world. However, at the time of writing a number of technical issues remain unresolved, and it is perhaps wise to treat these systems with a certain caution until they have proved themselves in the field.

Power cable links offer yet another alternative. An electricity producer, Norweb, has tested a system which creates a very high-speed Internet connection over the National Grid – in effect bringing information into and out of houses all over the country using a combination of the electricity supply and a small 'black box' that plugs into a computer. This has many obvious advantages over other systems, but at the time of writing the system is not yet commercially available.

Wireless links are currently a very slow way to use the Internet. Using current technology, mobile phone users are limited to 9,600bps. However, by about the year 2003 this should improve, and plans are in place for wireless networks offering between 128kbps and 4Mbps. If these appear on schedule, and prove to be affordable, they will effectively render BT's current connection schemes obsolete almost overnight. This will have a revolutionary effect on the way that the Internet, mobile phones, faxes and other communication systems are used.

Soundcards

These are used to add sound and music to your computer. All soundcards can record a sound and play it back if you connect them to a microphone and a pair of speakers. This can be useful if you want to add voice annotation to a letter, use voice-recognition software, or take advantage of the experimental international telephone-like services available on the Internet.

Many also include a music synthesizer. This adds a selection of more-or-less realistic instrument sounds that are used by games and other multimedia software. (Many web pages now include information that makes this synthesizer play a tune.) Older soundcards frequently offered a connection for a CD-ROM drive, but this feature is obsolete now that CD-ROM drives can use the same connectors as a computer's hard disk.

One final extra is a joystick and MIDI Interface. A joystick is a small extra that fits in one hand and is used in games. The MIDI (Musical Instrument Digital Interface) is a computer control system for synthesizers and music keyboards. If you decide the sound from your soundcard is a bit thin, you can add an external synthesizer to make it fuller and richer. If you want to use your computer to record and edit performances from an external music keyboard, you will also need a

MIDI interface. (You will also need an adaptor, as the connector on the back of most soundcards does not fit the MIDI standard.)

Over the years a soundcard standard has emerged, based on a range of cards from Creative Labs known as the Soundblaster series. In theory a 'Soundblaster-compatible' card should work with most software that needs a soundcard. In practice this is not always the case. If sound and music are important to you it is well worth getting a genuine Soundblaster card for the best possible results.

Soundcards vary in quality. Very old models use '8-bit recording', which is roughly equivalent to telephone quality and is adequate for speech and simple sound effects. All modern cards offer '16-bit recording' which approaches CD quality, although it's probably fair to say that in practice the sound from many cards doesn't quite reach true hi-fi standards.

A handful of cards offer 'digital input' and/or 'digital output', also known as 'S/PDIF' (Sony/Philips Digital Interface). A digital input can be used to make a perfect copy of music from a suitably equipped CD player on to a computer's hard disk. A digital output can provide ultimate audio quality when connected to a hi-fi extra called a DAC (Digital to Analogue converter).

Sound synthesizers also vary. Older soundcards use the old and very thin-sounding FM (Frequency Modulation) system, which was developed over a decade ago and uses the OPL3 and OPL2 set of chips. Newer soundcards use wavetable synthesis, which uses digital recordings of real instrument sounds, which are much more impressive and lifelike. You can sometimes upgrade older soundcards to wavetable synthesis with a *daughterboard*. This plugs into a socket on the soundcard and provides better sound.

The very latest soundcard designs include 'sampling memory', which lets you use your own recordings as musical instruments, and '3D sound'. The latter is designed to enhance the sound of games by making sounds appear to move above, below and behind the listener. Although the effect is noticeable with two speakers, it is far more striking with four, and the most recent soundcards include connections for four separate speaker channels.

Synthesizer technology has also improved. Home musicians can now buy cards which include synthesizers that are comparable to those available commercially. 'Software synthesizers' (also known as 'softsynths' are another new development. Instead of using a soundcard's hardware, these literally calculate the music in software as it plays. Windows 98 includes a softsynth made by the Roland company. Competitors Yamaha, meanwhile, offers a very-high-quality softsynth for around £30 that can be copied from its web site. This provides exceptionally good results for a very small outlay.

Amplifiers and speakers

With all soundcards you have the option of piping the sound through your existing hi-fi system. Sometimes it is more convenient to have speakers closer to your computer. Many multimedia systems are sold with speakers which stand on either side of the monitor or clip on to the sides. Speakers and soundcards are often sold together. When buying a soundcard you should always check if speakers are included. If not, check whether the soundcard has a built-in amplifier. Otherwise you will have to use your hi-fi, buy an external amplifier or buy powered speakers.

Apart from basic sound quality – which only your ears can gauge – it is important to check if speakers are shielded; this means that their heavy magnets will not affect a monitor if placed next to it.

A recent trend has been to offer more and more powerful speaker systems. 'Subwoofers' add extra bass to the sound. Some soundcards are now being sold with four or even five or six speaker systems, which attempt to mimic the all-round sound offered by an expensive home-cinema system. If you are considering one of these systems, it's worth noting that sound quality is very much poorer than that from a proper home cinema hi-fi. There may also be problems positioning the extra speakers, as some are designed to go behind the listener, and it's rare for people to have suitable shelving (or even a suitable wall) in the correct place.

CD-ROM drives

CD-ROMs look and work rather like conventional CDs, but instead of music, they contain pictures, text, sounds, video clips, software and other kinds of information. To use a CD-ROM you need to install an extra called a CD-ROM drive.

When buying a CD-ROM drive, the most important thing to check for is speed. Originally CD-ROM drives were designed to supply information at the same speed as music CD players, but this soon proved too slow for computer applications. Drives are now available that work up to 48 times ('48×') faster, although 40× drives are more common. These speeds are comparable to those offered by a hard disk, but the technicalities of CD-ROM technology mean that in practice most drives work at around 24× speeds most of the time.

All CD-ROM drives can play ordinary music CDs. If you have a soundcard and some speakers, the music will play through them directly – you will not even need to use your hi-fi. The sound quality is not quite up to hi-fi standards, but if you want some music while you work this is adequate. To play music you will also need some appropriate software. This is usually included as a standard feature of Windows 95/98.

CD-ROMs should also be multi-session – although almost all drives made today comply with this standard. This feature is specifically for use with the Kodak CD format that stores photographs on a CD. (This service is available as an extra at most high-street film developers.) The CD can be used again and again, so you can keep adding images from a new roll of film until the CD is full. CD-ROM drives that are not multi-session will only allow you to access the pictures from the first roll.

With the arrival of digital cameras (see pages 218–19) and affordable scanners, the future of the Photo-CD format is now in some doubt, although it's worth noting that the latter does offer much higher-quality images than a typical digital camera.

Drives designed in the early 1990s used one of the proprietary formats – usually Sony, Mitsumi or Panasonic – and were most often designed to work with compatible soundcards. More recent models use the IDE system which is more convenient as it requires less hardware – the CD-ROM can be connected in exactly the same way, to exactly the same hardware, as a hard disk – but it has an important side-effect. If you connect a CD-ROM drive and a hard disk using the same cable, the hard disk will be forced to transfer information at the same speed as the CD- ROM drive – typically up to ten times slower. To avoid this, make sure that the CD-ROM uses its own cable and connector. A handful of drives use the SCSI system instead. This does not suffer from the same drawback, but is not so widely available and tends to be more expensive.

Some older CD-ROM drives were designed to work with the Video-CD system, which offered the VHS-quality playback of commercial films and other videos on a computer's screen. This feature has not become the success that was originally hoped, and has been superseded by the appearance of DVD (see opposite.)

It is possible to buy multi-CD drives. These store a number of CD-ROMs in one unit, and are worth considering if you regularly need to access reference information from a variety of CD-ROMs.

At around £300, CD writers (also known as 'CD burners', 'recordable CD' or 'CD-R' drives) have now become affordable. These write information to special 'green' or 'gold' CD blanks, and make it possible to produce music CDs and CD-ROMs to your own requirements. These blanks cannot be re-used – information is stored on them permanently and cannot be changed. These drives also double as conventional CD-ROM drives, although they are very slow – the fastest drive currently available is a twelve-speed ('12X'). Information can be written up to 6-speed ('6X'), although slower speeds are recommended for maximum reliability. This is too slow for mass-production, but just about fast enough for anyone who wants to distribute a small number of home-made CD-ROMs.

CD writers require a fast PC that can produce the steady flow of information the writer requires. If the PC hiccups at all the writer will ruin a disk blank. Any medium-price modern PC should be fast enough, but older second-hand models almost certainly won't be.

A related development is the 'CD-RW' drive, which uses different – and more expensive – CD blanks that can be re-used. These drives are slightly more expensive than conventional recordable CD drives. The CDs they produce may not work in some conventional CD-ROM drives, and this limits their usefulness slightly.

Note that CD-R and CD-RW disks are more fragile than traditional CDs, and require more careful handling. CD-R and CD-RW drives typically use the SCSI system and are supplied with a plug-in connection card. Before buying one of these devices make sure that there is room in your computer for this card. However, a CD-RW drive can also be used to produce conventional fixed CD-Rs which can be read by any drive, as well as by a domestic CD player.

DVD

DVD (officially called Digital Versatile Disk, but more likely to be known as Digital Video Disk) is a next-generation CD-like system that appeared in computer stores during 1998. The disks can store up to 17Gb of information – enough for around 15,000 copies of the text of this book.

DVD was designed as a replacement for video tape, offering much better sound and picture quality in a more convenient package. While consumer DVD players (which look and work like hi-fi CD-players) are now well established, the computer world's equivalent is still suffering from teething troubles, and this technology is unlikely to become fully reliable before the end of 1999. One point to note is that DVD includes an anti-piracy feature which divides the world into a number of regions, with players and disks made specifically for each one. A 'Region 2' disk, for example, will not play in a 'Region 1' player. Not all computer DVD drives include this feature, which makes it possible to buy any DVD film from anywhere in the world and view it without problems.

Note also that most DVD systems also require extra hardware for best results. This makes the playing process quicker and more reliable than a software-only system. Most DVD drives do not include this extra hardware, although some manufacturers now supply a package which includes the drive itself and a suitable hardware extra. To confuse the issue further, some graphics cards have suitable hardware built-in. If you would like to add a DVD player to your computer, it can be very helpful to get the most up to date information about these various complications from a reputable and knowledgeable dealer before spending any money.

DVD-RAM drives, which can record as well as play, have also become available. These currently offer storage space of 5.2Gb on a single disk, which makes them a useful and relatively affordable back-up system.

Other drive types

Although floppy disks are rapidly becoming obsolete, no single technology has yet appeared to replace them. A variety of systems are now available, the most popular of which are the 120Mb 'a:drive LS120' from a number of sources, and the Zip and Jaz drives made by Iomega. The latter can store 100Mb and 1Gb respectively on small removable cartridges. These and various other systems offered by other manufacturers are relatively affordable and ideal for backups, although of course none has become a standard yet. If you are buying them solely for your own use this is not a worry, but if you are planning to use them to exchange information with friends and colleagues it is too early to tell yet which, if any, of these new systems will become the most popular and widely accepted.

Scanners

These copy pictures and photographs directly from a printed page into your computer. The quality range available stretches from simple black-and-white scanning (which is more than adequate for sending paper-based faxes) to full photographic colour, the latter rapidly becoming a new standard. As with other computer extras, scanner prices have plummeted, and equipment that was only within the budget of professionals at the beginning of the 1990s is now available for less than £200. Many scanners come with software for 'optical character recognition' (OCR). This attempts to read a page of text, rather than simply grabbing it as an image – so, for example, the words on the page can be copied into a word processor as if they had been typed. Although the results can sometimes be rough and ready, OCR software combined with a scanner can be a useful time-saving tool for applications where large amounts of text would otherwise have to be typed in by hand. Cheap OCR systems are unlikely to be reliable. You will need a good scanner and good OCR software if you want to use the system professionally. Otherwise, you will have to proofread copy after it has been scanned and make corrections yourself. With a budget system expect an accuracy of 95 per cent at best.

Scanners come in two types. A document scanner is a long, thin, plastic item with a slot at the front through which you pass the document. While less bulky than a flatbed scanner (see below), they tend not to offer comparable scanning quality and can also be surprisingly expensive. A flatbed scanner is more like a photocopier. You place the image on a glass plate under a lid and the scanner does the rest. Some flatbeds also include a transparency adaptor, so you can scan in slides as well as photographs.

Flatbed scanners are now very affordable and are used by both amateurs and professionals. Scanners can be connected to a computer in one of two ways – using the same connector as a printer, or with their own plug-in card, typically using the SCSI system. The latter offers much faster scanning and is the choice for more serious users.

The printer-connector option is much slower – a single A4 page can take more than 15 minutes – and may require a printer switch box. This typically costs around £15 and connects either the printer or the scanner to the computer.

Scanners are rated according to colour depth and resolution. The cheapest offer 8-bit greyscale, which means they can resolve 256 shades of grey. The best offer 24-bit colour, which makes them suitable for colour photographs. (A handful of professional-quality scanners offer 36-bit colour, which is better still but only relevant in a professional publishing context.)

Resolutions are specified in dots per inch (dpi) but most scanners use a mathematical process known as interpolation which fills in the gaps between dots and creates a higher effective resolution. 1200 dpi after interpolation is a good basic figure; 2400 dpi is used for more demanding work. Be warned that high-resolution scanning requires a lot of memory and hard disk space. A 2400 dpi A4 image scanned in full colour can demand up to 1.5Gb of the latter!

Check also that a scanner uses the TWAIN standard. This makes it possible for the scanner to scan images directly into most image processing software.

Mice

A mouse is a hand-held pointing device which fits under your palm. In order to use it correctly the connecting lead should be at the top of the mouse, by your fingertips, as opposed to under your wrist. As you move it from left to right and up and down, a pointer on the screen tracks your movements. There are one or more buttons under your fingers at the top of mouse. When you have moved the pointer to an active area on the screen you can make something happen by clicking one of these buttons.

IBM-compatible mice have two or three buttons (although the middle one is usually ignored by most software) and are connected to the computer's serial port, or directly to a special socket on the motherboard (the PS/2 standard). Mice vary mostly in comfort and ease of use. Some are sculptured to fit under your hand, while others are simply blocks of plastic.

A number of companies now offer 'wheel mice', which include a tiny wheel in between the buttons. This can be used to work the scrollbars at the side of a window. Many mice are also available in sculpted 'ergonomic' designs. As with keyboards, these are very much a matter of personal preference. One person's favourite can literally cause pain and cramp for someone else.

The latest designs are rounded and easy to use. Optical mice use a non-mechanical system to track movements, and are less susceptible to grime and dust. They are not widely available, although Microsoft plans to introduce an optical mouse towards the end of 1999. The best optical mice are more reliable and long-lasting than traditional mice, because they have no moving parts to accumulate dirt and debris.

In general one mouse is much like another, and unless you find the one you have been given intolerable, or feel the need to personalise your computer in some way, you will not need to change your mouse for another.

Trackballs are upside-down mice, and some users find them preferable, especially if they are working in cramped conditions without enough desk space for a standard mouse. As with mice, trackballs are available with a number of extra buttons and special features which make them easier to use.

Digital cameras

Digital cameras use no film. Instead, they store images in computer memory. These images can then be copied – 'downloaded' – to a home or business computer. No developing costs are involved, which means that images can be seen very quickly. This makes them ideal for anyone who wants to get images into their computer in a hurry.

The current generation of cameras offers much-improved optics and image quality compared to the first generation of cameras. However, it remains true that quality is usually equivalent to that on a film camera costing perhaps half or even a third as much. This makes most of these cameras more suitable for dabbling and for semi-professional work, than for professional photographers who need very high-quality results. (Cameras to suit professionals are available, but at prices that vary between £2,000 and £20,000. A standard digital camera is more likely to cost a few hundred.)

A number of systems are used to store and transfer images. A handful of camera designs write information on to standard floppy disks, which can be used in a computer in the usual way. More commonly images are transferred over a cable link, which can be slightly fiddly in practice. Camera memory is always limited. The best models can store up to 36 shots, although many models offer a trade-off between the number of shots that can be remembered and the detail and picture quality of each image. Sometimes it is possible to expand the memory in a camera by adding 'flash cards' – thin wafers that add extra memory in a very small space.

A useful feature on some cameras is the ability to preview and check images with a display on the back of the camera. If an image isn't satisfactory, it can be deleted immediately to make room for a new one.

A more advanced version of the same idea is the digital video camera. This has two applications – videophone links, which make it possible to see someone while you are talking to them on the telephone, and true digital video, which in effect offers a computerised tapeless camcorder. Videophone cameras are usually designed to sit on top of a monitor, and cannot be used without a connection to a PC. They offer poor image quality, can double as cheap still cameras, and at under £150 are relatively affordable. True digital video cameras have started to become more affordable. Apple's FireWire connection system makes it possible to transfer video directly from one of these cameras on to the computer's hard disk, where it can be edited further.

Advanced graphics cards

Where once graphics cards struggled to produce a detailed image in the maximum possible range of colours, now most cards take this task for granted. Progress has moved on to adding features for games, and in some cases for home video editing. In general, the card supplied with a PC when it is bought will be adequate for most uses, and the following will only be of interest to more demanding users.

Specialised games cards make it possible to play a game at a high resolution. They both speed up the rate at which images appear and also make the gaming environment appear more detailed. The technology used to do this is very complex, and a description of all the relevant details is outside the scope of this book. One point to note, however, is that cards develop at an overwhelming rate. The current market-leading card may be considered an also-ran as little as six months later. The only way to keep up with this technology is to watch out for comparative reviews in magazines.

Video editing systems are available as optional extras for some cards. These typically add a TV output, so that the picture can be made to appear on a conventional domestic TV set. They often also include *S-Video* connections, which can be plugged into a video recorder for transferring pictures with a minimum loss of quality. Not all cards include connections both ways. Sometimes it is only possible to get S-Video information into a card; for playback, the TV output is used. Finally, most systems include some form of editing software. (Adobe Premier is the best choice here, but is only available on more expensive systems.) There may also be a TV-tuner built-in, with a suitable aerial connection. This makes it possible to record video 'live' from standard broadcasts. Both TV tuners and adapters are sometimes sold as stand-alone extras for those who do not need all the other features offered by these cards.

Games accessories

The number and complexity of the hardware extras available for dedicated games players is increasing steadily. *Joysticks* allow game players to navigate around their virtual world by pulling and pushing a single controller. The most complex and expensive designs include extra buttons which can be pre-programmed to shoot weapons or move in a special way. Some also include 'feedback' – a built-in electric motor which sometimes shakes the joystick to make the gaming experience more tactile.

Steering wheels are a popular choice with players of driving simulations. These are literally smaller-than-normal plastic steering wheels which clip on to the front of a desk. Floor-standing brake and accelerator pedals are often also included.

Game pads are simple button pads similar to the ones used on games consoles, simply used to translate the console experience to a PC.

More advanced options include *motion-sensing headgear*. This uses a system which tracks head motion, and converts it into mouse or joystick movements that a game can make sense of. Some headgear also includes built-in headphones. The result can be an uncanny sense of realism. Anyone who doesn't mind looking slightly foolish at work may find that these items can sometimes replace the mouse as a pointing device.

Graphics pads

These are large, flat, plastic surfaces that are used in conjunction with a stylus. The stylus can be used as a pen, so you can draw, write or trace on the pad and the result goes straight on to your computer's screen. It can also be used as a replacement for the standard mouse. Graphics pads are used by artists and illustrators. The best pads are pressure sensitive – as you press harder, the stylus responds. You should always try out a pad for yourself before buying. This is a small market with few competitors. In tests, the most highly rated pads are usually those made by Wacom.

Pads are available in sizes from postcard-sized A6 to huge A2; A3 or A4 are adequate for most applications. Larger pads are not necessarily better. If they are too large you can strain your arms through excessive movement.

Network cards

Apple computers can be connected together very simply using the built-in network features and appropriate cables – Apple dealers will be able to advise you how to do this.

PCs are more complicated and require extra networking hardware. Although creating a medium-sized or larger network (typically involving more than five machines) is a job for an expert, it's possible to use the features in Windows 95/98, together with some network cards, to create a smaller working network very quickly and easily. A number of dealers now supply 'network kits' which include everything required to link two or more PCs for less than £100.

Network cards offer two speeds – 10Mb/s and 100Mb/s. 10Mb/s is offered by two very similar systems called 10baseT and 10base2 – the former is more popular. This speed is adequate for light use, such as copying a letter from one computer in an office to another, but rather slow for any applications that regularly use large amounts of information. For these more demanding applications the 100baseT system, which runs ten times faster, is recommended. 100baseT systems should ideally plug into the faster PCI slots in your machine, as the slower ISA slots can slow down the performance of the connection.

Networks based on network cards can sometimes be a little fiddly to set up. For someone who simply wants to connect two PCs together, it is quicker and cheaper to simply link the PCs using a USB cable and a copy of some suitable software, such as Travelling Software's LapLink.

The most recent versions of LapLink make it possible to transfer information from one PC to another, to control one PC remotely using the other's screen and keyboard, and even to print on the remote PC's printer.

Appendix III

Operating systems

Most software is designed to help you with a specific job – write a letter, send a fax and so on. An operating system, however, works on a more fundamental level. It manages the smooth running of your computer: it takes your commands, passes them on to the hardware and software, and then sends the results back to you.

By choosing the software first you will not need to worry about which operating system to use. It will be given as part of the software's required system specification, together with all the hardware details. Apart from the basics needed to get the software running, it is not usually necessary to deal with the operating system directly.

There is one exception: all software is written to match a specific operating system. Any new software you buy has to match the operating system you already have on your machine. If, for example, you have a spreadsheet that works with (the technical term is **runs under**) the popular Windows system, then buying software written for a different system, such as Unix, is a waste of time and money. It will not work. Find out which operating system your computer uses, and make sure that new software is compatible.

Ease of use

Operating systems work on two levels. The most visible level is the **user interface** which you use to work with your machine. It determines the 'look and feel' of your computer, and also how easily you can get work done.

Some operating systems use pictures on the screen to show what your options are. These systems are known as GUIs (Graphical User Interfaces) and are designed to be as easy to use as possible. Software that works with GUIs has on-screen 'buttons' and other controls. You use these with a mouse that is plugged into the computer – a palm-sized plastic object that sits next to your keyboard and controls a movable pointer or cursor on the screen. You select different options by clicking with the mouse. This means moving the pointer over a 'button' on the screen, and then pressing one of the two real buttons on the mouse to select it.

Most GUIs also include a drag-and-drop facility. To move a sentence or paragraph in a document you can simply highlight it with the mouse then 'drag and drop' it by holding one of the buttons down, moving the pointer to a new location and releasing the button. The sentence disappears from the old location and appears in the new one. This makes editing very quick and easy. Drag-and-drop features are used in all kinds of software.

Older operating systems work on a text-only basis known as a **command-line interface**. To work with one of these older systems you have to learn a set of commands, such as COPY, which moves information from one place to another, and DIR which lists all the information on your hard disk. To use these commands you type them on the keyboard, hit the RETURN key and the computer responds to your request. Editing tends to be much slower with this kind of operating system.

Text-only systems date from a time when computers were much less powerful, and text was all they could handle. This is no longer true today, and text-only systems are all but obsolete. However, they are still preferred for some kinds of work. They give you more control and have the advantage of working with cheaper and less powerful hardware.

The less visible level of an operating system is the system interface – a complex set of connections to the hardware. This standardises the way the hardware works. This part of the operating system is completely hidden from users.

Some operating systems let your computer do more than one thing at a time. You can start off a long calculation, compose a fax, send it, write a letter, print it out and log a phone call, all while the computer continues with the calculation 'in the background'. This useful ability is known as pre-emptive multi-tasking (usually shortened to multi-tasking.)

A multi-tasking operating system is – nominally – more reliable. Each task is managed so that it works independently of the others. If the task runs into problems or attempts something impossible, the computer as a whole does not hang or crash. The problem task can be stopped while the others carry on regardless.

A simpler version of multi-tasking is known as task-switching. This allows you to switch between different applications quickly and easily and can be very useful. You can be working on a letter, decide you need to check an address in your information manager, switch to it quickly, and then come back to the letter which remains exactly as you left it. Without task-switching you would have to unload the word-processing software, load in the information manager (time-consuming even on a fast machine), unload the organiser, load in the word processor and return to your place.

Older operating systems work on a strict one-job-at-a-time basis. The best they can manage is a feature called **print spooling**. This means you can print a letter without having to wait for the printer to finish – the printing itself continues in the background while you get on with other work. This feature is usually part of the software, rather than of the operating system.

Like other software, operating systems evolve and go through different versions. Some are radically different from their predecessors; for example, Windows version 1 and Windows version 3 are completely different operating systems. Others offer much smaller changes. It is important when looking at operating systems to include the version number, as the differences between versions can sometimes cause problems.

Only a handful of operating systems are available today. The ones you are likely to come across are listed below:

MS-DOS (IBM PC)

MS-DOS (Microsoft Disk Operating System) is the original PC operating system. It is still sold by Microsoft, the world's leading PC software company, even though it has now been made obsolete by Windows 95/98. MS-DOS was devised in the late 1970s but has maintained its position because so many people use it. MS-DOS (often shortened to DOS) is a command-line system. It can only do one thing at a time.

In terms of modern computing, MS-DOS is a throwback to the age of the dinosaurs. It can be something of a nightmare for beginners, as it does not appear user-friendly or accommodating. However, it is the lowest common denominator between different PC machines. A program written to use MS-DOS on a very early PC will work on an up-to-date model.

The one great advantage of DOS is that it is simple and unfussy. It will work on the oldest and least impressive hardware and will place minimal demands on it. In general, however, it is ham-fisted and obstructive. It was designed when computers were basic and slow, and users had to be forced to work them in a way that suited the computer, rather than the user. Graphics are minimal and crude, and the software can seem clumsy when compared with later examples that use a more modern operating system.

MS-DOS is no longer being developed. The last available version as a separate product is 6.22. Earlier versions (such as 6.0 and 5.0) are very occasionally sold by stores that cater to computer enthusiasts, but they are unreliable and should be avoided. Any new computer will be supplied with a recent version of Windows, rather than MS-DOS.

Windows 3.1 and 3.11 (IBM PC)

Like MS-DOS, Windows was created by Microsoft, although it is based on earlier products from Apple and Xerox. The name derives from the way in which the screen is split up into areas or 'windows' each of which has a frame. Each window can be moved, opened, closed, resized and hidden without affecting the others. This makes it possible to have a word processor in one window, a spreadsheet in another, some Internet software in a third, and so on. To switch between them you move the mouse pointer to the window you want to work with, click on it once and it becomes active.

Windows 3.1 and 3.11 (which are known generically as 'legacy Windows' or Windows 3.1x) are not quite true operating systems, because they exist on top of MS-DOS to make it easier to use and more appealing visually. Both are almost obsolete now, having been replaced by Windows 95 and 98 (see below). However, they are still available to special order and can also be found on second-hand machines, where they offer certain advantages for anyone on a tight budget. They can be used successfully on older, cheaper and less impressive hardware. Many businesses and large organisations still use them for these reasons. While less robust in some ways – if something

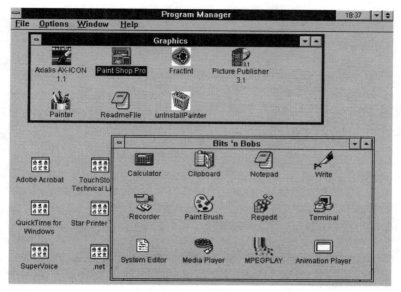

Windows 3.11.

goes wrong, they can stop a computer in its tracks until it is switched off and on again – they are also easier to troubleshoot.

3.11 is almost identical to 3.1, but has extra features which make it easier to use on a multi-user network. It is sometimes known as Windows for Workgroups (WfWG.) Both systems offer task-switching and very limited multi-tasking.

Windows 95

Windows 95 was a major rewrite of the Windows system released in 1995 that attempted to bring it up to date. It included all kinds of useful extras such as built-in Internet support, improved information handling, proper multi-tasking for Windows 95-compatible software and overhauled screen layout designs. Windows 95 was intended to be much easier to use. From a technical point of view, DOS (now up to version 7) had been hidden away even further, and Windows 95 could be used to work with applications written for Windows 3.1x, although with some reduction in effectiveness. It also included 'Plug and Play' features which made it easier to add new hardware to a PC, although these were still not as developed as they could be.

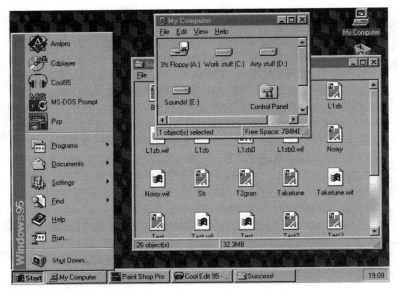

Windows 95

There were two versions of Windows 95. The more recent was known as OSR2 or Win95b, and offered some improvements over the original. OSR2 was never sold as a separate product, and could only be bought as part of a PC package. All its improvements are included in Windows 98.

Windows 98 (IBM PC)

Windows 98 – released during the summer of 1998 – was a minor update of the Windows system. Some of the parts of Windows 95 that didn't work properly were fixed, and a variety of other cosmetic changes were made. From a practical point of view Windows 98 was the first version that could work properly with USB computer extras (see pages 195–6). It also included a feature called FAT32, which was first introduced in OSR2 and made it possible to use larger hard disks more efficiently. Anyone who is still using either version of Windows 95 but doesn't find these two extras essential is unlikely to gain much from upgrading to Windows 98.

The most obvious difference is that Windows 98 uses a special version of Microsoft's Internet Explorer web browser to find and work with information inside the computer as well as outside it on the Internet. While this replaces the older and less flexible way of working available in Windows 95, it also makes much heavier demands on a computer's speed and power. This in turn makes Windows 98 a problematic upgrade for anyone who is using a computer built before 1998.

Microsoft originally planned to kill off this version of Windows as soon as it could, and replace it with a consumer-oriented version of its new Windows 2000 system (see below). However, Windows 98 has been temporarily reprieved because this proved impractical, and a 'Second Edition' (SE) version has been made available. This again fixes some of the more obvious problems in Windows 98, but otherwise offers little to consumers. When buying a new computer, check to see if this new 'SE' version of Windows 98 is being supplied.

Windows NT and 2000 (IBM PC)

Where Windows 95 and 98 – sometimes known in the computer press as 'Windows 9x' ('x' is often used as a wildcard in computer jargon) – are designed for consumer and very small business use, Windows NT

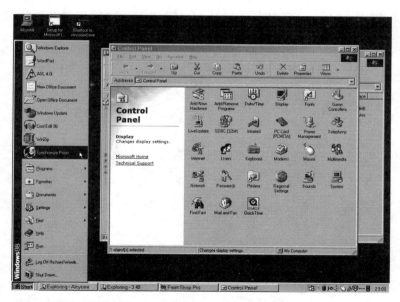

Windows 98 looks very much like Windows 95. The biggest difference is that it uses a browser-like system to find and display information.

('New Technology') has been aimed at more demanding professional users. From the user's point of view, NT looks and works very much like other versions of Windows. Internally, however, it works very differently. All versions include extra features which are designed to be used on networks of computers. It is also one of the few systems that can use more than one computer chip at once in the same machine – a feature known as Symmetric Multi-Processing (SMP) which is sometimes available on expensive, powerful hardware.

For a home or small business user, the extra expense, computer power and degree of skill needed to install and use Windows NT is probably wasted. It is also completely unsuitable for game players or other 'hobby' applications. But it can be worth considering for companies that need network security features and enhanced reliability.

NT 3.51 looked like Windows 3.1 externally. It was the first commercially successful version of Windows NT and, although it is still used in some companies, it has been superseded by the newer versions.

NT 4 is currently the most popular version. It looks like Windows 95, although it typically needs twice the memory (around 64Mb) to be used effectively. It also works with a much smaller range of hardware options (i.e. modems, graphics cards, sound cards, hard disk systems, and so on). Compared to NT 3.51 it offers enhanced network features. The 'server' version is expensive, and is designed to be used on the central computer in a business – for example the one that keeps client and other business records. The 'client' version is much cheaper and is designed for the individual computers used by employees.

Windows 2000 is the latest version of Windows NT. It is a complete rewrite of the NT system, and so much has changed that some Windows 9x and older NT software may no longer be compatible. Windows 2000 is designed for heavy-duty business use, such as maintaining the records of a very large company, as well as for smaller business systems. Sometime around 2001 Microsoft plans to create a consumer version of the product for home use, which will replace the existing Windows 9x series of products.

Note that NT users should make sure that they check with Microsoft for the latest 'service packs'. These are updates to NT that are supplied to fix various problems. They are available on CD from Microsoft for a nominal cost, or can be copied from the Internet. Business-oriented magazines often include them for free on their cover disks.

Windows CE (various)

Windows CE is the 'pocket' version of Windows, designed for small hand-held computers, and PDAs (see pages 257–9). It looks and works like a simpler version of Windows 95/98. The theory is that users who are familiar with Windows 95 on a larger home computer or laptop will be able to use WinCE right away with very little training. The many hardware differences between a true PC and a hand-held computer are carefully hidden so that users do not need to worry about them. WinCE also includes a greatly simplified version of Microsoft Office, with some or all of a word processor, spreadsheet, address book, presentation manager and even Internet, email and web-browsing facilities. Note, however, that compatibility is far from perfect, and some or all the information in a Windows CE computer may not translate fully to a larger Windows PC.

To date, WinCE has often seemed slow, given the much less powerful hardware available in hand-held units. It can also seem over-complicated when compared to operating systems such as EPOC, which is used in the Psion series of PDAs. As the speed and power of PDAs improves, it is likely that WinCE will become more popular and more usable. In the long term Microsoft also hopes that WinCE will start to be used in various other consumer electronics products, including cars, fridges, and microwaves.

OS/2 and Warp (IBM)

Warp was IBM's competitor to Windows 95. Despite an 18-month lead and a number of technical advantages (such as the ability to run software written for Windows 3.1), Warp became a historical curiosity instead of a serious alternative, although a professional version of Warp, known as OS/2, can occasionally be found in a business setting. Neither OS/2 nor Warp can be recommended even when supplied with a second-hand machine. They are only included here for completeness.

Unix (all computers)

Unix is widely considered (with reason) to be a computer professional's operating system, and hence something of a challenge for non-technical users. Unix is a command-line system, and much of its notoriety stems from the way in which command names seem to be obscure and confusing. Fortunately, a graphical extension called X-Windows is available which works rather like Windows or the Macintosh Operating System. Unix is always fully multi-tasking.

Although Unix is used mainly on powerful machines in large companies, on smaller machines it tends to be the preserve of the hobbyist. Consultants may recommend it for certain applications, as at best it can be much more powerful and reliable than Windows, and perhaps even Windows NT. It is not recommended for beginners.

Linux (various)

Linux is a version of Unix that was developed as a co-operative effort by computer hobbyists on the Internet. Unlike other operating systems, Linux is supplied with a licence which makes it clear that it is completely free. You can copy a version to your computer from the Internet and install as many copies as you like on as many machines as you like without owing a penny to anyone. (Compare this to systems such as Windows, which are usually charged on a per-user basis, causing very significant expense to businesses.)

Commercially packaged versions of Linux on CD – Red Hat, Slackware and SuSE are among the most popular – are now widely available in larger computer stores under similar licence terms. These include the core Linux software and typically also feature plenty of extras, including Internet software, simple games, and so on. (Corel supplies a free version of its Wordperfect Office Suite with some of these commercial packages.) A Windows-like system called Gnome is also available, which makes Linux easier to use for beginners.

Compared to Windows, Linux will work well even on very old hardware. (A 386 computer with 8Mb of memory is a recommended minimum system.) It also uses available computer power very much more efficiently, which makes it useful for scientific and mathematical research. In general, it seems to be more reliable and robust than Windows. From a computer professional's point of view, Linux is unique in that it is supplied with its *source code* – the actual raw programming details that are used to put it together. This makes it ideal for customised business projects, or for anyone who wants full control over what is happening inside their computer. Unlike Windows, which is a completely prepackaged system, Linux allows, and even encourages, users to change it to suit their own needs. Improvements are typically posted on the Internet, so that others can benefit from them.

The main drawback of Linux is that it is currently too complex for complete beginners to set up – although, once running, it is no more difficult than Windows to learn and use. It is also unlikely to work with unusual hardware. Finally, it lacks some of the safety features that Windows includes to prevent beginners damaging their hardware. It is perfectly possible to accidentally set up Linux so that it destroys a monitor. While this is very unlikely – and the newer commercial packages do their best to make it as unlikely as possible – this level of control makes Linux inappropriate for anyone who lacks a good working knowledge of computer hardware and software. This may change in the near future, however, and it's likely that a simplified and accessible version of the system aimed at beginners will appear sometime during 2000 or 2001.

BeOS (IBM PC and Apple)

Created by an ex-Apple employee, BeOS is a very specialised operating system which is aimed at anyone who works with music, art or video. It is designed to use the available hardware more efficiently than other operating systems, and so effectively turns existing computers into more powerful machines. However, the range of software available for the system is currently very limited. At the time of writing it is too early to tell whether BeOS will be able to carve enough of a niche for itself to survive, and it is only included here for completeness.

Mac OS (Apple only)

Apple's proprietary operating system, which is designed to work exclusively on Apple's own machines, has swerved an unsteady and unpredictable course during the 1990s. But at the end of the decade it finally appears to have settled into a more predictable and rationally planned niche.

At the time of writing, Apple is selling version 8.6 of its operating system. This is due to be upgraded first to the interim version 8.7 – sometimes known as 'Sonata' – and then to a completely new system, called MacOS X (pronounced 'ten'), scheduled to appear early in

2000. This is already available in a form suitable for professional computer users who want to use a powerful Macintosh at the centre of a business network, but it is currently unsuitable for less demanding home or light business use. The 'consumer' version adds true multi-tasking and a number of other technical improvements, as well as the ability to customise the 'look and feel' of the system far more than earlier versions.

In the meantime, Version 8.7 will add a number of minor enhancements to MacOS. One of the most interesting is the 'Sherlock II' system, which can be used to find information on the Internet. Unlike Internet search engines, which look for web sites that include specific words or topics, Sherlock can search for goods and services and also check for product availability. It is specifically designed to make Internet shopping easier.

Note that it is possible to buy products known as 'Windows emulators' for MacOS. These effectively turn the Mac into a simulated PC that can use most standard Windows software. Because of the simulation process, the software runs rather more slowly than on an equivalent real PC, but for dabbling, and even for more serious business applications, Windows emulators give Mac users a chance to work in the best of both worlds.

THE FUTURE OF WINDOWS

At the time of writing, Microsoft's future is uncertain. It is involved in a anti-trust (anti-monopoly) lawsuit with the US government over alleged illegal business practices designed to take unfair advantage of the success of the Windows system. If the government wins the case, and is able to fight its way through the resulting appeals, it will be in a position to demand that Microsoft changes the way it does business. In practice this could result in a number of changes, including breaking up Microsoft into a number of independent smaller companies, making it possible for other companies to develop and sell their own versions of Windows, or some other as-yet-unexpected eventuality. What this will do for consumers remains unclear, but it is likely that by the end of 2000 the operating system market will be rather more complex and volatile than it is now. And it is possible, if by no means certain, that Windows will no longer be the dominant product for PC users.

Appendix IV

The IBM PC

When you start looking at different computer makes and models, you will find that by far the most readily available and widely publicised brand of computer on the market today is the IBM-compatible PC.

PC stands for 'Personal Computer'. In this context it means a computer that is designed to be used by one person at a time and to fit conveniently on a desk. This can apply to any small computer, but in practice the letters 'PC' have become synonymous with IBM-compatible machines.

IBM-compatibles are manufactured from standard parts manufactured in the US and South-East Asia. Smaller dealers simply assemble these to order. Larger manufacturers, notably IBM, Dell, Compaq and Gateway, put together their machines from parts they have designed and manufactured themselves. Whatever their origin, all PCs conform to the same design standard originally defined by IBM (International Business Machines). In practical terms this means that any software that is 'written for a PC' will work on any of these machines. It also means that it is easy to exchange information between machines.

Over the years the IBM PC standard has undergone a number of revisions. Newer models can do everything that the older models could and usually much more quickly. Each aspect of the design has been refined and updated, and this process continues today. The full range of machines is still available, although the older models can only be bought second-hand.

Instead of brand names, PCs are distinguished by the model of computer chip at their heart. This master chip (also known as the processor or central processing unit (CPU)) is rather like the engine in a car – it is the main component that does most of the work. All the other parts of a computer exist to get information into and out of this chip. Some computer chips work faster than others. A chip's speed is quoted in MHz – millions of cycles a second. This means that a chip that runs at 10MHz will run just over twice as fast as the same model of chip that runs at 5MHz. Unfortunately, this does not mean that the computer will work twice as fast – the speed of a computer system as a whole depends on a number of other factors. However, the processor speed does give a basic indication of a computer's power.

Here is a guide to the PCs you will see advertised, together with ratings out of ten for cost (a higher rating means a cheaper machine), performance (a higher rating means a faster computer) and value for money (a higher rating means a better price/performance ratio).

Note that second-hand prices are variable, and the ones shown below can only offer a very rough indication. Sellers often lack a realistic idea of what an older machine is worth. Put simply, all computers but the very latest are worth very little compared to their purchase price. The constant stream of improvements in new machines also means that there is a huge backlog of outdated technology available. With this in mind, it is always worth looking out for technology of a more recent generation when buying second-hand. The difference in price between an old 486 model and an old Pentium machine is likely to be only around £25–£50. But the Pentium is a significantly faster and better computer.

8088/8086 (4.77MHz, 10MHz)

Cost: 10/10
Performance: 1/10
Value for money: 1/10
Suggested applications: Very simple word processing, accountancy and (at a push) spreadsheet and database work. Very unsatisfactory for Internet use.
Pros: Very, very low cost (typically £50 or less).
Cons: Slow, dated and not powerful enough for anything other than the simplest and most undemanding tasks. Getting new software and spare parts for these machines is likely to be a serious problem.
Expansion: ISA bus slots – on some machines only.
Floppy disks: 5.25-inch as standard, 360K 3.5-inch disks available occasionally.
Hard disks: Usually no more than around 30Mb if fitted at all.
Typical memory supplied: 640K maximum.

These first-generation machines appeared in the mid-1980s and are hopelessly outdated in modern terms. They are worth considering only if you are working to the tightest of tight budgets and need a computer for very simple tasks such as writing letters and basic bookkeeping. They are suitable for those who want to dabble and learn the basics without a large outlay. You may sometimes see them advertised as 'PC-XT' compatibles. They cannot run Windows software. They cannot usually be used for WYSIWYG word processing, and attaching a laser printer or a high-quality bubble-jet printer may also be problematic.

80286 (6MHz – 20MHz) (286)

Cost: 9/10
Performance: 2/10
Value for money: 2/10

Suggested applications: Word processing and office work. Not recommended for Internet use

Pros: Reasonable computer power at a modest price (£50 or less).

Cons: Now very dated and not able to cope with the latest software. Difficult to upgrade to a full modern specification.

Expansion: ISA bus. (A few Compaq and IBM machines may offer EISA and/or MCA bus expansion as well.)

Floppy disks: 5.25-inch as standard, although most machines can easily be upgraded to 3.5-inch disks.

Hard disks: Sometimes standard, not usually more than 120Mb.

Typical memory supplied: Usually 1Mb, occasionally 2Mb.

These are the very oldest machines that can do useful work in an office and are all but obsolete in modern terms. New software will not be compatible with these machines, although some suitable older shareware is available on the Internet. If bought second-hand with software already installed, they can handle simple word processing and other office work. Internet use is not recommended. These models are sometimes known as '286s' (this also applies to other chips in the series – thus '386' and '486' are the short-form names of computers built around 80386 and 80486 chips). These machines can run MS-DOS at a reasonable speed, and Windows 3.1 very slowly. They are not suitable for Windows 95, 98, NT or 2000.

80386SX & DX (16MHz – 40MHz) (386)

Cost: 8/10
Performance: 3/10
Value for money: 3/10

Suggested applications: Suitable for business use if not using Windows 95/98. Suitable but very slow for Internet use.

Pros: Now £100 or less second-hand.

Cons: Very sluggish compared to recent machines.

Expansion: ISA bus slots.

Floppy disks: SX: Equal likelihood of 5.25-inch and 3.5-inch disks. DX: Usually 3.5-inch 720K, although sometimes 3.5-inch 1.44Mb disks are standard.

Hard disk: SX: Often, but not always, standard; usually between 100Mb and 200Mb. DX: Usually standard, between 120Mb and 340Mb.

Typical memory supplied: SX: 1Mb, 2Mb, sometimes 4Mb. DX: Typically 2Mb, sometimes 4Mb or even 8Mb.

These machines were the top-line models in the early 1990s. The SX version is significantly slower than the DX and is best avoided. They can be upgraded with an 80387 coprocessor chip to speed up arithmetical calculations, and can run older Windows 3.1x software, but not software written for Windows 95. Technologically, these machines are obsolete and it is impossible to upgrade them. They are not recommended unless they suit a buyer's needs 'as seen' with all appropriate software included.

80486SX & SX2 (25MHz – 66MHz)

Cost: 8/10
Performance: 3/10
Value for money: 2/10

Suggested applications: Light office work. Can work with older Windows software but slow with Windows 95/98. Suitable but slow for Internet use

Pros: Good value for simple office tasks.

Cons: Very slow at arithmetical work (such as spreadsheets).

Expansion: ISA and VLB slots.

Floppy disks: 3.5-inch 1.44Mb standard.

Hard disk: Standard between 250Mb and 540Mb.

Typical memory supplied: 4Mb, sometimes 8Mb.

These machines are best avoided, even on the second-hand market. They are outperformed by 486 DX models (see below), which will be sold for a very similar amount.

80486DX, DX2, DX4, DX5 (33MHz – 150MHz)

Cost: 8/10
Performance: 4/10
Value for money: 5/10

Suggested applications: Good basic business machine, now outdated technically but still a competent performer when used with suitable software. Adequate for Internet use.

Pros: The faster models especially are good budget machines with plenty of power.

Cons: A touch sluggish when working with Windows 95 software. Difficult to upgrade to a modern specification. Not suitable for very latest multimedia software

Expansion: ISA and VLB slots. Some machines offer PCI slots.

Floppy disks: 3.5-inch 1.44Mb standard.

Hard disk: Standard, between 250Mb and 540Mb.

Typical memory supplied: 4Mb, sometimes 8Mb.

The DX4/120 and DX5/150 models are faster than a slow Pentium machine. On the second-hand market they offer reasonable value for anyone whose needs are modest. For Windows 95 16Mb or even 32Mb of memory are strongly recommended. As an upgrade this will offer better value for money than a faster processor chip.

Pentium P60 and P66 (60MHz and 66MHz)

Cost: 8/10
Performance: 4/10
Value for money: 4/10

Suggested applications: Average office work. Adequate for Internet use.

Pros: Faster than an equivalent 486 processor, especially for work which involves lots of numerical calculations (for example working with large spreadsheets).

Cons: Not good value compared to other Pentiums.

Expansion: ISA and PCI slots.

Floppy disks: 3.5-inch 1.44Mb as standard.

Hard disk: Typically 420Mb fitted as standard.

Typical memory supplied: 8Mb, sometimes 16Mb.

The 60MHz and 66MHz Pentiums were introduced at the end of 1994, but were soon left behind by faster models. These early chips may suffer from the Pentium bug (see note at the end of this Appendix). Not recommended under any circumstances, as other Pentium models offer much better value for money.

Pentium (75MHz – 200MHz)

Cost: 7/10

Performance: 5-6/10

Value for money: 7/10

Suggested applications: Office and home use and advanced applications such as large spreadsheets, image editing and sound and video work. Adequate for Internet use.

Pros: Now firmly in the recent category, these models are reasonable, low-cost, second-hand machines.

Cons: Sluggish compared to more recent machines.

Expansion: ISA and PCI bus slots.

Floppy disks: 3.5-inch 1.44Mb as standard.

Hard disk: 540Mb, up to 1Gb (SCSI).

Typical memory supplied: 8Mb, 16Mb, sometimes 32Mb.

Although these computers are all but obsolete, the faster models – from 133MHz upwards – are still perfectly usable for word processing, light office work and occasional Internet use. Intel deliberately killed off this range in mid-1997 to make way for its new Pentium MMX computers. However, only game players and dedicated Internet users are likely to notice much of a difference between MMX and non-MMX computers

Pentium MMX (166MHz – 233MHz)

Cost: 6/10

Performance: 6/10

Value for money: 6/10

Suggested applications: Serious business and home use, including games and other multimedia applications, and sound and video editing. Ideal for the Internet as it is now, but likely to be left behind when on-line video becomes popular.

Pros: Reasonable second-hand machines.

Cons: Overspecified for many uses. MMX features only make a difference with suitable software.

Expansion: ISA and PCI slots. Recent models include USB and AGP.

Floppy disks: 3.5-inch 1.44Mb as standard. Some systems now supplied with LS120 120Mb drives as well.

Hard disk: 1Gb to 3Gb, plus 24× CD-ROM drive.

Typical memory supplied: 16 Mb, 32Mb, occasionally 64Mb.

These machines are second-generation Pentium chips, with enhancements for multimedia applications. These enhancements are irrelevant for most business uses, but may make a difference for home and leisure uses. Normally only very slightly faster than equivalent Pentiums, they come into their own with MMX-ready software. As second-hand machines they can comfortably handle all simple business and domestic applications. However, they may struggle with recent games and with demanding work such as video and audio editing and computer animation.

Pentium Pro (150MHz – 200 MHz)

Cost: 5/10
Performance: 6/10
Value for money: 3/10

Suggested applications: Originally designed for very demanding professional computing tasks, but now obsolete.

Pros: Relatively fast compared to the original Pentium series.

Cons: A quirk in the design makes these models poor value for users of Windows 95 and 98.

Expansion: ISA and fast PCI.

Floppy disks: 3.5-inch 1.44Mb as standard.

Hard disk: 1Gb upwards, 24× or faster CD-ROM drive usually available as standard.

Typical memory supplied: 8Mb to 32Mb.

The Pentium Pro has been replaced by the Xeon range for professional work. Because it was aimed at a narrow range of specific professional applications, it offers questionable value on the second-hand market.

Celeron (266MHz – 466Mhz)

Cost: 5–6/10
Performance: 5/10
Value for money: 8/10

Suggested applications: Less demanding work, including office work and Internet use.

Pros: Much cheaper than an equivalent Pentium II model, and often only slightly slower.

Cons: Not ideal for games and very demanding work.

Expansion: ISA and PCI slots. Recent models include USB and AGP.

Floppy disk: 3.5-inch 1.44 Mb as standard.

Hard disk: 8–10Gb, plus 32 CD-ROM drive.

Typical memory supplied: 32Mb to 64Mb.

The original 'Celeron A' range of chips was based on a very crippled Pentium design. It was supposed to offer low power at a low price, but the slow speed and relatively poor value for money persuaded Intel to kill the design and replace it with the technically more advanced and less crippled standard Celeron, which is often significantly cheaper than a Pentium II but offers very similar performance. Celeron machines are ideal for undemanding home users, but are a little sluggish with the latest games.

Pentium II (233MHz – 450MHz)

Cost: 5/10
Performance: 7–8/10
Value for money: 8–9/10

Suggested applications: All general-purpose computing work, including demanding applications such as multimedia design and editing.

Pros: Fast, and now reasonably good value.

Cons: None.

Expansion: PCI, USB and AGP. ISA is no longer available on some models.

Floppy disks: 3.5-inch 1.44Mb as standard. Some systems are now supplied with 120Mb LS-120 drives, or the Iomega Zip system.

Hard disk: 3Gb to 10Gb, 40× CD-ROM or sometimes DVD drive as standard.

Typical memory: 32Mb, 64Mb, occasionally 128Mb.

Intel is attempting to kill off these computers towards the end of 1999 and the beginning of 2000. They can therefore offer excellent value for money, especially now that computer prices in general are much lower than they were in 1995. Realistically, only the latest games will stretch the capabilities of these models. For office and simpler home applications, most of their power will be wasted.

Pentium III (500MHz – 900MHz)

Cost: 1–2/10
Performance: 8–9/10
Value for money: 5–6/10

Suggested applications: All computing work, including demanding applications such as multimedia design and editing.

Pros: Very fast.

Cons: Expensive.

Expansion: PCI, USB and AGP. ISA is no longer available on some models.

Floppy disks: 3.5-inch 1.44Mb as standard. Some systems are now supplied with 120Mb LS-120 drives, or the Iomega Zip system.

Hard disk: 9Gb to 20Gb, plus 40× CD-ROM or DVD drive as standard.

Typical memory supplied: 64Mb, 128MB, occasionally 256Mb.

These chips contain a 'next-generation' version of MMX called KNI (Katmai New Instructions). Despite Intel's advertising campaign suggesting that these models can speed up access to the Internet, the reality is that most users will notice barely any difference between the performance of a Pentium II and a Pentium III running at the same speed. As with MMX, software needs to be specially rewritten to take advantage of the KNI features. So far only certain games, a small selection of multimedia editing titles (such as Adobe's Photoshop) and Microsoft's Office 2000 suite include the changes. Eventually it is hoped that KNI will also speed up other applications, such as voice recognition, although it is too early to tell to what extent this will be true in practice.

THE PENTIUM BUG

In computer-speak, a 'bug' is a design flaw and, whether found in hardware or software, can cause reliability and/or accuracy problems. Bugs cause your computer to stop working or give you the wrong answer to a calculation.

Early versions of the Pentium processor (specifically those produced before February 1995) included a bug which gave the wrong result for certain long-division calculations.

For most users this bug is more of an irritation than a major worry. The error introduced is slight – of the order of a few pence in a calculation working with tens of thousands of pounds – and happens only with a small range of numbers. For engineering, medical and other professional applications the chip should be replaced. This is a free service from Intel.

You should use a simple test program called CPUIDF.EXE, which is available directly from Intel. For more information call Intel's customer support line on 0800 374838.

The Apple Macintosh

The Apple Macintosh (the 'Mac') computer has a long and colourful history. Unlike the IBM PC, which has always been something of a corporate design, the Apple Mac was conceived as an attempt to make a computer that was easy to use and appealing to non-business people.

Apple machines are the computer of choice for many artists, graphic designers and publishing houses. They are less popular with businesses, which tend to choose the more widely used IBM PC-compatible machines.

The Apple Mac offers a number of important advantages for absolute beginners. Firstly, it is undoubtedly easier to use and set up. Upgrading a PC is usually best left to a specialist, but almost anyone can upgrade a Mac. Older PCs need to be set up after some new hardware has been installed, but a Mac will often accept the upgrade and work out what needs to be changed for itself. This can save time and temper in a professional setting, and can also help build confidence among users.

All modern Macs include networking facilities as standard. It is possible to set up a simple network – which can share information among users and make the best use of common resources such as printers – for little more than the cost of a few cables. A simple email facility, called QuickMail, is also available, and this can be used to exchange messages between different computers on one site.

All Macs are built to a high standard, whereas PCs can vary greatly in build quality and reliability. The Mac looks good and works well.

After the range became established, Apple split the product line into two areas. Domestic Macs are aimed at home users and professionals working at home. Professional Macs are targeted at publishing houses and professionals who need power and can afford to pay for it.

Domestic models tend to cost roughly as much as an equivalent PC. Professional models are usually significantly more expensive.

At the top end of the market many Apple Macs are fitted with extras which speed up certain kinds of work. These specialised upgrades have no equivalent in the PC world, and so it is difficult to compare the two kinds of computer on a like-for-like basis. These top-level Macs are recommended for computer-intensive work such as image manipulation, photo-retouching and professional magazine publishing.

The best way to decide whether or not a Mac system is suitable for you is to find a local Apple dealer – many advertise in *Yellow Pages* or in local directories – and try out a system for yourself. Explain your needs to the dealer, try out some relevant software and then do the same with a similarly priced PC system.

Over the decade and a half or so that the Mac has been available, Apple has released a regular stream of new product announcements and name changes. A complete list would take up many pages, so a summary is presented here.

Mac Classic series – Classic, Colour Classic, 128, 512, SE, SE/30 and Plus

These are the original Macs in the original all-in-one case. Memory is minimal – a mere 128K in the '128' version – and no more than 4Mb in the SE/30. Hard disks are either small or absent. These models are suitable for word processing, but otherwise belong in the 'vintage' category. There are no internal expansion slots.

Mac II range – Mac II, IIx, IIcx, IIci, IIsi, IIvi and IIvx and IIfx

These were powerful machines in their day, especially the IIfx, but are now somewhat dated. They were aimed at professional users. Memory was expandable up to 32Mb in some cases and hard disks are standard. NuBus slots were included to allow for expansion.

Mac LC range – LC I, II & III, LC460, LC475, LC520 and LC630

These are all domestic Macs and are now very dated. The LC was roughly equivalent to a Classic. The LC II was only slightly more powerful. The others are dated second-hand machines and are suitable for light business use. The 630 was sometimes fitted with a TV tuner card and NICAM stereo decoder system.

Performa range – Performa 630, 5200, 5300, 6200, 6500

These are the previous-generation domestic Macs. All except the 630 offered Power PC performance at a reasonable price. The 5200 and 5300 were single-box models that contained the computer and colour monitor in a single case, which helps reduce unsightly cabling. The Performas were designed very much as home entertainment centres, and CD-ROM drives, TV tuner cards (which could also grab 'stills' from TV programmes) and NICAM stereo decoders are either available as options or included in the basic price. The 6500 was the only Performa model to use a PowerPC chip, making it still usable today, although it is very slow by modern standards.

Quadra range – Centris 610, 650, 650AV, Quadra 605, 610, 650, 700, 800, 840AV, 900 and 950

These were aimed at professional users and were the top of the line until the PowerMac models were introduced in 1994. The AV models included extra hardware to record and play back sound at CD quality.

PowerMac range – 6100, 7100, 8100; 7200, 7500, 7600, 8200, 8500, 9500; 4400, 8600, 9600

These machines significantly boosted the performance of Macs by switching to a new and more powerful chip called a 'PowerPC'. The 6100, 7100 and 8100 were the original models, and are now very out of date. More recent models, especially the 9600, are still very usable today, although they have been eclipsed to some extent by the latest G3 models.

Original G3 range

With the G3 range, Apple decided to give up its complicated naming scheme and distinguish models according to the speed of the processor chip and the available memory. These models used the 720 and 740 chips. Although outdated, they are still usable today.

'Blue' G3 range

The very latest Apple models use a striking new blue-and-white case design. Inside, a fast 750 chip makes these computers unusually powerful. Otherwise, though, the trend is to increasingly PC-like technology, with IDE drives being used instead of SCSI, and a PC-standard graphics card instead of a proprietary model. Note that the 'Blue' series lacks a SCSI connector, which means that users of older Apple equipment may need to buy a SCSI card if they upgrade to a blue G3. The G3 also lacks a floppy-disk drive; USB floppy-disk drives have to be bought as an extra.

'iMac' range

The domestic equivalent of the G3, the iMac comes in a very striking translucent case, available in a range of colours that (oddly) are named after different kinds of fruit. It returns to the original Apple all-in-one design, with a built-in screen. The iMac is aimed at first-time buyers, and is sold with a collection of software and other extras, including a built-in modem and network connections. As with the G3, there is no floppy-disk drive; if one is needed it has to be purchased separately. At the time of writing there are four versions of the iMac, the most recent being the 'revision D' model, which includes a faster main processor chip. Most buyers seem to be very happy with their iMacs – apparently because of the combination of styling and convenience. It's worth noting, though, that at the time of writing iMacs are only average games machines; more dedicated players may find them frustrating, and may find a G3 is a better choice.

PowerMac clones

For a short period, Apple licensed its technology to a number of other manufacturers. This is no longer the case, and these 'clones', as they were known, are now only available second-hand. In general, however, they are a poor choice, as servicing and spares can be problematic.

Powerbook 100 series – 100, 140, 145, 145b, 150, 160, 165, 165c, 170, 180, 180c, 190, 190cs

These were first-generation portable Macs. All are now obsolete, although they can still be used for word processing and note-taking. Models with the 'c' suffix included a colour screen.

Powerbook Duo series – 210, 230, 250, 270c, 280, 280c

These were 'docking-station' computers; most extras were external and could only be accessed by plugging the computer into a 'docking port' when it was deskbound. Unlike the other models they were lighter and easier to carry around than the other Powerbooks, and could be used as normal desktops if connected to a docking station (see Appendix VII). This allowed a normal keyboard, a floppy-disk drive and a printer to be connected.

Powerbook 500 series – 520, 520c, 540, 540c

These were Powerbooks with the same speed and power as the old Quadra range. They have a 'PDS' (Processor Direct Slot), which means that in theory they can be upgraded to a more modern specification. In practice, however, suitable extras are no longer readily available. Unlike earlier Macintosh portables, these use a trackpad system, which responds to finger pressure.

Powerbook Power PC series – 1400 range, 2400 range, 3400 range, 5400 range and G3 range

These latest Powerbooks use the PowerPC chip, and are as fast as some of the PowerPC desktop models. They are far too powerful for the kind of simple word processing and contact management for which most notebooks are used. On the other hand, these machines make it possible to continue with almost any kind of work away from the office, including DTP and CAD. The G3 range is the most recent, and also the most expensive.

Appendix VI

Other brands of computer

In terms of sales alone, IBM-compatibles and the various versions of the Apple Macintosh account for almost all of the market. There are other brands, however, most of which date back to the early 1980s, when the computer market was split between machines that were used for serious work and those that were used for games and entertainment. Although most of these are no longer available new, they are still available on the second-hand market.

The main disadvantage of these brands is a lack of service and support, and the fact that they have become increasingly marginalised as the home-computer market has matured. IBM-compatibles and Apple Macs are an industry standard, and information and software for both are all widely available. These other brands therefore cannot be recommended except perhaps for someone who would like to dabble with computers without making a huge investment.

Acorn Archimedes

Descendants of the original BBC Micro of the 1970s, the Archimedes range sold well to schools and colleges up until the end of the 1990s. Technically these computers were far more advanced than the more popular PCs of the day, and they were also very much easier to work with. The most recent models included a 'PC on a card' which gave users the best of both worlds. Unfortunately, Acorn lacked the marketing resources needed to push them effectively, and the company bowed out of the market in 1998; spares and extras have subsequently become very thin on the ground. Despite their technical credentials, it is no longer possible to recommend these computers as second-hand machines.

Atari

The Atari ST series was originally designed as a games machine, but found favour in the professional music market, largely as a result of the chance inclusion of the music industry-standard MIDI control system.

The Atari range never lived up to its potential as a business machine. The early games-oriented machines had a clunky, rubbery keyboard which was integrated with the main system unit, and this made them unappealing to anyone who needed to do a lot of typing. The floppy disk drives had to be bought separately and were housed outside the main system unit. This often led to a tangle of wires.

The models that are worth serious consideration for business use are the Mega ST and Mega STE ranges. Both have a more usable detached external keyboard and come with a built-in floppy disk. Hard disk drives are available as an extra. One of the best features of the Atari range was the excellent black-and-white monitor, which is more than adequate for prolonged use and matches or even betters some of the monitors available today.

In terms of software, Write On! and First Word Plus are good choices for word-processing applications, while Calamus offers powerful DTP features as well as simple word-processor style editing features. First Word Plus is adequate for light-duty work, but does not have any of the features needed for professional use.

Other applications are not widely available. Although spreadsheets and communications packages do exist, they can be hard to find. Most Atari machines are sold second-hand with large collections of games or music software. To find an Atari machine for serious use it is best to look in some of the mainstream computer magazines and other Atari-specific journals.

Amiga

The Amiga started life as another games machine. It found favour with some programmers, but on the whole was more of a leisure than a business computer. For all this it had some impressive features, and in some ways was more advanced than comparable computers at the time.

Commodore Business Machines, which marketed the Amiga, foundered in 1994. In spring 1995, Escom, a high-street retailer and PC manufacturer, bought the rights to the Amiga range. However,

Escom, too, ceased trading in 1996. A number of attempts have been made to resurrect these computers since then, but to date none has been entirely successful. As a result, this machine is now something of a museum piece, and spares are becoming increasingly difficult to get hold of.

Amstrad Word Processor Range

These machines, which are known as the PCW range, were very popular when they were released in the mid-1980s. Combining basic word-processing software with a keyboard, monitor, disk drives and printer, they were the ideal all-in-one solution for anyone who wanted to write letters but did not have the expertise to take on a complete computer system. However, they are true computers, rather than just word processors, and can handle a range of applications beyond simple word processing.

The technology used in the PCW range is more typical of the 1970s than the 1980s and thus they are very slow. Print quality tends to be poor, although it is possible to connect a more modern bubble-jet printer in place of the dot-matrix or daisy-wheel originals. The software is based on the CP/M operating system which is an early ancestor of MS-DOS. Locoscript is the word-processing software. A version of this is available for the PC, so adventurous PCW users can make a relatively painless transition to a much faster system.

The biggest problem with the PCW range is the non-standard floppy disk format used on earlier models. These use 3-inch disks rather than the more usual 3.5-inch variety. Supplies of these disks are now drying up, but a number of companies offer a 3.5-inch disk upgrade option which allows normal disks to be used. Another disadvantage is price: a PCW system may well prove more expensive than an equivalent vintage PC.

Existing PCW users planning to upgrade should be wary of 'easy upgrades' to PC systems. Although these offer a relatively painless way to get PC power while maintaining a familiar PCW style and approach, some of these are being sold at hugely inflated prices. When considering one of these systems be sure to shop around first and see if the equivalent is available at a much more reasonable price.

Amstrad PCs

In the mid-1980s Amstrad released a range of PC-compatibles which created their own mini-standard at the lower end of the market. Much of this was due to marketing – these were the first machines that were widely available in the high street. Technically they were simply cheap IBM-compatible machines.

The 1512 and the 1640 are now very much in the 'vintage' category. Many people still use them for word processing and simple tasks. They cannot run modern software or easily be upgraded. But they were popular in their time and are widely available on the second-hand market. Although limited and slow, they are suitable for light use and are a good choice if you need a computer but have a tiny budget. If possible choose a model with a hard disk.

Emulators

Atari, Amiga and PCW owners can to some extent replicate their machines inside a standard PC or Mac. A special piece of software called an 'emulator' simulates the older machine in software. Many emulators are produced as amateur projects. While these are available for free, they may not be 100 per cent reliable. However, commercial products are sometimes also available (for example Cloanto's AmigaForever product).

The advantage of emulators for users of older computers is that they can keep all their old information and software, while using them in a more modern environment. This is of particular interest to PCW owners, who can now fearlessly buy a 'proper' PC at the usual price from all the usual sources, instead of buying from a PCW specialist and perhaps paying far more than is necessary.

Appendix VII

Portable computers

A good option for the business user is a powerful, expensive computer at work and a relatively cheap portable machine for use everywhere else. It is rare that a portable can take the place of a proper office system, as the small screen and limited battery life mean that its uses are restricted in a practical context. But for light use – letters, invoices, faxes and so on – a cheap portable can be ideal. Expensive portables, which include extras such as a pair of speakers and a CD-ROM within the case, are an excellent choice for making presentations. Most portables can be hooked up to an external display, which means it is possible to prepare a presentation at home or even on the road, and then present it on location.

Portables are becoming more and more popular. Battery technology is improving all the time, and as batteries get smaller and lighter portables will replace desktop machines. Some of the most exciting developments will be in the field of on-line services. It is now possible to buy modems that work with the cellular phone network, and this means that users can send and receive email messages away from their base of operations. This is likely to transform the way that people communicate with each other.

For now, portable computing is recommended for anyone who needs to be away from his or her base, be it home or office, while maintaining access to records and other information stored back at base. It is also recommended for users who find existing monitor designs difficult to work with. Portables use a different display system that does not flicker in the same way, and some users find this easier.

Portables come in a variety of shapes and sizes. The larger machines are now dated and almost obsolete; newer models are getting smaller and lighter each year. Within the portable family you will find the following kinds of machine:

'Luggables'

Like all portables, this includes a computer, a screen and a keyboard all in one case. On these models the keyboard clips down on to the base unit to create a box the size and often the weight of a pilot's briefcase.

These machines are too heavy to be carried long distances and much too large to be used in trains or on planes, but they can easily be taken home after a day's work or placed on a desk in a client's office. Unlike 'true' portables they need to be plugged into the mains supply to work – batteries are not included and are not an option.

There are very few luggable computers available these days, and their only advantage over a desktop machine is the absence of wires. Anyone looking for a portable can find a similarly specified but much more manageable machine for less money.

Portables

'True' portables are still unwieldy, although they can be carried quite a distance. They tend to be large and bulky and, like luggables, are rapidly being superseded by more modern designs. Because many of these models are now obsolete they cannot be expanded in the way that more modern machines can. Battery life is poor and, like luggables, they are better suited for desk work rather than for use on trains and planes. They do have batteries, however, so in theory can be used anywhere. Like luggables, these machines are now extremely rare.

Notebooks

Notebook machines are a much more manageable size and weight. They are usually more or less A4 size, but offer features which are similar to those found in desktop machines. All-in-one models which include extras such as modems and CD-ROM drives within the one case, are now available, although it is doubtful whether these are light enough to be easily carried a long way. Modern notebooks are expandable using the PCMCIA system, and this allows tiny extras such as modems and soundcards – some of which are literally credit-card size – to be plugged into the case. Notebooks have become the portable standard since the early 1990s and are now often known as 'laptops'.

Sub-notebooks

These are even smaller versions of the standard notebook design. Sub-notebooks are an excellent choice for a general-purpose information manager and portable word-processing tool. They can be used for most of the tasks a desktop computer can, but they are light enough to carry around with ease.

At the time of writing, there has been a spate of very slim, style-conscious, light machines. With these machines it is important to check which extras – such as a floppy-disk drive, or a CD-ROM drive – are included inside the case and which need to be used and carried externally (and perhaps even bought as extras).

Electronic organisers, palmtop computers, and Personal Digital Assistants (PDAs)

Those who do not want the size, weight and expense of a true laptop can choose one of a growing range of smaller computers. At the bare minimum, these include an electronic notepad, address book, diary and planner, and clock with alarm and time-zone facilities. More advanced models include email and web browsing facilities, although these are very limited compared to those available on a full-size or laptop PC and usually need to be used over a slow and expensive mobile phone connection. Some models can also be enhanced by adding and installing extra software.

The very smallest models have no keyboard. Instead, notes are entered by 'writing' on the display with a stylus. Some of them use a form of hand-writing recognition to make sense of the writing; others expect users to learn a form of written shorthand with separate and distinct letter shapes. Another common option is a tiny 'virtual keyboard', with letter keys that appear on the display and are selected with the stylus.

More advanced models use some form of mini-keyboard. These are usually quite hard to work with for long periods, although they may be adequate for note-taking. The most sophisticated – but also large and expensive – offer a true keyboard that is only slightly smaller than that on a standard laptop.

All models offer some form of exchange system that makes it possible to copy information to and from a PC for backup purposes, and (in some cases only) integrate it easily with an existing address book or diary. Note that only a small subset of the available organisers offers the same facility for users of Apple computers.

The following models are popular:

The 3-Com Palm series These are tiny units, approximately the size of a wallet, with a large display panel/writing area which is operated with a stylus. The software is very simple, and users are required to spend some time learning how to 'write' individual characters before they can start to use the machine. Simplicity, low cost and ease of use have made these models very popular. An infra red link makes it easy to exchange electronic business cards with other Palm users. A surprisingly large range of software is available for these machines.

Pocket Windows CE models These are made by a number of companies, and offer similar features to the Palm range. However, they use a simplified version of the Windows system, which includes 'pocket' versions of a Windows-standard word processor, address book, and so on. Handwriting recognition is usually only available as an extra. Otherwise there is little or no extra software available. To date, these models have not had the success of the Palm series.

The Psion series The Psion 3 has been a popular PDA since the early 1990s. The more advanced Psion 5 has built up a similar following since it was released in 1996. Psion machines are popular with business users because of their very slick design, flexibility and ease of use. Email and data-exchange software is included as standard, together with a relatively sophisticated word processor, spreadsheet and database. A wide range of software is available. Uniquely, Psion includes features which make it possible for users to write their own software to suit individual needs. At the time of writing Psion is expanding its range with a colour model, as well as one with an improved keyboard.

Larger Windows CE models These are also made by a number of manufacturers and, like their pocket Windows CE counterparts, use a variant of the Microsoft Windows system. The main difference is that they offer a built-in keyboard. The quality, usefulness and value for money of these machines varies hugely. At worst they are very heavy compared to smaller organisers, and have poor displays and poor keyboards. At best the very largest offer a reasonable alternative to a PC laptop, by including all the features required for note-taking and simple office work in a package with a high-quality keyboard, a reasonable display and a much longer battery life.

Expanded mobile phones A very small number of portable phones include a built-in PDA. Nokia and Alcatel are two names to watch for. To date they have offered products which include a notepad, address book, web and email software, and fax facilities, sometimes with a small typewriter-style keyboard. The case typically hides the PDA features when the unit is being used as a phone. While these models are very much heavier and bulkier than most phones, anyone looking for a PDA with mobile facilities will them find worth considering.

Cellular communications

Although on-line services such as the Internet are just starting to become popular, the real revolution will happen when email and other communication systems are freed from their reliance on physical phone lines. Portable modems that use cellular technology to provide an integrated communication system are now available without using telephone lines. However, cellular modems are relatively expensive and slow compared with their more conventional equivalents. But as the technology develops and systems become cheaper it is very likely that portables will come to replace desktop machines altogether, and that it will be possible to arrange meetings and dinner dates away from the phone, directly from organiser to organiser. At the time of writing the wireless/cellular networks are hinting that much higher speeds and cheaper access may become available around 2002. If this proves to be the case, cellular communications may even start to compare favourably with fixed telephone lines. As and when this happens, it will make the Internet accessible from everywhere, rather than mostly from homes and offices as it is now.

GPS

The Global Positioning System (GPS) offers a kind of electronic compass which uses a network of satellites to define positions on the Earth's surface to within 100 metres. Certain route planners (see page 110) are now sold with an option which can be connected to a GPS receiver to create a 'live' road map that literally shows you where you are. GPS hardware for laptops is relatively affordable (around a few hundred pounds) and is already being used by certain haulage companies and fleets of sales reps. One drawback is that few route planners are completely geographically accurate, so a map may show your car in a field when you are really on the adjacent motorway.

Docking stations

Some portables can be plugged into a larger base unit – a docking station – when used on the desk. This base unit contains extras – expansion slots, an option for a better keyboard and perhaps a better display – which will not fit into a standard portable. The idea is that when 'docked' the whole system becomes a substitute for a proper desktop unit.

Docking stations are now extremely rare and are only available for a very small number of PC and Apple laptops. Most laptops now include all the facilities that would once have required a docking station, so the idea is becoming obsolete.

Buying tips

When buying a notebook you should remember to check with your dealer the level of support and service offered. Will the dealer's service scheme cover you if something goes wrong when you are on the road?

Check what software comes with the portable. A very useful extra is a data exchange program which enables you to transfer information to your main PC. On some machines this will need additional hardware. Other features to check for include:

Maintenance and service options Laptops and portables are not currently outstandingly reliable. According to some estimates, as many as one user in three will suffer some kind of failure during their first year of use. As a result, technical support is even more important than usual. Check to see what support is offered, and how long it will take to get the work done in total. If possible, also phone the support line to see how easy it is to get through during office hours. A permanent engaged tone is unlikely to bode well.

Weight How easy is it to carry the portable? Is it as portable and light as an organiser, or is it more 'luggable' and unwieldy?

Display quality Try the computer out and look closely at the display. Watch out for mouse pointers that disappear when you move them, and for overall brightness and clarity. Will the display still be visible in bright sunlight? In general, TFT (thin film transistor) displays give the best results but are between £100 and £300 more expensive. Colour is now standard on all laptop models, although for technical reasons this usually means 64,000 colours, rather than the more useful 16.7 million. This in turn makes accurate image-editing a problem.

Size and resolution are also important. Some displays now offer a resolution of 1024 x 768, which is ample for most work. In general, a 12-inch display is usually adequate, although 13.3-inch and even 14-inch displays are available at extra cost. When checking the displays, look for *stuck pixels*. These are tiny dots, the colour of which is fixed because of a manufacturing flaw. An ideal display would have no stuck pixels at all, but for reasons of cost most manufacturers accept a small number – typically five or less – as an unavoidable side-effect. Any more than this and the display can be considered faulty.

Keyboard Does the keyboard suit you? Check the 'feel' – its stiffness and clickiness – and also whether or not you think you can work with the keyboard layout. There is much less room on a portable than on a desktop machine so the keys have to be fitted into a smaller space and this inevitably means that some keys do double or even triple duty. The ideal layout is one that is not too dissimilar to your current desktop machine, if you have one. Beware of 'bargains' that offer a US keyboard layout instead of the UK standard. On these machines the £ key may be absent, or only available with an obscure combination of keystrokes.

How does the mouse work? On portables, mouse pointers come in all shapes and sizes. The most popular are *trackpads*, which track finger pressure on a special rectangular area. Cheaper track pads are prone to static, which has the annoying effect of sometimes keeping the pointer moving after you remove your finger from the pad. More expensive models work more reliably. *Trackballs* are inverted mice. The ball is fixed in place, but can be rotated by hand. *Trackpoints* are tiny plastic stubs that usually sit between the G, B and H keys on the keyboard.

If you are left-handed, check to see how conveniently placed the pointer system or the mouse buttons are. Some models have a definite right-handed bias, which may prove inconvenient over long periods.

Battery life Battery life is uniformly poor on laptops. Four hours is exceptional; three hours is good; two hours is average. Older laptops used nickel cadmium (NiCad) and nickel magnesium hydride (NiMH) batteries, which were heavy and also offered poor charge/discharge characteristics. (NiCads, for example, had to be fully discharged before recharging – a 'top up' was likely to shorten battery life.) New lithium ion ('lion') designs offer improved power capacity with lighter weight and without these drawbacks.

Externals, connectors and built-in extras On some machines a floppy disk drive is an optional, and external, extra. If you can connect your laptop to a desktop machine you may not find this is a problem. Other extras to check for include soundcards and speakers (these are almost always built into laptops now, although the speakers are often very poor), CD-ROM drives, DVD drives, zip drives, network cards and TV/video connections (the latter are very useful for presentations) USB ports are now standard on laptops.

It can also be worth checking the number of available PCMCIA slots. Some extras – such as combined modem/network/cellular modem cards – can use all the available slots. If your laptop features less than the usual complement of slots, you will not be able to make use of these.

Basic specification and expansion options Processor chips, memory and hard disk size should be selected in the usual way. Note that the memory and hard disk units used in laptops are smaller than usual, and so more expensive. It makes sense to get a generous specification when buying, rather than finding yourself forced to upgrade at a later date.

Infra-red links The very latest organisers include an IR information transfer system. This makes it easy to exchange information with other organisers and suitably equipped PCs.

Using laptops abroad

Below are some practical points worth considering when using a laptop on your travels.

The first is power – always make sure that you travel with suitable power adaptors for the country or countries you are visiting, and that your laptop's power supply can work with the local voltages. General-purpose adaptors are available in many airports and travel stores.

Similar considerations apply to foreign telephone systems. If you plan to use your modem abroad, you will need a suitable phone adaptor. You will also need a modem that can be 'homologised' to work with the local telephone system, so that it can create and respond to the correct dialling and other tones that are used there. Not all modems do this, and if you plan to travel widely it is essential to make enquiries about this.

Although in theory airport X-ray machines are safe, in practice they have been known to cause occasional data loss, especially with older hardware. So, where possible, try and avoid putting your machine through this process. It can also be worth stocking up on spare batteries for long flights – and you should not use your laptop during take-off or landing, as it can interfere with a plane's radar and communications systems.

The Internet and bulletin board systems

The Internet

The Internet originated as a series of experiments designed to create a computer network that could survive nuclear attack. From these rather unpromising beginnings it has evolved into a global computer network linking people in almost every country in the world.

The most useful service available on the Internet is email. Other networks may have a mail gateway to the outside world but are geared towards exchanging mail internally. With the Internet, however, you can send mail to anyone who has an Internet mail address anywhere, no matter what kind of computer the addressee uses or which system he or she subscribes to.

To access the Internet you need to open an account with an **Internet Service Provider (ISP)**. This allows you to connect your computer directly to the Internet. You can also access all the other Internet services listed in Chapter 6. Some providers offer a service to a certain geographic area, but the majority offer local-call access from anywhere in the UK using special telephone numbers.

Finding a service provider

The number of providers is growing all the time. For an up-to-date list of ISPs look in one of the Internet magazines listed in Appendix XIV. More detailed information on the Internet is given in *The Which? Guide to the Internet*.

When choosing a provider, it is important to check what kind of software you will be given, and also how good the technical support is. The software should be easy to use, easy to install and offer the full range of services. The most important elements are news (Usenet),

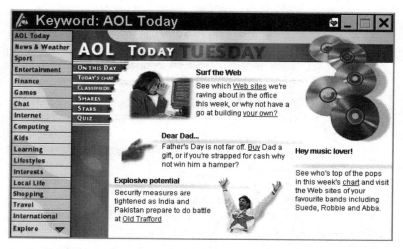

America OnLine is a popular on-line service

email and access to the Web. All providers now offer web space as well. This can be used to publish your own web pages, which will then become visible to everyone on the Internet. Note that some providers prohibit commercial use of this facility, and that the amount of space available is always limited (although in practice most people are unlikely to need more than 5Mb for their pages) .

While some providers charge a flat rate per month, typically between £5 and £15, others now offer a completely free service. (Instead of charging you, they take a percentage of the phone bill that you run up while using their service.) The range of companies offering free connections includes many household names, including Dixons (which pioneered free connections with its Freeserve service), various banks, football clubs, supermarket chains, and so on. A few have started to offer free calls at certain periods, such as evenings or weekends (they aim to make money from advertising on their main web site). Such providers are obviously worth investigating, especially for dedicated Internet users.

In general, service from different providers, both free and paid for, can be especially variable. The slowest and least efficient can have a disastrous effect on your phone bill; not only can it take a number of tries to get a connection, but the connection itself can be very slow. For anyone who uses the Internet for more than occasional email, the importance of finding a fast provider cannot be overstated. In tests, slower providers can literally take four times longer than the fastest to deliver the same web page. *Internet* magazine publishes a regular league table of the best and worst services available.

On-line services offer both an Internet connection and access to a range of information and services which is not available elsewhere. To date there are no free on-line services. The best example is perhaps AOL (America OnLine) which offers huge quantities of information on every subject imaginable, as well as the ability to send internal emails to other members, and also 'chat' with them live (in practice this means typing messages live on a one-to-one basis). AOL is popular with beginners, although more experienced users sometimes find its approach too watered down and simplified.

Which? launched its own Internet service – Which? Online – in November 1996. For a fixed monthly fee, Which? Online offers unlimited Internet access plus exclusive access to regularly updated *Which?* information from its magazines and books. In addition to this, there are discussion forums where *Which?* experts are on-line to give personal advice and guidance, plus details of its campaigns, product recalls and safety information.

Cable?

If your home is wired for cable TV, you may be able to avoid the phone charges associated with Internet use. Some cable providers offer free local calls for some or all of the day, which makes them ideal for Internet access (although a handful prohibit this because it places a strain on their services). If in doubt, check with your cable company. If the service is available it can save you a fortune in phone bills.

At the time of writing, the network computer (NC) remains more of an interesting idea than a practical option for home users. NCs, if and when they appear commercially, will be small, simple computers that can be used to read and send email, view information on the Web and perhaps watch TV-like broadcasts over the Internet. NCs themselves will be much less complicated than existing personal computers, easier to use and to maintain. The technical complexities which currently baffle many users will be hidden away, albeit at the expense of reduced power and flexibility.

A number of companies, including Apple, Microsoft and Sun, have announced plans to produce practical NCs. However, these are unlikely to become popular until the Internet becomes much faster. At the moment there is no chance at all of delivering live TV-like 'broadcasts', although this is likely to become possible in the early years of the next century.

It is suggested that buyers should avoid NCs until the technology has had a chance to settle down and prove itself. Until practical examples become widespread, it is prudent to treat NCs (which may be known commercially as 'set-top boxes') as an interesting experiment rather than a practical alternative to the personal computer.

Bulletin board systems (BBSs)

Although BBSs are being superseded by the Internet, they are still popular with a die-hard collection of enthusiasts, and are likely to be with us for some time to come.

There are hundreds of BBSs in the UK, many of which have a distinct area of interest of their own, ranging from the formal and professional to the extremely strange and disturbing. Some are lively and sociable and may sometimes organise face-to-face social events; to a large extent it depends on the enthusiasm, energy and friendliness of the owner of the board known as the **sysop**. BBSs come in two varieties. The first are run by hobbyists, enthusiasts and computer clubs. These are usually free, although there may be a small annual membership fee (not usually more than £30) for some services. Most hobbyist boards are run on an informal basis. When dialling in for the first time you may be asked to fill in a questionnaire.

The second kind of bulletin board is a strictly commercial venture. These often advertise in computer magazines and usually offer two telephone access numbers. The first puts you through to a section of the BBS where you can see what is available. The second – on an 0891 telephone number or other charge-by-the-minute basis – is used when you want to copy information to your computer. Commercial BBSs do not usually offer anything more than a free bulletin board, and the 0891 access system can make them expensive.

BBSs in theory and practice

Bulletin boards are used for playing games, exchanging messages and software. Games are often multi-player and can prove costly in terms of phone bills. Many boards include large public areas which contain shareware and freeware software, as well as other information such as pictures and computer art, sounds and so on. All of these can be accessed via the telephone to your computer, often for free.

Messages are the lifeblood of any board and are organised into conferences, each of which has a topic (computers, football, politics and so on). You may find that you will not be given access to some conferences until you subscribe. Apart from general chatter about topics of the day, you can also use the message facilities to get technical help. Many board users are computer professionals who will sometimes offer advice when they come across a struggling newcomer.

Bulletin boards tend to attract younger, computer-literate, male users and to the more mature user the exchanges can seem inane.

Most boards are connected together in loose networks. These allow messages to be passed between users of different boards – internationally if need be – as well as within the board itself. The most popular network is FidoNet. FidoNet allows you to exchange mail with anyone on another FidoNet board anywhere in the world. But unlike the Internet, mail and messages exchanged this way move slowly. They are transferred between boards at night. It can take a while for a message to get through the system, and you can expect a delay of up to a week before you get a reply.

Some boards also offer an Internet service. Unlike a true electronic mail account, which works almost instantaneously, BBS Internet mail is sent and received at set times – usually once or twice a day. This means it can take a couple of days to get a reply, instead of a couple of hours. But for anyone dabbling with email this is a good opportunity to learn the basics at minimal expense.

To access a bulletin board you will need a piece of software known as a **terminal emulator**. This turns your computer into a dumb keyboard-plus-screen remote window into the BBS computer at the other end of the phone. Terminal emulators are available as shareware from any good shareware source.

Once you are familiar with the basics, you should get hold of an **off-line reader** package (OLR). OLRs let you pull your messages down the phone to your computer in one packet. Once you have disconnected from the line, you can read them and prepare your replies before connecting again to send them back to the board. This is far more cost-effective than the on-line method of reading and replying to messages while actually connected to the board. OLRs are also available as shareware. Off-Line Express and Telix are among the most popular programs.

Finding a BBS

Finding a board can be problematic. Hobbyist boards tend not to advertise and sometimes suffer from limited life-spans. This means that lists have to be updated on a monthly basis. Ideally you want access to a board within your local call area. This can be good socially and also makes for cheaper telephone bills. Calling long distance is possible, but can soon get expensive if you use the board a lot. An up-to-date list of all UK boards – known as the RobList – is carried on many boards. A good way to get hold of it is to join a local board, then explain to the sysop that you are a beginner and would like a copy of the list. The best place to find information about BBSs is now on the Internet – a web search for 'UK BBS' will produce the relevant details.

Appendix IX

Tackling computer DIY

This appendix is intended for readers with a practical bent who have become familiar with the basics of computer ownership and would like to know how to save money on upgrades and modifications. While it may be quicker to pay a local dealer to maintain and modify a computer, it certainly will not be cheaper. Service charges can vary from £25 to £50 an hour. 'On-site' modifications (an engineer comes to you) are likely to be even more expensive, if they are available at all.

Besides the financial incentives, there are practical reasons why computer DIY can be worth mastering. If something goes wrong you are able to be less reliant on outside support, and therefore less at risk of 'down-time' – time wasted while your computer is not working properly. And as with conventional DIY, some people find the process of learning these new skills offers a satisfaction all of its own.

Of course, this approach will not suit everyone. However, if you are practically minded and capable of basic domestic DIY, very little about computer DIY should faze you. In this Appendix the tasks have been graded according to difficulty and experience, and it is strongly recommended that you master the simpler ones before attempting the more advanced.

Most of the information given here applies to recent IBM-compatible PCs, such as those built from 1995 onwards. Certain tasks are also relevant to Macintosh and PowerPC computers, and – to a lesser extent – to older PCs.

The electronics inside the different models of Apple computers are not as standardised as those in PCs, and for reasons of space it has proved impossible to include the relevant details here. Because Apple system components are not available to the general public, it is not possible to build an Apple computer from scratch.

Older PCs and also laptops require more detailed instructions before they can be upgraded. The possible options, especially those covering hard disk drives, new processors and motherboards, are too complex to be listed in full here. If you own an older PC and would like to find out more about upgrading it you may wish to start by discussing this with a knowledgeable dealer who can advise you on which options to pursue.

Consumer issues

PCs can and do behave in quirky and unpredictable ways that require trained professional help to sort out. For obvious reasons, it is impossible to cover every single eventuality in a book like this. Any modifications carried out by the reader are done so at his or her own risk.

Warranties

Opening up your computer may or may not void the warranty. This depends very much on the policy of the dealer or manufacturer. A few companies have a cast-iron policy that states that any unauthorised work voids the warranty immediately. Other dealers, especially some of the larger and better-known names, will continue to offer warranty support if they can talk you through the upgrade process themselves. Some do not seem to mind either way. Before attempting any work detailed in this Appendix, **always check to see where your dealer stands on this issue and** *read the small print.*

Getting support

Most dealers who sell upgrade hardware will be happy to provide basic telephone support to customers who are attempting their own modifications and upgrades. Smaller, local computer stores may do this at no cost to you, and some medium-sized dealers may even offer free technical support lines on a special telephone number. As usual, it pays to do as much research as possible – if you appear to be 'one of the trade' you will be treated with more respect than someone who is a complete beginner. But even beginners can get useful support this way.

Finding spares and upgrade hardware

These are advertised throughout the computer press. One of the best sources is *MicroMart* magazine, which contains advertisements from a large number of component specialists who tend to sell more cheaply than some of the larger industry names. Before buying any extras it is essential to check that they are suitable, preferably by reading through magazine reviews. If in doubt about which particular brand or model of extra is best, it can pay to phone a selection of suppliers and ask their opinion. This can help to weed out those suppliers who can't provide technical backup. For example, if you are trying to choose a hard disk drive, a supplier who says 'We supply whatever brand we have in stock at the time' is best avoided. One that can quote different makes and model numbers and recommend one or more items is much more likely to be worth dealing with, and may also be able to provide useful technical support.

First steps – a practical primer

Before you start work on your PC, *you should read through this section carefully*. It introduces the most useful practical points involved in computer DIY, explains some of the more advanced jargon, and describes how you can work on your computer safely.

Tools

The following should be sufficient:

- A small Phillips (crosshead) screwdriver
- A small standard screwdriver
- A pair of pliers
- A small torch or Anglepoise desk lamp
- A grounding strap (see opposite)
- Notebook and pen or pencil.

Many people assume that they will need to use a soldering iron or complex electronic test equipment. This is not true. All basic upgrades and modifications consist of nothing more complicated than clipping or screwing the correct parts into place and – occasionally – pushing plugs and cables of various kinds into suitable sockets. Most of the items in question are designed so that it is impossible to do this the wrong way – for example, memory modules will only fit into their sockets the correct way round. Where this is not the case, parts are clearly marked to show which way round they should be fitted.

The most challenging aspects of computer DIY are not electronic, but mechanical. It can be a very tight squeeze inside a computer's case, and on some machines certain vital areas will be hidden under other parts. (The most common example is the main memory, which often seems to be hidden underneath the power supply.) This can turn a simple upgrade into a challenging three-dimensional jigsaw puzzle.

For this reason it is always worth opening up your PC before attempting this kind of work, to acquaint yourself with its innards and try to foresee possible problems. You may decide that the work you were planning looks too complicated and is best left to a professional. This is a perfectly sensible decision to make. While you are unlikely to damage your PC if you follow the precautions outlined below, you may find yourself in a situation where putting the computer back together may not be as straightforward as it first appeared. To avoid this, it is an excellent idea to make notes and sketches as you work, especially where you suspect that reassembly may be less than obvious.

Static electricity

The electronic items used in computers are extremely sensitive to static electricity. While most people have experienced a jolt of static after getting out of a car or walking across a carpet, it takes much less than this to damage an electronic device. Your fingers can build up a charge of tens of millions of volts without any obvious symptoms, and when this is earthed through a computer chip the results can be disastrous and expensive.

Before starting work on a computer, it is important to invest in a **grounding strap**. This is a strip of special plastic that conducts electricity, which you wear as a bracelet round your wrist. The strip plugs into a wall socket which 'grounds' static before it can do any damage. (Note that only the earth lead in the socket is connected to anything!) These straps are available from larger computer stores and from electronics hobby shops, such as Maplin Professional Supplies.

All computer spares are sold in bags made of a similar plastic. It is important never to remove an item from a bag before you are ready to use it, and never to place it on a non-conductive surface of any kind (particularly not a carpet or a plastic kitchen table top) while you are working. Always put chips and circuit boards on the metal parts of the frame of your computer when you are working with them, or on top of the bag they were supplied in. Try to avoid touching any of the exposed electronics with your fingers, even if you are using a grounding strap. It can even be worth buying a grounding tray – a plastic conductive tray which can also be connected to earth, and provides a completely safe working area for static-sensitive components.

Power

Always work with the power switched off and the mains lead disconnected from the wall socket. You should never attempt to plug in or unplug anything inside a computer's case while the power is switched on. Apart from being potentially fatal, this is guaranteed to cause irreparable damage to your computer.

Turning off the power at the front of the computer is **not** a safe equivalent. Dangerous mains voltages can still be present in the area around the power switch and the power supply.

Backups

Wherever possible, back up all the information in your PC before attempting any of these tasks. While it's unlikely that anything will go wrong, accidents do happen, and you may be left with a completely dead machine. Having a backup copy of everything can save the day in situations like this.

What's inside the case?

When you open up a PC, you should be able to see three main parts. The **motherboard** is the large circuit board that holds most of the electronics. In modern PCs, the processor chip, which is the most prominent item on the motherboard, will be hidden by a small fan or a large metal structure with fins called a **heatsink.** This board also holds the memory (RAM).

Everything inside the PC is connected to this board with cables. Arranged in a row at right angles to the board, plugged into a line of long thin sockets – known as the **expansion slots** - are various extras such as a soundcard, a graphics card and perhaps an internal modem if one is fitted. Expansion slots present two rows of metal 'teeth' inside a plastic strip. These teeth grip the corresponding bare metal terminals on an expansion card.

On ISA slots the teeth are fairly wide apart. On VLB and PCI slots they are much closer together. (All ISA slots are electronically identical, but on some PCs the PCI slots differ. You may find that a particular item will only work in a certain slot; this will be noted in the documentation.) In all cases these slots back on to **blanking plates** – small metal plates fitted to the back of the computer with a single screw.

The **drive cage** sits behind the front panel of the PC. This is where the hard disk drive(s), the floppy disk drive and the CD-ROM are fitted. When adding a new drive, free space must be available in this cage for it. These spaces come in two sizes – 5.25-inch for larger hard disks and CD-ROM drives and 3.5-inch for floppy disk drives and standard hard disks. You can fit a 3.5-inch item into the larger space with the aid of an adaptor pack, which your dealer can supply. The number of free spaces for each size of item varies depending on the case your PC came in. Full tower cases will have plenty of free spaces of both sizes, while slimline cases may not have any. Before attempting to add a new CD-ROM or hard drive to your PC it is essential to check that a suitable space is available.

The **power supply** is the large metal box with the fan at the back and a nest of brightly coloured (mostly red, black and yellow) thicker cables protruding from the front and leading to large, flat, plastic power connectors. Cards that slot into the motherboard draw their power from it directly and do not need any further power connections. However, certain extras have to be connected to the power supply by hand. You will need a free power connector for this. If none seems to be available, ask your dealer for a power cable splitter. This splits a single connector into two. You can then connect one back to an existing item, the other to the new extra.

Power connectors are designed to fit tightly into their sockets, and you will need to use considerable force to detach them. This reduces the chance of their becoming loose by accident. However, it does mean you need to take care when trying to disconnect one. A triangular notch on the connector's socket makes it impossible to fit them back to front.

Ribbon cable

Many computer extras – such as hard disks – use **ribbon cable.** This is a long flat strip of cable fitted with thin plastic connectors which have two rows of tiny sockets. The cable is made of a number of much finer cables laid flat and welded together at their sides. One edge will be marked in some way, typically with a red line, or with a fine mist of red paint. This marking tells you which way round the cable fits into its socket. It is often referred to as 'Pin 1'. The plugs that match these connectors have two corresponding rows of tiny pins. 'Pin 1' will be indicated in some way on the circuit board near the plug – with an arrow, a dot, or some other marker.

One of the biggest problems with computer DIY is getting ribbon cable to behave itself. The connectors can easily be pulled out of their sockets by accident, they can be fitted wrongly, either by plugging in one row of pins instead of two, or by misaligning the connector so that some pins are left unconnected. In some instances – especially when working with a full tower case – the cable is simply too short, and the only solution is to move the item it connects to closer to the motherboard. Or the cable may need to be twisted and threaded in a clumsy way through the PC.

If something doesn't seem to be working, always double- and even triple-check that you have the ribbon cable fitted properly. Getting it wrong will not usually cause any permanent damage, but it may mean that your PC refuses to start. This can be heart-stopping for beginners, but it can usually be solved by refitting the connector properly.

Jumpers

Some computer items use small plastic-coated links that have to be pushed on to or removed from tiny pairs of pins. These links are known as **jumpers,** and have to be fitted or removed by hand. Jumpers perform different functions on different items of hardware – for example, on a motherboard they are often used to set the correct operating speed for a given processor chip. Documentation supplied with the item will explain how and where jumpers should be fitted. Thankfully, this rather crude technology is slowly becoming obsolete, but jumpers are still found regularly on items such as hard disks.

Where a pair of pins should be left unconnected, it is standard practice to fit the jumper so it only covers one pin of the pair. Never detach jumpers from an item completely, just in case you need to change the operating settings for the hardware again. Jumpers are very easy to lose, and replacements are hard to find.

Drivers

Many items of computer hardware require **drivers.** These are small items of software supplied on floppy disk or CD-ROM that tell your computer how to 'talk' to the hardware. These are specific to the hardware involved – for example, each kind of soundcard comes with its own unique set of drivers. Always follow the installation instructions *exactly* as specified.

If you buy an item marked 'OEM' in a computer magazine, you may not get any drivers with it at all. In theory, OEM ('Original Equipment Manufacturer') items are aimed at computer manufacturers. In practice the OEM label simply means that you get the same product for less money, albeit in a plain box instead of a colourfully decorated one, and most often with no supporting documentation or software.

The way around this is to copy the latest drivers from the Internet. This can often be a useful thing to do even for non–OEM 'consumer' items. By the time an item has been shipped, stored and sold, it may be months old, and the drivers supplied with it may no longer be the most current.

All the major manufacturers have their own web sites. Sometimes you may need to do a web search to find them, but you are likely to find the most recent drivers, as well as frequently asked technical-support questions. Copying the drivers to your PC is a relatively simple procedure which takes more than 20 minutes to half an hour. Usually it is simply a case of clicking on a web link and telling your PC where to store the resulting driver information. Once it has been copied, you can install the drivers in the usual way.

It is not just hardware extras that require drivers. Motherboards sometimes benefit from a driver update. In theory, Windows includes all the drivers that are needed. In practice, these may not be up to date, and so it can be worth visiting your motherboard manufacturer's web site, and that of the manufacturers of the chipset it uses (often, but not always, Intel), to see if any updates have been made available. Doing this can sometimes solve serious problems, such as mysterious random crashes.

Simple tasks

The following tasks are very straightforward, and a relative novice should be able to tackle them successfully.

Installing a soundcard

This is a relatively simple procedure, especially on PCs that are not already heavily burdened with extras. The step-by-step approach given below can be applied to most circuit-card upgrades.

1. Turn off the power to the PC, open the case and identify the expansion slots.
2. Pick a suitable expansion slot. (You may find that in some slots the soundcard is blocked by the processor chip. This is an unfortunate design flaw in some PCs that limits your choices.)
3. Remove the blanking plate from the slot you have chosen. Keep the screw to hand.
4. Push the card into the expansion slot. You might have to use a fair amount of force, but be careful not to apply too much as the motherboard may crack. Try lining up the card and then wiggling it into place. The row of bare metal terminals fits into the teeth of the slot, and the metal bracket on the card takes the place of the blanking plate. Make sure that the card is pushed in fully.
5. Double-check that the card is slotted in properly. Most of the metal on all of the card's terminals should be hidden by the plastic strip of the expansion slot. The terminals should be pushed in evenly, so that the bottom of the card is horizontal. If it is uneven, take the card out and refit it.
6. Fit the blanking plate screw so it holds the card's bracket in place.
7. Keeping clear of the PC's innards, turn on the power and install the drivers. Test the card by connecting speakers, microphones, and so on.
8. If everything seems to be working, turn off the power, and refit the PC's case.

Where an existing soundcard is present, remove the old soundcard before installing the new one. This is simply a case of pulling the old card out of its slot. The same slot can be used for the new card. You may also need to remove (uninstall) the old drivers as described above, before installing the new ones.

Installing a graphics card

To install a faster graphics card follow the same procedure as for a soundcard. The card slots into one of the PCI or AGP slots instead of the ISA slots, but otherwise the procedure is identical. (If your PC has VLB slots instead of PCI slots you will probably find that it is impossible to find a suitable card, as VLB graphics cards are very, very difficult to find now.)

Installing graphics card drivers can often be a fiddly process. It is useful to make sure that you always have the very latest drivers to hand (see page 277). Drivers aside, graphics cards in PCs use part of Windows known as DirectX, which is supposed to make games and other demanding software work more efficiently but often causes problems of its own.

When you install new hardware or software, it sometimes assumes that you also want to install a version of DirectX. However, the version that comes with the product may be *older* than the version you already have installed. Or the installation may reinstall older drivers for some other part of the system, such as the graphics or sound card.

If you run into any of these problems, first make sure that you have the latest versions of both DirectX (which is available for free on the Microsoft web site) and the relevant drivers to hand. Then try reinstalling one or the other till the system appears to be stable again.

Installing a faster IDE CD-ROM drive

If your PC dates from around 1996, the existing CD-ROM drive may be on the slow side. Faster drives are relatively inexpensive and very easy to fit. Note that the procedure below only applies to IDE CD-ROM drives. These are connected to the motherboard, usually by way of a ribbon cable that goes via one of the hard disk drives.

If your PC was made before 1995, the drive probably will not appear in this frame, and you may find that the CD-ROM drive is attached to the soundcard instead of the motherboard. This makes the process more complicated. Treat this as similar to 'Installing a bigger hard disk', an advanced task described on pages 284–8.

Like hard disk drives, CD-ROM drives can work in 'master' or 'slave' mode. This is a way of connecting two items to the same cable so that they can work together. To ensure your new CD-ROM works properly, you have to set it up the same way as the one that is currently installed. This usually involves setting a jumper on the drive. You can tell how it has been set up by looking at the 'identification frame' that appears after you switch on your computer. This is a list of hardware settings and includes master/slave information for your hard disk(s) and CD-ROM drive. If your CD-ROM doesn't appear here, you will need to check the jumpers on the back of the drive after you have removed it and read through the drive's manual to discover which way it has been set up. If all else fails, contact your original supplier for help.

1. Turn on your PC, and watch for the 'frame' that appears. Look for the item near the bottom left of the frame that refers to the CD-ROM drive. Note whether the word 'master' or 'slave' appears.
2. Turn off the power, open the PC's case, and identify the drive cage (see page 275).
3. Find the CD-ROM drive. Undo the screws that hold the drive in place on the metal frame of the cage. Keep the screws in a safe place.
4. Remove the connectors at the back. Tie them or tape them together to stop them disappearing into the rest of the PC.
5. Slide out the old drive.
6. If the word 'master' appeared in step one, slide in the new drive. If the word 'slave' appeared, find the jumper that sets slave mode operation. (This will usually be on the back of the drive near the connectors. You may need to refer to the drive's manual or talk to a technical support person to find it.)
7. Slide in the new drive, and screw it into place. Refit the connectors.
8. Turn on the PC. If the CD tray slides out immediately, or if your PC does not work or appears to stop after a minute or so, you may have plugged in the ribbon cable at the back of the drive the wrong way round. Turn off the PC and refit the cable correctly.
9. If the PC still refuses to start, you may have failed to set the 'master' or 'slave' operation properly. Double-check the jumper and set it appropriately.
10. When the PC is working properly install the drivers and check the system by trying out a CD. If it works, refit the case.

Intermediate tasks

The following tasks require more detailed specialist knowledge and are prone to technical or mechanical complications. They are within the reach of adventurous beginners, but are realistically best left to those with more experience.

Adding more memory

Computer memory is supplied in the form of long thin green or brown wafers called SIMMs (Single In-line Memory Modules) or DIMMs (Dual In-line Memory Modules) which have varying numbers of attached black plastic chips. These wafers fit into slots, which use a similar but smaller version of the 'teeth and terminals' system used for expansion cards. (Note that memory slots do not have any blanking plates, and the memory 'cards' themselves are very much smaller than a typical expansion card.) Four or six slots will be available. Modern PCs use slots with 72 holes for SIMMs and 168 holes for DIMMs. Older models have 30 holes which are used with a larger, now nearly obsolete, kind of SIMM.

SIMMs are supplied in pairs, and each pair can offer 1Mb, 2Mb, 4Mb, 8Mb, 16Mb, 32Mb or 64Mb of memory. (Note that the physical size of the SIMMs doesn't vary, even though the memory capacity does. However, the number of attached black plastic chips will.) By fitting different-capacity SIMMs into different pairs of sockets you can expand the memory up to a limit set by the design of the motherboard – typically 128Mb or 256Mb. DIMMs are usually fitted singly. (Some portables use yet another type of memory called SO – Small Outline – DIMMs. They are much smaller than the DIMMs used in desktop PCs and again need to be fitted in pairs.)

Installing more memory can be straightforward enough to count as a beginner's task, but a number of problems can complicate the process. Perhaps the most aggravating is discovering that the memory has been hidden by the power supply. In this situation the task is perhaps best left to someone with extensive PC experience, as typically you will have to unplug all the cables from the motherboard and lever it out of the PC's case so that you can get at the relevant slots.

The other problem is working out what kind of memory you have installed already, and deciding whether there is room to fit more. Once all the slots are filled some memory has to be removed before more can be fitted. As an example, one popular upgrade is to remove two SIMMs that offer 8Mb in total and replace them with two that offer 32Mb.

All memory modules of whatever variety are graded according to speed and memory type. When fitting new memory always use the same type, and a speed that is equivalent to or better than your existing memory. Speeds are measured in nanoseconds (nS) and vary from 60nS to 80nS. Faster memory will work perfectly well in slower computers, so if you always use 60nS you should have no problems. Types include standard, EDO and SDRAM. You may need to refer to your PC's manual to work out which to use, or you may even need to call the manufacturer's technical support line.

1. Turn off the power, open the PC's case and find the memory. You should be able to see a number of wafers slotted in vertically somewhere on the motherboard. The memory is often situated near to one of the edges of the board.
2. If it is easily accessible, either find two free slots or remove two of the existing SIMMs. To do this push the clips at each end of the slot outwards until the memory moves freely. Then lever it out.
3. Slot in the new SIMMs. Make sure they click into place firmly. If they do not, turn them round and try again.
4. Switch on the PC and watch for the memory test that appears almost immediately. The numbers should stop at the total amount of memory you have fitted. (Note that 1Mb = 1024Kb, not 1000Kb. So, for example, if you fitted 80Mb of RAM this counter would stop at 81920Kb.)

Installing a faster processor chip

Before starting this task, you may want to consider whether or not installing a faster processor will be a cost-effective upgrade. In terms of value for money, expanding your PC's memory to 64Mb or even 128Mb is much more likely to make a noticeable difference to your work than replacing a 300MHz Pentium II chip with a 400MHz Pentium II. However, if you have already expanded your memory to a reasonable amount and still feel your computer is sluggish, then a faster processor is a valid alternative.

As with adding more memory, this upgrade can be a relatively simple task, or it can involve the disassembly and reassembly of most of the PC. This depends on the motherboard that is installed. Most motherboards will only work with a given range of processor chips, and some will only work with a subset of that range which works within a certain speed band. If you want to fit a better chip inside your computer, and you find your motherboard cannot cope with it, you will need to replace the motherboard as well. For example, if your current PC is a Pentium, and you want to fit a Pentium III you will need to buy and install a new motherboard. While this has its attractions – you will end up with a much faster PC without the hassle of copying all your information from one machine to another, or buying a new case or even a whole new system that you don't want or need – installing a new motherboard is an example of advanced DIY and should not be attempted by someone with limited experience.

However, if your motherboard *can* work with a faster chip than the one you have now, the upgrade is relatively straightforward. If you are not sure if your motherboard is compatible, then ask your supplier. Guessing the answer and getting it wrong can leave you with a useless – and very expensive – dead processor chip.

A handful of newer motherboards are 'jumperless' and can assess automatically what kind of processor chip needs to be fitted. If you have a jumperless board – check the documents that came with your computer or ask the retailer – you can skip the steps below that refer to changing the jumper settings. Otherwise you will need manually to set any jumpers to match your processor chip's model and speed rating. Information about how to do this is invariably included with the manual supplied with the motherboard.

1. Check your motherboard's manual to try and identify the jumpers that set the processor chip's speed. If you cannot find these, refer to your original PC supplier. If you still can't find them, STOP! You will not be able to perform this upgrade and should consider buying a new motherboard.
2. Turn off the power to the PC, open the case, and locate the jumpers on the motherboard. You may find they are hidden under a nest of cables. If so, carefully push your way through the cables until the jumpers become visible. Be especially careful not to pull out any of the cables by accident.
3. Set the jumpers to the speed of your new chip.
4. Remove the old chip. On PCs where the processor is hidden under a square heatsink, unclip the processor from the socket using the plastic or metal arm next to it; lift out the old chip. On PCs which use a long slot, pull the whole unit out of the slot, removing any mechanical restraints first.
5. If your new chip uses a clip-on heatsink, fit it first.
6. Insert the new chip (you won't be able to fit it the wrong way round). On PCs with a plastic socket, lower the arm to clip it firmly

into place again. On PCs with a slot, refit the mechanical restraints if present.

7. Turn on your PC and check for signs of life. If everything seems to be working properly turn off the power and refit the case. Otherwise turn off the power, double-check the jumper setting, double-check any connectors around the chip, and make sure that the new chip has been seated firmly.

Advanced tasks

These tasks require a reasonable amount of technical background knowledge and should be attempted only by those who understand the issues and principles involved. If you are a complete beginner you are strongly advised to do some thorough research first to familiarise yourself with the various technical and mechanical settings involved. Getting these settings wrong can create a PC that appears to have stopped working. At the very least you should understand enough of the theory to be able to retrace your steps in case of trouble.

Installing a bigger hard disk

Typically, new PCs are supplied with a single hard disk drive. This can fill up remarkably quickly, and almost everyone who uses a PC finds that a larger hard disk soon becomes essential.

Most PCs built after 1995 can be fitted with up to four hard disks and/or CD-ROM drives. These are fitted to two connectors on the motherboard – one labelled 'primary' and one 'secondary' – using pieces of ribbon cable. The two drives that can be attached to each of the primary and secondary cables are further distinguished by being set up as either the 'master' or the 'slave'. As explained earlier, this is simply the way the PC tells them apart even though they use the same piece of cable.

These designations appear on the information frame when you turn on your PC. The primary master, primary slave, secondary master, and secondary slave disks are listed there together with their capacity and their 'mode' – a measure of the way they transfer information. (Modern hard disk drives use 'Mode 4'. CD-ROM drives use 'Mode 1'. These are identified automatically, and you don't need to worry about what they mean.) If any of these designations appears blank it simply means that there is no drive connected in that position.

In most PCs you are likely to find a single hard disk drive as the primary master, and a single CD-ROM drive as the secondary master. If your PC has been set up like this you should fit your new hard drive as the primary slave.

Occasionally you may find that the main hard disk is the primary master, and the CD-ROM is the primary slave. If your PC has been set up like this, you should complain to the manufacturer. The rule of thumb with drives of any sort is that if two drives share the same cable, information will move at the speed of the slower drive. Since a CD-ROM drive can be as much as ten times slower than a hard disk, the speed of your whole PC will suffer as a result. Ask your dealer to modify your PC to make sure that the hard disk is the primary master, and the CD-ROM drive is the secondary master before you proceed any further – and install your new drive as the primary slave as above.

Setting jumpers and connecting ribbon cables is still only part of the story. The PC needs to be told about the specification of the new hard drive once it has been fitted. And the drive itself needs to be prepared ('formatted') before it can be used.

The first part of this process requires an exploration of what are known as the 'BIOS settings'. (BIOS – short for Basic Input Output System – is pronounced BYEoss.) These appear on a set of special screens that can only be accessed after you turn on your PC. When you see a message that says 'Hit DEL to enter SETUP', hit the delete key and the main BIOS screen will appear. (Some systems use a key other than delete; the message will indicate which key to press.)

The BIOS settings are the heart of the PC, and changing these settings can cause your PC to appear to stop working. These settings have to 'match' the exact hardware used in your PC, otherwise the PC may not work, or will only work erratically. If you change anything by accident, or don't know the numbers that match your hardware and type in the wrong ones, your PC will most probably not get any further than the 'Hit DEL to enter SETUP' message when you turn it on. This is unlikely to cause any permanent damage, but if you can't work out for yourself what the correct setting should be, you will need to get professional technical support to get your PC working again. Changing these settings should not be undertaken lightly! All the settings – and there are over a hundred in a typical PC – are arranged on different pages. Each page shows the settings for a specific part of the PC – for example, the speed of the memory, the specifications of the hard disks, and so on. The first BIOS page is an index to the other pages. To look at, or change, anything on one of the other pages, move the highlight to a page's name with the arrow keys and hit the 'Enter' key. This will show all the settings for that page. To select a setting, use the arrow keys again. To change it, use the 'Page Up' and 'Page Down' keys (when you have to choose one of a fixed list of options) or the number keys (when you have to type in a number). To get back to the main index page hit the 'Esc' key. (Note the mouse will not work while any of these pages are shown.)

Because these settings are so critical, you have to confirm any changes you make before they take effect. If you change something on these pages by accident, as a last resort you can always turn off your PC immediately to recover the original settings. A more elegant solution is to learn how to confirm or cancel the changes. The 'save and exit' option on the main index page confirms the changes. The 'exit without saving' option cancels them, leaving all the settings unchanged. As a double-check each of these brings up a further question, asking you to confirm your confirmation, or cancel the cancellation. Respond with a 'y' for yes and 'n' for no, depending on which you require. If you hit 'enter', the changes will not be confirmed.

Always make a note of the old BIOS settings before changing them. If you get into trouble you can get back to where you were by going back to the relevant pages and typing in the old settings again. While this may not always solve the problem, it is invaluable information to have to hand if you need to make a technical support call.

Although there are a number of BIOS pages, there are two particular pages to look out for. The first will be called something like 'Basic CMOS setup'. The other may be something like 'AUTO IDE HDD identification' (the wording may vary). The first is where you set the numbers that define each hard disk's operation by hand. The second attempts to guess the correct numbers automatically. Details of how to use these options are given below.

The second part of the setup process requires **partitioning** and **formatting** the new drive. Partitioning divides up the drive into sections (known as **logical** partitions) which appear as separate letters in the list of hard drives – for example d: and e: can both be on the same disk drive. You will be forced to partition your drive if it is over a certain size. If you don't, you will waste a large proportion of the drive's available storage space. The size depends on the version of

Windows you are using. You will discover what the maximum size is on your machine when you attempt to create partitions on the drive for yourself. Formatting prepares the drive so that Windows can store information on it. In effect, it creates a framework for the information and makes it possible for Windows to keep track of where all the information is stored on the drive's surface.

One final practical note – when buying a larger drive, always ask for mounting screws and ribbon cable to be included. Otherwise you will be sent a bare drive with no way to fit it into the PC, or connect it to the motherboard. If you do find yourself with a drive but no screws or cables, a small local computer store will usually be able to help you with these extras.

1. Restart your PC and note which of the primary or secondary, master or slave designations are free.
2. Turn off your PC and open the case. Identify the drive cage. Check that there is space available inside the cage for a new drive, and whether or not you will need a mounting bracket to fit a small drive into a 5.25-inch mounting space.
3. Install the new drive into the cage. Fit a power connector and the appropriate ribbon cable, making sure that the latter is fitted the correct way round. (When the cable is plugged in, Pin 1 always goes nearest the power connector.)
4. Turn on the PC and hit the relevant key to enter the BIOS setup screens. Find the IDE auto-detect page if one is available. This scans each hard drive in turn and reports back the correct settings for it. Where more than one setting is available the one marked 1(Y) is usually the correct one. Hit 'Enter' to scan the next drive. Where no drive is fitted, the scan will report back with a row of zeros. Hit 'N' to skip a failed scan – unless the scan has found a CD-ROM drive, in which case hit 'Y'.
5. If there is no auto-detect option, go to the Main CMOS Setup screen and type in the numbers by hand. You will find these in the manual that comes with the hard drive. If this is missing, or if you are not sure which numbers to type in, call your hard disk supplier's technical support line and ask them to talk you through this part of the process.
6. Hit 'Esc' to take you back to the main BIOS screen, and then 'Save & Exit.' This last option is designed to confuse you and make you

think twice about what you are doing, so that you don't save a new setting by accident. Confirm with 'Y' or 'N', as appropriate, to make sure that the new settings are saved.

7. Your PC will now restart. If you have entered the settings correctly it should start up as normal. If not, it will stop and wait at the screen that says 'Hit DEL to enter SETUP.' Hit the delete key (or whichever is appropriate for your machine) and double-check the settings. Save them as before.

8. Once your PC restarts properly, you will need to be in DOS to partition the disk. If running either version of Windows, quit to DOS.

9. Type FDISK. Follow the prompts to set a physical partition and then one or more logical partitions on the new drive. **Be very, very careful here. If you delete a partition on an existing drive, all the information on it will be lost and you may also cripple your PC by deleting the operating system.** The latter is not fatal; the operating system software can be reinstalled. However, there is no remedy at all for the former – except to avoid the problem in the first place.

10. Restart the machine and format the new hard disk. You can do this from within Windows or DOS, using the relevant format commands. Again, be careful – if you format the wrong drive you will lose all the information on it.

11. When the new hard disk is ready, close the case again. You can now start to copy information to it, or install new software.

'Cloning' an existing hard disk

Sometimes it is more convenient to move all your information to a larger hard disk and then install that as a replacement for your current one. This approach means that in addition to having extra space, your main disk will be faster and newer than the original, and all your software and settings will remain unchanged. The most convenient way to do this is to use a program called Partition Magic. This can copy, format, and otherwise maintain disks of all types. To clone a disk:

1. Fit the new hard disk using a spare connector. Make sure it is set to the correct master/slave setting as usual.

2. Do not format it or partition it. Instead, start Windows, then start Partition Magic.

3. If you have more than one partition on the original disk, use Partition Magic to create the same number of partitions on the new disk.

4. Copy all the partitions from the old disk to the new one.

5. Resize the new partitions ad lib, to give yourself extra working space.

6. Make sure that the partition that now contains the operating system is marked 'bootable' (the documentation supplied with Partition Magic will explain how to do this, and why it is important).

7. Turn off the PC, and fit the new disk to the connector used by the old disk, setting it to the correct master/slave setting (this will usually be 'master' mode).

8. Restart your PC. The operating system should start as normal, only you should now have more disk space available.

9. If everything appears in order you can optionally turn off the PC again, then fit the older hard disk to a different connector, to give yourself more disk space. (Note that, if you have more than one partition on the disks, doing this will change the order in which the various disks and partitions appear within Windows. This is usually undesirable, and will – almost inevitably – cause problems. However, if you simply use all the partitions other than the first to store information rather than for software – for example, if you have a large collection of music, images, animations or video clips – then this becomes less important.)

Installing a new motherboard

This is a rather more complex process than installing a new hard disk. In effect, you will be taking your old PC apart and putting it back together again. Do not attempt this unless you have plenty of experience.

There is usually little reason to buy a new motherboard unless you buy a new processor chip at the same time. When buying a combination, check to be absolutely sure that your motherboard is compatible with the chip you have in mind, and also with its clip-on heatsink (remarkably, it is possible to buy a heatsink from a dealer that cannot be fitted successfully to certain motherboards sold by the same dealer). Check also that it matches the kind of memory you are using.

If you have a lot of extras installed ensure that there are at least as many ISA slots on the new motherboard as in your existing PC – otherwise you may find that you run out of slots, and so have to do without one of your extras. Also check that you buy the same size of motherboard – either AT, or ATX. Otherwise you will need to buy a new case and transplant your entire PC to it, motherboard, disks and all.

When fitting a new motherboard you will need to keep track of all the connectors on the back of the PC, including the parallel (printer) port and the serial (mouse and modem) ports. If your PC offers USB you will need to keep track of these connectors too. While not difficult, it pays to identify the relevant connectors on your new motherboard so that you don't miss anything out. As with other jobs, you may find that fitting all of these inside the case is a tight squeeze. Unfortunately this is an occupational hazard, and you may need to use your powers of ingenuity to swap the different connectors around until they can all be fitted in correctly.

1. Restart the PC, enter the BIOS screen and make a note of all of the drive settings. You will need to supply your new motherboard with this information later.
2. Shut down the PC, turn off the power, open up the case.
3. Disconnect all the wires and cables from the motherboard, making a note of what they are connected to. Do this slowly and carefully.
4. Either remove the cables and connectors, or tie or tape them to the inside of the case so that they do not get in the way. Pay particular attention to the two big power connectors at the edge of the motherboard.
5. Remove all expansion cards from the board.
6. Remove the screws that hold the old motherboard in place and remove the board itself. You will usually need to jiggle around the small plastic pins that hold up the board to do this.
7. Place the old board on a static-safe surface, such as a static-protective bag.
8. Remove the memory from the old board and install it in the new motherboard.
9. Install the new board using the plastic pins and appropriate screw fittings you have saved from the old board. The position and number of pins and screws may well be different to that on the original board.

10. Refit the expansion cards.

11. Referring to the motherboard's manual, set up any jumpers on the new board to match the processor chip you have chosen, and install the processor and its heat sink.

12. Refit all the connectors, bearing in mind the notes above.

13. Double-check that the expansion cards are seated firmly in their slots, the jumpers are set correctly, the memory is fitted correctly, and that all the connectors are attached properly – especially the power connectors for the board. Triple-check these connectors using the diagram in the motherboard's manual.

14. Turn on the PC. Enter the BIOS setup screen. Set the hard disk specifications. All the other settings – include those you haven't checked yet – will usually work correctly.

15. Check to see if the PC starts. If nothing at all happens, double-check the BIOS settings, the processor jumpers on the motherboard, and all the hard disk connectors. If you get memory errors or the PC seems very erratic, you may need to change the BIOS memory setup. Get a support person to talk you through this.

16. If the PC starts up with a beep but stops at the 'Hit DEL to enter SETUP' screen, repeat step 15, leaving out the jumper check.

17. When all is working properly refit the case.

Very advanced tasks – building a PC from scratch

If you have mastered the earlier tasks, then building a PC from scratch should present few problems. However apart from putting the PC together, you will also need to install an operating system (OS) from scratch. In doing this, you have two options. If the operating system is supplied on floppy disk (which is unlikely if you are installing a modern OS such as Windows 95/98) then start by installing MS-DOS, and install the other OS over the top. If the operating system is supplied on CD-ROM you will need to install MS-DOS, install the drivers for the CD-ROM, and then run the installation program from the CD. The rest happens automatically.

The following is a 'shopping list' for constructing a DIY PC. If you buy all these items together you should be able to negotiate a discount on the total. Remember to check for compatibility – for example, that the motherboard is designed to work with the processor chip you have in mind. Most retailers will be able to help you make these decisions.

Surprisingly, the DIY route may not save you money. Even with a discount, the total price is likely to be greater than that for an off-the-shelf PC. However, you will end up with a machine that you know inside out, and will be able to repair if something goes wrong.

Some suppliers are now offering complete PC kits, which include all the relevant parts, complete with instructions, for a slightly greater discount. If you have computer DIY experience these can be worth considering as an alternative to buying everything separately. Even so, the benefits of building your PC from scratch are in the realm of personal satisfaction and acquiring new skills rather than financial gain.

Hardware (main PC unit)
- Motherboard
- Processor chip
- Memory
- One or more hard disk drives
- CD-ROM drive (optional, but strongly recommended)
- Soundcard (optional)
- Graphics card
- Floppy disk drive
- Case

Hardware (other)
- Keyboard
- Mouse
- Monitor
- Modem (optional)

Software:
- Working copy ('boot disk') of DOS on floppy disk. You will also need a part of DOS called FDISK on the same floppy.
- Main operating system, such as Windows 95/98 (If the operating system is on CD-ROM, you will need drivers for the CD-ROM on floppy disk as well.)

1. Open up the case.
2. Fit the motherboard. This is supported on small plastic pins and screwed into place with one or more screws. Make sure the board is well supported.
3. Fit the memory on to the motherboard.
4. Fit the processor to the motherboard. Fit the heatsink to the processor.
5. Set any drives that require it to slave mode, and fit them all into the drive cage. You may find that you need to remove part of the cage (typically the 3.5-inch part) to make it possible to fit screws on both sides of all the drives. If this is so, simply refit that part of the cage when you have finished. You may need to remove one or more metal blanking plates. These are plates fixed to the front of the drive cage behind plastic panels, and can only be removed permanently. Push out the plastic panels at the front of the PC where you need access to the drives – i.e. the floppy disk and the CD-ROM.
6. Plug in all the relevant power connectors. Be especially careful with the power connectors to the motherboard as you can plug something in the wrong way round and cause damage. Double-check the connections in the manual before proceeding.
7. Plug in the ribbon cables for the hard drive(s), floppy drive, CD-ROM, printer and serial ports, mouse, and any other connectors on the back.
8. Fit the graphics card into an expansion slot.
9. Plug in the mouse, monitor and keyboard and turn on the PC. Check for signs of life. If nothing happens, double-check every single cable and connector and also the graphics card, and try again. Your PC won't start properly, but you should get a single 'beep' and a message that says 'Hard drive failed...'
10. Restart the PC, and set up the BIOS so it recognises the hard disk(s) and the CD-ROM drive. Restart the PC again with the MS-DOS floppy in the slot.
11. Run FDISK to partition the hard disk(s), and then FORMAT to format them.
12. Restart the PC, install MS-DOS to the hard disk, and then install the CD-ROM drivers.
13. If installing an operating system from a CD-ROM, run the SETUP program on the CD-ROM. Everything else should

happen automatically. If the operating system is on floppy disks, then you will need to swap these in and out by hand as it loads.

14. Shut down the PC, and install the other expansion cards and drivers for all of the cards. (Up to this point the graphics card will have been working in a 'bare minimum' way that doesn't make use of all of its facilities. Installing the drivers for it will allow it to operate at its full potential.)

15. Install your favourite software.

Trouble-shooting games

Games can be notoriously difficult to get working. Typical problems include lack of sound, lack of CD music, stuttering, slow animations and even complete crashes which freeze the PC. Sorting out the many possible problems is not an easy task. Before attempting anything more complicated, it is a good idea to start by making sure that you have the very latest drivers for all the hardware you are using. This includes the latest version of Microsoft's DirectX (see page 279).

Next, visit the game manufacturer's web site and see if there are any updates (sometimes known as 'patches') for the game itself. This is one area in which the Internet is invaluable. Usually there is literally no other way to get the same information, so without access to the Internet you may, unfortunately, be left with a non-working game and no chance of fixing it. Manufacturers will often include a list of frequently asked questions about the game on their web site, and one of these may solve any problems you are experiencing. Typically, you will also find details of a contact email address or phone number here, or else in the manual for the game. Over time manufacturers build up a database of common problems, and if you contact them directly they can sometimes help.

However, it is always possible that your particular problem will be new to the manufacturer, especially if the game is relatively new. At this point, your options are very limited. It can sometimes be worth looking at the more obscure settings offered by your graphics card and experimenting with any setting that uses terms such as 'Direct Memory Access' or 'Bus Mastering' (if these exist, they may be hidden away behind a button labelled 'advanced').

If, after everything you try, the game still fails to work, you are perfectly within your rights to take it back to the shop you bought it from and ask for a refund.

Appendix X

The Year 2000 problem

On 31 December 1999 at 23:59:59, many computer systems all over the world will stop working properly. The problem is partly historical, partly practical and partly financial. Many large computer systems still use software written in the 1960s and 1970s. At that time memory was expensive, and to save space programmers used two digits instead of four to represent the year. For example, 1997 is stored as '97'. After the year 2000 this number becomes '00', and arithmetic using this representation becomes unreliable. A bank account, for example, may suddenly be credited or debited with a century's worth of interest.

In the acronym-loving computer world, this has become known as the 'Y2K' problem ('2K' is a technical abbreviation for '2000'). Industry predictions of the outcome of this problem range from the expensive – as companies suddenly find they have to hire troubleshooters to fix their systems – to the life-threatening. In practice, it now seems likely that some companies will not be able to make the required changes in time. Since many systems, including power distribution, banking, telecommunications and travel, rely on software that needs to know what date it is, it's possible that the first few weeks of 2000 will be an unusually interesting period for many people.

For the PC user, the results are unlikely to be dramatic. It is still important, however, to find out whether or not an individual PC is 'Y2K compliant' and hence able to cope with the next century correctly. There are three things to check:

Hardware needs to work accurately. All personal computers have a built-in clock, which carries on working even when the computer is turned off. This clock includes the date as well as the time, and it needs to be able to represent dates after the year 2000 with no problems. Even if the clock chip doesn't work properly – and many don't – the part of the computer known as the BIOS (Basic Input Output System) may compensate for this automatically. If it does, not only will the year 2000 appear as it should, but the BIOS will also know that 2000 is a leap year and thus includes an extra day on 29 February.

Operating systems, such as Windows 95/98, need to be aware of the problem and know how to continue to display the time and date properly.

Software, especially that which handles dates and times, also needs to be checked to make sure it handles the change correctly. This is particularly important for databases and spreadsheets.

Practical hardware tests and checks

As 2000 approaches, many PCs will start being sold as 'Y2K compliant'. In theory this means they should work properly at the level of hardware, operating system and software. In practice, this may not be true. It's useful to be able to check for yourself whether or not a PC will continue to work properly.

The easiest way to do this is to set the clock by hand to just before one of the problem-prone dates, turn off the PC so it has to rely on its own internal hardware clock. When turned on again it should show the correct date. This is a simple test and is quick enough to be practical in a shop. The relevant dates, and the results shown if the computer passes, are:

Before	After
31 Dec 1999	1 Jan 2000
28 Feb 2000	29 Feb 2000
29 Feb 2000	1 Mar 2000

In each case set the time to 23:57:00 before shutting down the computer, and wait for *not less than four minutes*. Anything other than the results shown above proves that the computer is not Y2K compliant.

In some cases the computer may pass these tests even though its clock chip does not work properly. This is because Windows 95/98 can make the relevant adjustments automatically. Windows 3.1x will usually adjust accurately too, although in some cases it seems to show dates incorrectly. MS-DOS will not be able to do this, and if you use MS-DOS rather than Windows you will need to make sure that all of your hardware works correctly.

If the computer fails, even with Windows running, or if you use MS-DOS, you have six choices:

Ignore the problem A perfectly valid option if you don't use date-sensitive software. If you are primarily interested in using your computer for playing games or for word processing, then the problem may not bother you at all. It certainly won't harm your computer. However, if you use a date-based backup system you will need to take steps to fix it.

Set the date by hand The vast majority of PCs will continue to work correctly as long as you manually change the date to the new century sometime on or after 1/1/2000. Unfortunately, this 'fix' will not work on a small minority of PCs: for example, most of those that use version 4.50g of the AWARD BIOS will continue to have date problems even if you do this (you can see which version of the BIOS is being used by watching the very first screen that appears when you turn on your PC). But for many people, a single manual change of date will be all that is needed to solve the problem. Note, however, that this does *not* apply for a computer that is running at the centre of a network, and so needs to provide a reliable time and date to other machines. It is also not recommended for users of Windows NT.

Use a software 'patch' This is a small piece of software that needs to be run once. It is a simple fix and probably the best route for most people. Commercial patches will be widely advertised as the date approaches, but it's very likely that someone will produce a shareware or freeware product that does the same thing for a fraction of the price, or even for free. Watch out for these low-cost solutions on the Internet, and also on magazine cover CDs. Information on relevant software fixes is also available from Which? Online at *www.which.net*

Buy a hardware solution Cards that plug into a PC and ensure that the clock works correctly are available. These are rather an expensive way to go about fixing the problem, but there will – very occasionally – be situations where a software patch will not work.

Install a new motherboard. This is not a job for a beginner (see pages 272–4). A shop is likely to take between one and three hours to do the job for you. The cost, including the new board, is unlikely to be less than £300, making this an expensive option. However, it may be worthwhile if the PC is being upgraded with a new processor chip and improved hardware at the same time.

'Flash BIOS' upgrade. Some motherboards include a 'flash BIOS' option, which means they can be upgraded using a special piece of software supplied on a floppy disk or copied from the Internet. However, there are dangers inherent in attempting this. Very few consultants and dealers will consider this option, because it can be very difficult to ensure that the software is exactly right for any one particular motherboard. Many boards are modified slightly by their manufacturers, and sold with a very specific version of the BIOS designed to work with that particular board. Upgrading to a different version may cause the computer to stop working. This solution cannot be recommended unless you have been assured by a dealer – preferably in writing – that it is an appropriate solution for you.

Software checks and tests

Even if the clock works properly, some software may still fail to function correctly. The latest office suites from major manufacturers are known to be Y2K-compliant, and you should have no problems with these, especially if you always type in the full four-digit year when you use their spreadsheets and databases for calculations.

Older versions may or may not be compliant. The full details of which products may cause problems in which circumstances are too complex to print here, but in short most software from the larger manufacturers seems to work correctly most of the time, although there may be very specific circumstances which cause software to give the wrong answer. If you are worried about whether or not your current software is Y2K-compliant you should contact the manufacturer's technical support line.

The situation with software produced by smaller companies is more complex. This is a particular problem for shareware, because of the huge range of very variable software that is available in this form. If in doubt, check the software if you can – again by changing your computer's clock if necessary – well before you find yourself in a situation where you need to be sure it's working reliably. You can then move to a different package if you need to.

More information

The Internet is by far the best source of up-to-date information on the subject. A search for 'Year 2000' or 'Y2K' using any of the popular search engines will show even more detail.

Also look out for special features in all the computer magazines.

If you have experienced any problems with products or services as a result of the Millennium bug, *Which?* would like to hear from you. You can report any problems with products on (0645) 830232 and any problems with services on (0645) 830234. These are *not* advice lines.

Other useful web sites:

The Year 2000 site at *www.year2000.com* includes plenty of background information and links to other sites.

British Computer Society *www.bcs.org.uk/millen.htm*

National Computing Centre *www.ncc.co.uk/y2k.html*

Site with links to manufacturers *www.compinfo.co.uk/y2k/ manufpos.htm*

The government's Millennium Bug Campaign aims to help businesses of all sizes.

The Millennium Bug Campaign is run by Action 2000, sponsored by the Department of Trade and Industry. Among other goals, it exists to provide direct support for small and medium businesses, with, for instance:

- a national hotline on (0845) 601 2000
- a guidebook and help sheets
- a web site on *www.open.gov.uk/bug2000.htm*

Whatever the size of your business, act sooner rather than later.

Computers, your health and the environment

Can computers damage your health? It seems bad working practices (sitting in a fixed position at the keyboard for long periods, making awkward or repetitive movements with your arms, head or body) contribute to a variety of ailments ranging from eyestrain to pain and discomfort in the limbs. Fortunately these are easily preventable. Taking time to ensure that your desk, chair and screen are positioned correctly can save days, even months of frustration and fatigue.

Health issues

Repetitive strain injury

Repetitive strain injury or RSI is a blanket term used to cover a collection of strain- and sprain-related health problems. Although there is some disagreement in the medical profession about whether or not RSI really exists, and if so exactly what causes it, a number of RSI sufferers are in no doubt that it is a work-related health issue. In extreme cases it can cause significant loss of flexibility in the hand and fingers.

If caught early and treated, the effects can sometimes be reversed. But there is no guarantee that this will be possible; the damage produced by some kinds of RSI may lead to a permanent incapacity.

From the point of view of working at a screen RSI seems to be related to tendonitis and carpal tunnel syndrome (CTS), a disabling injury which can affect anyone who uses their fingers or wrists for long periods. Concert pianists and professional keyboard players have been known to suffer from CTS, which can sometimes be treated by surgery, though not always with success. It is much wiser to avoid the problem in the first place.

Keyboard

One of the biggest problems facing anyone who uses a keyboard every day is the way that the standard QWERTY keyboard is arranged. Conventional touch-typing can place severe strain on the wrist and finger joints. The hands can be cramped and often unsupported for long periods, the fingertips can be in almost constant use, and the finger joints may be held in a strained position as well as being continually flexed.

One simple but effective solution is a wrist support. This is a simple foam pad placed in front of the keyboard on which the wrists can be rested comfortably between bouts of typing. Whilst typing the wrists should not rest on anything. A wrist support is highly recommended for anyone who works with a computer keyboard on a regular basis.

A more adventurous solution is to use another keyboard layout. The Dvorak keyboard – named after its inventor, John Dvorak – uses a different and more logical letter arrangement. Not only is it faster to work with, it is also easier to learn and produces less strain when used over long periods. Most keyboards come with keytops that can be detached with nothing more complicated than a small screwdriver, so the keyboard can be rearranged into the Dvorak layout. Some software, such as Windows for the PC, includes support for the Dvorak system as well as the QWERTY layout.

Another alternative is ergonomic keyboards. These are designed to fit the hands better and provide built-in wrist support, although they still use the standard QWERTY layout. Apple sold an ergonomic design in the mid-1990s but this is now only available second-hand. Microsoft's ergonomic keyboard is still current.

A company called Maltron offers ergonomic keyboard designs for the UK market. These look even stranger than the Microsoft and Apple models, and cost between £200 and £400, which makes them very expensive. However, many users report that these keyboards can make a difference to anyone with persistent RSI.

Opinions about ergonomic keyboards are mixed. Some users find they make a huge difference, others find they do nothing at all. Try out a keyboard at your local computer store and see for yourself before you decide whether or not to pay the extra.

VDU emissions

A computer screen is also known as a VDU or visual display unit and, like a television, emits radiation, although levels likely to be generated are well below those set out for limiting risk to health. A simple but expensive way to avoid the problem is to buy a good portable computer. These have screens which do not produce the same kind of hard radiation. Unfortunately these screens are still very expensive. The next best option is to choose a monitor that has been fully certified to the MPRII or TCO95/99 standard. This ensures that any stray radiation is below background levels (see page 189).

A glare filter – a plastic, glass or mesh panel that fits over the front of the VDU – will not affect 'hard' radiation such as X-rays, as these need proper shielding, but advanced models can help with static electricity. This tends to collect as charge on the screen – hence the 'crackling fingers' effect – and can, in extreme cases, have an effect on the operator's face and skin. If this is a problem, you may consider investing in an air ioniser. This adds a complementary charge to dust particles that balances out the positive charge from the screen. Glare filters can also be helpful in improving display quality and contrast, and hence in lessening eyestrain. Generally speaking, correct position will do more for glare than a bolt-on filter. However, the problem of glare should be treated at source, for example, angling the screen, rearranging the work station, using window blinds, and other options before resorting to glare filters. Before buying a monitor look very thoroughly at it, with a glare filter fitted if you feel you need one. A good – or a bad – monitor can make a huge difference to the amount of stress you feel when using your computer.

Printers

Early laser printers produced ozone, a gas which can be harmful in high quantities. Some newer models use a slightly modified printing system which is ozone-free. Always make sure that the printer you are using is in a well-ventilated area.

Another health hazard is toner spillage. The toner for most printers is a very fine powder and can be messy if spilled. Spills – which are unlikely unless the toner case is broken – should always be cleaned up immediately, wearing protective gloves. Be careful not to have your head too close to the powder when cleaning up spillage. Inhaling this powder can be uncomfortable and harmful. It is best to wear a simple dust mask if you think there is a risk of inhaling the dust.

The problem with dot-matrix and daisy-wheel printers is one of noise. Many computer accessory stores sell acoustic hoods, which you place over the printer to deaden the sound. These are strongly recommended for daisy-wheel printers in particular and worth considering for dot-matrix designs.

The print head on a dot-matrix model can become very warm. When changing a ribbon avoid touching the print head until it has cooled down. Bubble-jet printers are relatively safe. Apart from the very minor problem of ink spillage if you try to refill an ink cartridge, bubble-jet and ink-jet printers have no notably unhealthy side-effects.

Noise

Your computer should run quietly. The cooling fan should not be distractingly loud. Although this may seem like a minor point, unwanted noise can aggravate stress levels. If you plan to spend a long time in front of your machine make sure that it is quiet enough to enable you to work with some tranquillity. Also, arrange your work to ensure you leave the screen for frequent short breaks *before* the onset of tiredness.

Posture

To prevent long-term problems you will need to maintain a good posture and relax regularly while working. Take short, frequent breaks from keyboard work. A helpful scheme to follow is a one-minute break every ten minutes, a ten-minute break every hour and a forty-minute break (at least) every three hours. Stress-management consultants and some alternative health practitioners are sources of advice on how to relax while still working effectively.

EC directives

The European Union's set of directives designed to prevent operator discomfort while working with DSE (display screen equipment) became mandatory on 1 January 1997. If you are an employer you are required to follow these. In outline this means you must:

- provide a monitor which has clearly formed and well-defined lettering, no reflective glare and negligible radiation
- provide a footrest for anyone who asks for one
- provide a document holder which can be positioned so as not to require unnecessary movements

HEALTH

Monitors
Clean! (And easily cleaned)
Low radiation, MPRII-rated
Adequate letter size and display contrast
Comfortable flicker rate (i.e., 72Hz or better for smaller screens, 90Hz or better for screens larger than 19-inch)
Comfortable on-screen colour scheme
Tilted and swivelled to a comfortable viewing position
At the right height
Fitted with a glare filter if necessary
Located out of direct sunlight, with brightness and contrast set comfortably

Keyboards
Fitted with a wrist support
Easily movable
Weighted to prevent sliding
Optional Dvorak layout
Optional ergonomic design

Desks
Worktop at a comfortable height: this varies from person to person. First get the height and position of the chair right and then either raise the desk surface and/or use a footrest. Concentrate on the body position and adjust accordingly
Matt, non-reflective surface
Sufficient free space (at least 6 sq. ft.) around the computer for papers, etc.
Located out of direct sunlight
Supplied with a comfortable footrest if necessary
No unnecessary obstructions underfoot (such as papers, wastepaper bin)

Chairs
Stable, moves easily
Good back support, including the lower back

ECKLIST

Fully adjustable; should be adjustable to a height which allows the forearm to be horizontal to the desk in order that the fingers fall naturally on the keys. This may mean you need to use a footrest

Document holders
Easily adjustable; should be at the same height as the screen and on the same plane

Printers
Acoustic hoods where necessary
Located in a well-ventilated area
Toner spills are cleared up immediately

System units
No buzzes, squeaks, squeals or hums
Accessible without user having to strain

Lighting
No glare or direct lighting from any source shining into user's eyes

Electrical
All power connections made safe
Unavoidable trailing wires placed under flat rubber floor conduits
When ceasing work always switch off at the unit then at the mains supply at the socket

Air ionisers
To remove positive ions from the immediate environment if necessary

Working practices
Regular breaks of at least ten minutes an hour, spent walking around rather than stretching at the desk
Regular relaxation periods, based on professional relaxation techniques.

For further information contact the Health and Safety Executive

- provide a wrist support that enables the operator to adopt the correct posture.

These regulations can be ordered from good bookshops and though, in part, quite vague, they will go some way to ensure that as an employer you are aware of health issues and of your responsibility to act on them.

How 'green' are computers?

You may see computers advertised as 'green', and in this context the word means something very specific. 'Green' features imply a range of power-saving options. The computer only draws maximum power while you actually use it. After a period of inactivity it starts to shut down – the monitor, the main processor chip and perhaps the hard disk go into a low power 'standby' mode. This saves electricity and – in theory – has less of an effect on the environment.

To get a computer with power-saving features, you should watch out for the 'Energy Star' rating. This was introduced by the US government in an attempt to save energy on a national basis, but is now available in the UK as well. A computer with a full set of Energy Star features will use less electricity than one without. But the differences are likely to be minor.

Legal aspects of computer use

The Data Protection Act

If you maintain any kind of information about living people on your computer, you may be liable to register with the Data Protection Registrar. This is a relatively painless process which costs a standard fee of £75 for three years. The penalties for not registering are much stiffer – up to £5,000 plus costs in a Magistrates Court, or an unlimited sum in the Higher Courts.

There are a small number of exemptions. If you use your computer for writing letters, and the information you keep is used solely for that purpose, then you will not need to register. But if you start to include personal details – and these can include a name and basic contact details – you become liable for registration. Even if you do not need to register, according to the Act you should ask the people whose information you hold if they have any objections.

The other main exemption is the information used for payroll calculations. If you keep this, and use it for no other purposes than this then you are exempt. However, if you start to maintain credit histories and other details, such as payments to the Child Support Agency, then you will need to register.

You should register even if the information is kept on a computer that you do not own. If you contract out the maintenance of a list of details to a computer bureau, then you are still the person 'in control' of the records and should register accordingly.

Once you are registered, you must follow the code of good information-handling practice set down in the Act in the eight Data Protection 'Principles'. Broadly these state that personal data must be:

1. obtained and processed fairly and lawfully
2. held only for the lawful purposes described in the data user's register entry
3. used only for those purposes, and disclosed only to those people, described in the register entry
4. adequate, relevant and not excessive in relation to the purpose for which they are held
5. accurate and, where necessary, kept up-to-date
6. held no longer than is necessary for the registered purpose
7. accessible to the individuals concerned who, where appropriate, have the right to have information about themselves corrected or erased
8. surrounded by proper security.

If you are registered you will have to convince the Registrar that you are not collecting information unnecessarily. This can sometimes have surprising implications. In one case the Registrar was called in to deal with a video hire shop that was collecting the passport and driving licence numbers of its customers as a security measure. The Registrar advised the shop to stop this practice, as collecting this information was inappropriate in the circumstances. Registration will require you to look at the records you keep and to ensure you have good reasons why you need to continue keeping them.

Following changes to data protection rules across Europe the UK recently passed new data protection laws. The Data Protection Act 1998, expected to be brought into force at the end of 1999, will replace the Data Protection Act 1984. The new law will still require those using personal data to follow a code of good practice based on data protection 'principles' set out in the new Act, but it increases some obligations on data users, gives individuals some new rights of access to information and changes registration requirements to a simplified system of notification. For information about the new law or the current Data Protection Act contact the Data Protection Registrar (see Addresses).

Software piracy

Software piracy ranges from the organised black-market copying of software and manuals, to the use of illegal copies of a word-processing package in an office because 'no one need ever know', to the installation at home of a single copy of software obtained from a friend who bought it legally.

If you use pirated software – and some estimates suggest that almost half of all the software in use in the UK today is pirated – you are liable for prosecution. Although the police tend to concentrate on organised pirating operations, if you use a disk supplied by a friend, in theory you are still committing a theft and are liable for any proceedings.

Software is usually sold on a licence rather than an outright purchase basis. This usually means that your rights are limited to:

- using the software on one machine at a time
- making backup safety copies

You are not allowed to:

- use the software on two different machines at once (e.g., desktop and laptop)
- pass copies to a friend
- sell the software on, even second-hand.

Any of these actions could leave you liable to prosecution. Passing copies to a friend is particularly dangerous. All software includes a unique serial number. If copies with your number turn up in an investigation then you will be held responsible.

In general, then, it is unwise to pirate or to use pirated software. This applies especially in an office situation, where the software is spread across a network or is installed on a number of PCs. This kind of semi-organised piracy is being vigorously pursued by the industry, and agencies such as FAST (Federation Against Software Theft) even run a hotline service where the public can provide tip-offs about piracy (see Addresses). In short, the best advice is – don't.

What to do with your old computer

What do you do with an old computer? Getting rid of it can be a headache. You could just throw it away – leave it outside the house with the other rubbish, or take it to the local tip or recycling centre. However, by throwing away the computer you could also be throwing away any value that it may still have.

Second-hand value

Many computers still hold a second–hand value. But you must be realistic in your pricing. A machine that cost £1,000 five years ago is likely to be worth perhaps a tenth of that today. It can be more appealing to prospective buyers if the computer is sold as a complete package with all software and a printer included. You could advertise it for sale in the local newspapers and in newsagents' shop windows. Another option is advertising it on the Internet, for example on auction services such as eBay (*www.ebay.co.uk*).

Selling the parts

More experienced users may want to consider dismantling the computer and selling the pieces individually. Breaking up a computer in this way is only worth considering if it is so outdated that it is unlikely to interest anyone looking for a complete second–hand machine. Depending on size, hard disks are worth between £10 and £100 second hand. Experienced buyers will want to know if there are any damaged or 'bad' sectors or flaws on the surface of the disk that will affect its ability to hold information reliably. The Partition Magic package can check for these, and a hard disk that is completely free of them can be sold with some confidence. Other components can also be sold off one by one. Cases are worth up to £30, again depending on size and 'form factor', floppy disk drives around £5, and CD-ROM drives between £10 and £20, depending on speed. Processor chips can fetch up to £300, depending on speed and age, although in older machines a more realistic asking price might be between £10 and £50. Used motherboards, especially obsolete ones, are very hard to dispose of, and are unlikely to fetch more than between £10 to £20.

If you do decide to sell your computer in bits the best place to advertise all the parts is in the local free advertising papers, and in computer specialist magazines such as *MicroMart* and *PCMart*.

Deleting information

Before disposing of a computer, it is important to remove any sensitive information from it. Normally deleting the information (which in Windows 95/98 means making sure that it is also removed from the 'recycle bin') will offer enough security. However, business users and those with confidential personal information should be aware that deleted information can be reconstructed, albeit with some time and effort. Anyone worried about business or personal details falling into the wrong hands may want to use a 'professional' delete tool, which not only removes the information but makes it utterly irretrievable. For example, Norton Utilities has a military-standard deletion tool which removes all traces of deleted information so thoroughly that not even removing the hard disk from its case and surrounding it with specialised electronic equipment makes it possible to retrieve it.

Donating to charity

You may want to consider donating an old computer to charity, or to a local school. Secondary schools tend to standardise on systems from one manufacturer, and so may be less keen to take an older machine. However, primary schools are often less fussy, and it can be worth asking head teachers if they are interested in a free machine.

In the UK, Computers for Charity and Gifts In Kind are two organisations which specialise in taking away old machines and passing them on to worthwhile causes. Details are given at the end of this appendix.

Computers for Charity
Tel: (01288) 356045 (9-5 Mon–Fri, 9–12 Sat)
Fax (between 09:00–17:00): (01288) 359320
Email: Graham.pitt@ukonline.com
Web site: http://web.ukonline.co.uk/graham.pitt/cfc/

Gifts In Kind
Email: productdonations@GiftsInKind.org

Further reading

Although most computer magazines cover the same territory, there is a huge difference in readability, usefulness and value. At one end of the market are the unashamedly technical magazines aimed at readers who already have a good grasp of the subject and need the latest information to keep up with the rest of the industry. At the other end are the magazines which specifically cater for the uninitiated. In between are the new family-oriented lifestyle magazines. A recent development is titles specialising in the Internet.

Many magazines include software in the form of one or more floppy disks or a CD-ROM on the cover. These can be an invaluable source of product demonstrations and free software. Magazines sometimes publish separate CD-ROM and floppy-disk versions of the same issue. However, the latter are becoming rare as most magazines have taken to assuming their readers have CD-ROM drives.

You will also find free booklets which give further information on some aspects of computing. These can be an excellent source of information for beginners and a very good way to equip yourself with a 'free' set of tutorials and a reference library. What follows is a brief survey of the magazines available in December 1997.

Monthly professional PC titles

These are usually heavy on advertising and make few concessions to the absolute beginner. Many articles will be all but incomprehensible to anyone without a good grasp of the subject, although there will sometimes be a couple of pages – but no more – devoted to absolute beginners. A handful of titles try much harder to present information in a way that does not exclude readers without a technical background.

Computer Buyer (Dennis Publishing)
An all-round general-purpose title, although sometimes perhaps too technically advanced for complete beginners. The main emphasis is on hardware and software news, comparisons and reviews. The comprehensive Buyer's Guide is unusually good.

Computer Shopper (Dennis Publishing)
There are useful sections devoted to computers other than the PC and Mac but much of the content is highly technical. A regular beginners' feature ('Ivan Iwannado') does its best to demystify a different part of computing each month, but is perhaps still a little technical for absolute beginners. The large question-and-answer section is a reliable source of technical hints and solutions. *Computer Shopper* has a very low cover price.

PC Direct (Ziff Davis UK)
This magazine is aimed particularly at mail order buyers of PC equipment. Otherwise it is very much a typical PC enthusiast's monthly title.

PC Magazine (Ziff Davis UK)
PC Magazine specialises in in-depth comparative reviews. Hardware reviews are presented in simple bar-graph form and software reviews include usability and productivity studies.

PC Plus (Future Publishing)
This magazine has the usual opinion, news, reviews and educational sections. Like the others, it is best suited to readers who have a grasp of the basics rather than absolute beginners. It has recently started to include regular free booklets, which can be extremely useful, and there is an informative, if not quite comprehensive, buyer's guide which lists most of the widely available software and hardware products in any month.

PC Pro (Dennis Publications)
This title is aimed at the computer-literate professional user. It includes a comprehensive buyer's guide and list of industry contact numbers and addresses.

Personal Computer World (VNU Publications)
This is one of longest-running computer titles on the market. Apart from the usual blend of industry news and product reviews there are also company profiles and interviews, as well as occasional more general computer or information technology-based features.

What PC? (VNU Publications)
This is a very basic and straightforward monthly which is unusually useful to beginners. Each month a new topic, such as printers or portable computers, is covered in some detail. While not as thorough as some of the more professionally-oriented monthly magazines, it is a good place for complete novices to find explanations of jargon and other useful information.

Fortnightly

Computer Active (VNU Publication)
Among the best of the beginners' titles, *Computer Active* includes news, reviews, step-by-step how-to workshops and a range of other general PC interest features. The contents seem to be chosen as much for practical as technical interest, and the magazine as a whole tries hard to be accessible to non-experts – it is recommended by the Plain English Campaign.

PC Mart (Maze Media)
A fortnightly paper containing classified ads. Good source of bargains and computer book reviews but not much solid buying advice.

Monthly PC leisure titles

Leisure titles concentrate on games and entertainment. They are written in a much friendlier and chattier style than the professional titles, and this can make them much less intimidating to beginners. They are also likely to include reviews of non-business multimedia software such as animated story books for children, encyclopedias, and other general knowledge and specialist-interest software products.

A relatively recent development is a range of leisure titles aimed at home and family users. These cover a wide range of computer-related subjects and include many articles pitched at beginners.

Mobile Computing (European Publishing)
Concentrating exclusively on news and reviews of laptops, PDAs and palmtop computers, *Mobile Computing* also includes information about using mobile phones with the Internet, and occasional technical features of relevant but more general interest.

PC Advisor (IDG Media)
Aimed specifically at beginners and family users, it is very reasonably priced and also reasonably comprehensive. However, the presentation is perhaps not as clear and focused as it could be.

PC Answers (Future Publishing)
This is a general leisure title.

PC Basics (IDG Media)
A slightly more technically oriented title than other beginners' titles, *PC Basics* includes how-to columns, reviews, news and a technical answers section.

PC Format (Future Publishing)
This title concentrates on games and is aimed largely at younger readers, but also includes general-interest articles, interviews with writers, artists and musicians as well as computer professionals, and reviews of leisure software.

PC Gamer (Future Publishing)
A title devoted exclusively to PC gaming, and aimed at younger readers. It offers plenty of game reviews, hints and instructions on how-to find the built-in cheats in popular games, and complete game puzzles solutions. However, there is not much general PC advice.

PC Gaming World (Ziff Davis)
Aimed at slightly older readers, this title includes the standard blend of reviews, previews, cheats, solutions, and occasional game-related technical features.

PC Guide (Future Publishing)
Originally a family-oriented monthly, this has now changed course and become a more general interest PC magazine, with simple 'how-

to' features for beginners and information and stories about colourful and creative computer applications that affect everyday life, such as computer-generated special effects in films.

PC Home (IDG Media)
Similar in style and content to *PC Format*, but without the general-interest articles. Concentrates on games and multimedia titles.

PC Review (Future Publishing)
Although *PC Review* resembles other leisure titles, it has a wider coverage and includes more news and general semi-technical features. Most of the pages are devoted to games-related subjects, but there are also useful reviews of other general-interest titles and hardware.

Total PC (Paragon Publishing)
A fairly standard combination of reviews, features, upgrade information, and occasional general interest articles. More technically minded than many leisure titles.

Windows Made Easy (Paragon Publishing)
Aimed at the relative beginner, *Windows Made Easy* consists almost entirely of heavily illustrated step-by-step tutorial features describing a range of more or less obvious, common and useful PC tasks.

Monthly Apple titles

Apple titles tend to carry far less advertising than PC titles. Some PC monthlies are more like phone directories, which can make them unwieldy to read and store. Apple-specific monthlies are much more typical of other magazines.

As befits their readership profile, Apple magazines tend to concentrate on creative and artistic applications. But there is usually plenty for the home and business user too.

MacFormat (Future Publishing)
MacFormat covers the full range of Mac software from business to games and creative applications. There is a wide range of reviews, hints and tips and the content is suitable for beginners.

MacWorld (IDG Communications)
A good choice for the professional Apple user. Tends to cover traditional Apple areas of image processing, DTP and creative design.

TotalMac (Paragon Publishing)
Essentially a CD-ROM of shareware with a magazine attached, *TotalMac* includes plenty of low-cost and trial software, although the accompanying descriptions in the magazine are perhaps a little minimal.

Fortnightly Apple titles

MacUser (Dennis Publishing)
MacUser is one of the more informative Apple titles. It covers a wide range of software, not just the usual graphical and artistic applications, and there is even a 'getting started' section for beginners, although this tends to be aimed at Apple users with some basic experience rather than complete novices.

Weekly titles

MicroMart (Trinity Publications Ltd)
Cheap, printed on cheap paper, it includes some of the best computer bargains around. This is one of the best available sources for cut-price hardware and software bargains. Also has pages of free classified ads.

Internet publications

Internet (EMAP publications)
Internet includes features aimed at both beginners and more experienced users, although the style is always approachable and non-technical. The title is distinguished by its comprehensive directory section which includes an Internet glossary, full details of UK service providers and a huge selection of Internet locations and services.

InternetWorks (Future Publishing)
A business-oriented Internet title that concentrates on setting up Internet facilities for a medium-sized company, and other topics of business interest. Rather specific and technical for beginners, but can occasionally be a source of useful tips.

.net (Future Publishing)
Includes 'how-to' introductory features. There are useful lists of places to look for software and a directory of ISPs in the UK.

Practical Internet (Paragon Publishing)
Covers a broad range of Internet-related topics and takes a more accessible and less glamorous approach to its subject matter. It is aimed at a general audience and includes a mix of news, comments, tips and suggestions on where to find useful information on the Web.

The Web (IDG Communications)
Although aimed at a more technically minded audience, *The Web* mostly concentrates on useful practical tips about how to use the Web for fun and profit. Some general interest features are also included.

Wired (Wired Ventures Ltd)
Wired is more of a lifestyle and general-interest than a technological monthly, and more than any other it captures the flavour of interactions on the Internet.

The magazine market is rather volatile, and titles appear and disappear regularly. For the latest information visit the web sites of the major publishers, as listed at the back of the book. (The Ziff Davis and the *Wired* sites are particularly interesting as they include topical industry news and commentary.)

Books

It can be worth taking your time to browse when buying computer books, because they can save you money in the long run. Many titles are expensive – expect to pay anywhere from £15 to £50 – but this should be taken in the context of other computer-related training materials. A one-day training course can cost you between £150 and £500, and will not necessarily tell you any more than a book will (although you will be able to ask questions). So good books are a wise investment, and you may find that if you work through a well-written off-the-shelf tutorial you will not need to take a training course at all.

A trip to any bookshop will show that there is an almost unlimited number of titles available. It is impossible to recommend specific titles, as your choice will depend on your own needs and learning style. For example, many computer books for novices take a humorous approach, and some readers respond well to this. Others simply find it annoying. The depth of the information presented and the overall layout vary tremendously too.

When starting from scratch you should budget up to £150 for books to get you started, although a basic familiarisation text will cost you £25. This will give you a good range to choose from, and you should be able to find everything you need to master the basics of the subject.

As a rough buying guide points to watch for include:

Style The most effective titles are those that take a step-by-step tutorial approach. Some books take a different tack and are meant as reference works. They may well contain everything you need to know but it will not be presented in a simple, easy-to-follow way. Unless you are already proficient in the applications covered, reference-style books are best avoided.

Accessibility If you can get to the end of the first chapter without understanding a word – and this is possible, even with some of the titles aimed at beginners – consider another title instead. Some authors fall into the trap of using jargon without explaining it first. This can be annoying and confusing, and does nothing to help you master the subject. An accessible book will make the subject seem easier rather than harder.

Relevance New versions of software are being released all the time, so you will need to check that a book on a specific software title applies to the version you have.

Many computer books are written and printed in the US, and therefore use American expressions. Apart from the culture clash, this can sometimes render information inaccurate. Many Internet books, for example, include lists of Internet service providers. You should definitely look for an English title here, as American lists will not apply. In general, though, most US titles are suitable for the UK market.

Free software Some titles include free software. Check for a description in the book to see whether this will be genuinely useful to you.

Addresses

The UK's telephone numbering system is being reorganised. As part of the reorganisation, six geographic areas across the UK have been given new area codes beginning with 02. These are Cardiff, Coventry, London, Northern Ireland, Portsmouth and Southampton. You will be able to use the new area codes from 1 June 1999 and both the new and old area codes will be in use until 22 April 2000. After that date only the new area codes will work when dialling.

Each of the six areas will have a three-digit area code (starting with 02), followed by an eight-digit local telephone number.

Business software manufacturers

Although most of these manufacturers can be contacted via email, this is usually reserved for contacting specific employees rather than for general public enquiries. Telephone in the first instance or try the relevant web site.

Connect Software
3 Flanchford Road
London W12 9ND
Tel: 020 8743 9792
Fax: 020 8743 8073
Email: connect@moneysoft.co.uk
Web site: www.moneysoft.co.uk

Intuit Service Centre
PO Box 139
Chertsey
Surrey KT16 9FE
Tel: (0800) 585058
Fax: (01932) 578522
Web site: www.intuit.co.uk

Lotus UK
Lotus Park
The Causeway
Staines
Middlesex TW18 3AG
Tel: (01784) 455445
Fax: (01784) 469342
Email: postmaster@lotus.com
Web site: www.lotus.com

Microsoft Ltd
Microsoft Campus
Thames Valley Park
Reading RG6 1WG
Tel: (0870) 6010100
Fax: (0870) 6020100
Web site: www.microsoft.com

Novell UK
1 Arlington Square
Downshire Way
Bracknell RG12 1WA
Tel: (01344) 724000
Fax: (01344) 724001
Web site: www.novell.com.uk

Pegasus Software Ltd
Orion House
Orion Way
Kettering
Northamptonshire NN15 6PE
Tel: (01536) 495200
Fax: (01536) 495001
Email: mailbox@pegasus.co.uk
Web site: www.pegasus.co.uk

Quantum
Cowley Bridge Road
Exeter EX4 5HQ
Tel: (01392) 429424

Sagesoft Ltd
Sage House
Benton Park Road
Newcastle upon Tyne NE7 7LZ
Tel: 0191-255 3000
Fax: 0191-255 0308
Email: info@sage.com
Web site: www.sagesoft.co.uk

Tas Software
29 East Street
Epsom
Surrey KT17 1BS
Tel: (01372) 727274
Fax: (01372) 721414
Email: sales@tassoftware.co.uk
Web site: www.tassoftware.com

Health

HSE Books (Health and Safety Executive)
PO Box 1999
Sudbury
Suffolk CO10 6FS
Tel: (01787) 881165
Fax: (01787) 313995
Web site: www.open.gov.uk/hse/
hsehome.htm
For free copies of leaflets IND(G)36
Working with VDUs and IND(G)243
Computer Control,
telephone (01787) 881165

PCD Maltron Ltd
15 Orchard Lane
East Molesey
Surrey KT8 0BN
Tel/Fax: 020 8398 3265

Insurance brokers

Association of British Insurers
51 Gresham Street
London EC2V 7HQ
Tel: 020 7600 3333
Fax: 020 7696 8996 8999
Email: info@abi.org.uk
Web site: www.abi.org.uk

Burnett & Associates
39-41 Victoria Road
Woolston
Southampton SO19 9DY
Tel: (01703) 442227
Fax: (01703) 442210
Email: info@burnett.co.uk
Web site: www.burnett.co.uk

First Domestic
Swan Court
Wimbledon
London SW19 4AA
Tel: (08705) 490000
(First Domestic offers a combined
insurance and support service)

Royal & Sun Alliance Engineering
17 York Street
Manchester M2 3RS
Tel: 0161-235 3000
Fax: 0161-235 3001
Email: marketing@eng.royalsun.com
Web site: royalsunalliance.co.uk/
engineering

Tolson Messenger
148 King Street
London W6 0QU
Tel: 020 8741 8361
Fax: 020 8741 9395
Email: vwheatcroft@tolsonmessenger.
co.uk
Web site: www.Tolsonmessenger.co.uk

Internet service providers

America OnLine (AOL)
Gilde House
East Point Business Park
Fairview
Dublin 3
Ireland
Tel: (0800) 2791234
Fax: (0800) 2797446
Email: Ukgen@aol.co.uk
Web site: www.aol.co.uk

**Cix Ltd (formerly WinNet
Communications)**
1 Sundial Court
Tolworth Rise South
Surbiton
Surrey KT5 9RN
Tel: 020 8255 5000
Fax: 020 8255 5101
Web site: www.cix.co.uk

CompuServeUK
1 Redcliff Street
Bristol BS1 6NP
Tel: (0870) 6000800 (customer
support)
(0990) 000200 (sales)
Email: mail.compuserve.com
Web site: www.world.compuserve.
com

Demon Internet
Gateway House
322 Regents Park Road
London N3 2QQ
Tel: 020 8371 1234
Fax: 020 8371 1201
Email: sales@demon.net
Web site: www.demon.net

Which? Online
Freepost
Hertford X
SG14 1YB
Tel: (0645) 830256
Email: which@which.net
Web site: www.which.net

User groups

PC-Users' Group
Archgate Business Centre
825 High Road
London N12 8UB
Tel: 020 8492 5729
Fax: 020 8445 1434

Parents Information Network (PIN)
PO Box 16394
London SE1 3ZP
Tel: 020 7357 9078
Fax: 020 7357 9077
Email: post@pin-parents.com
Web site: www.pin-parents.com

Voice dictation systems

Dragon Systems UK Ltd
Millbank
Stoke Road
Bishops Cleeve
Cheltenham
Gloucestershire GL52 4RW
Tel: (01242) 678581
(01242) 678575 (sales and
marketing)
Email: alan@dragon.co.uk
Web site: www.naturalspeech.
com

Pre-printed computer stationery

Paper Direct
Nuffield Road
Harrowbrook Industrial Estate
Hinkley
Leicestershire LE10 3DG
Tel: (0800) 616244
Fax: (0800) 716563
Email: sales@paperdirect.co.uk

Viking Direct
Bursom Industrial Park
Tollwell Road
Leicester LE4 1BR
Tel: (0800) 424444
Fax: (0800) 622211
Web site: www.viking-direct.co.uk

Shareware libraries

Atlantic Coast Plc
The Shareware Village
Station Road
Colyton
Devon EX24 6HA
Tel: (01297) 552222
Fax: (01297) 553366
Email: sales@atlantic-coast.com
Web site: www.soft-shop.com

The Public Domain and Shareware Library (PC)
PO Box 131
Crowborough
East Sussex TN6 1WF
Tel: (01892) 663298
Fax: (01892) 667473
Email: info@pdsl.com
Web site: www.pdsl.com

Support providers organisation

Computing Services & Software Association
20 Red Lion Street
London WC1R 4QN
Tel: 020 7395 6700
Fax: 020 7404 4119
Email: cssa@cssa.co.uk
Web site: www.cssa.co.uk

UPS and surge protector components

Farnell Electronic
Components Ltd
Canal Road
Leeds LS12 2TU
Tel: 0113-263 6311 (sales)
0113-279 9123 (product support)
Fax: 0113-263 3411
Email: sales@farnell.com
Web site: www.farnell.com

Suppliers

Maplin Professional Suppliers (MPS)
Freepost SMU 94
PO Box 777
Rayleigh
Essex SS6 8LU
Tel: (01702) 554000
Fax: (01702) 554001
Email: sales@maplin.co.uk
Web site: www.maplin.co.uk

Others

Data Protection Registrar
Wycliffe House
Water Lane
Wilmslow
Cheshire SK9 5AF
Tel: (01625) 545745
Fax: (01625) 524510
Email: data@wycliffe.demon.co.uk
Web site: www.open.gov.uk/
dpr/dprhome.htm

Federation Against Software Theft
(FAST)
1 Kingfisher Court
Farnham Road
Slough
Berkshire SL2 1JF
Tel: (01753) 527999
Fax: (01753) 532100
Email: fast@fast.org
Web site: www.fast.org.uk

Magazine publishers

Dennis Publishing
19 Bolsover Street
London W1P 7HJ
Tel: 020 7631 1433
Fax: 020 7636 5668
Web site: www.theden.co.uk
Web sites for specific magazines
Computer Buyer: www.com-buyer.
co.uk
Computer Shopper:
www.compshopper.co.uk
MacUser: www.macuser.co.uk
PC Pro: www.pcpro.co.uk
Maxim: www.maxim-magazine.co.uk
PC Zone: www.pczone.co.uk

Future Publishing
30 Monmouth Street
Bath BA1 2BW
Tel: (01225) 442244
Fax: (01225) 446019
Web site: www.futurenet.co.uk

IDG Media
Media House
Adlington Park
Macclesfield SK10 4NP
Tel: (01625) 878888
Fax: (01625) 850652
Web site: www.idg.co.uk

Maze Media
2 East Hill
Colchester
Essex CO1 2QL
Tel: (01206) 861574
Fax: (01206) 862537

McGraw-Hill
1 Wimbledon Bridge House
1 Hartfield Road
Wimbledon
London SW19 3RU
Tel: 020 8543 1234
Fax: 020 8540 3833
Web site: www.mcgraw-hill.com

Paragon Publishing
Paragon House
St Peter's Road
Bournemouth BH1 2JS
Tel: (01202) 299900
Fax: (01202) 299955
Email: subs@paragon.co.uk
Web site: www.paragon.co.uk

Trinity Publications Ltd
First Floor
Edward House
Tindal Bridge
Edward Street
Birmingham
West Midlands B1 2RA
Tel: 0121-233 8712
Fax: 0121-233 8715
Web site: www.micromart.co.uk

VNU Business Publications
VNU House
32–34 Broadwick Street
London W1A 2HG
Tel: 020 7316 9000
Fax: 020 7316 9003
Web site: www.vnunet.co.uk

Wired
Email: info@wired.com
        subscriptions@wired.com
        rants@wired.com
Web site: www.wired.com

Ziff-Davis UK Ltd
International House
1 St Katherine's Way
London E1 9UN
Tel: 020 7903 6800
Fax: 020 7903 6000
Web site: www.zdnet.co.uk

Index